Sustainable Development and Learning

This book examines the difficult and wide-ranging issues relating to how we understand our environment, and our place in it, and how we choose to act.

This comprehensive text provides an overview of these developing key issues, illustrating how – through schooling, higher education, professional training and development, and awareness-raising – people can being about change, as well as engaging in debate and critique of the issues. The book builds on existing work across a number of fields, as well as on original international research, in order to model the complexity of the problems, the institutional contexts in which they arise, and the interrelationships between these.

Areas explored include: the policy context, the links between sustainable development and learning, the economic and moral interdependence of humans and nature, the management, assessment and evaluation of learning, and globalisation. The book suggests ways in which those responsible for learning can target their efforts appropriately, matching straightforward solutions to simple problems, and designing complex interventions only where these are needed.

This text will be a valuable resource for anyone studying Masters degrees and MBAs that focus on environment or sustainable development, and for professionals dealing with problems on a day-to-day basis. Though a free-standing text, its analysis is supported by a companion reader: *Key Issues in Sustainable Development and Learning: a critical view*.

William Scott and **Stephen Gough** are members of the Centre for Research Education and the Environment at the University of Bath. The Centre collaborates with NGOs, education and research associations and the business sector in research, development, evaluation and teaching.

Sustainable Development and Learning

Framing the issues

William Scott and Stephen Gough

With a Foreword by Sir Neil Chalmers,
Director of The Natural History Museum

Routledge
Taylor & Francis Group

LONDON AND NEW YORK

First published 2003
by Routledge
2 Park Square, Milton Park, Abingdon, Oxon, OX14 4RN

Simultaneously published in the USA and Canada
by Routledge
270 Madison Ave, New York NY 10016

Routledge is an imprint of the Taylor & Francis Group

Transferred to Digital Printing 2006

© 2003 William Scott and Stephen Gough

Typeset in Baskerville by
BOOK NOW Ltd

British Library Cataloguing in Publication Data
A catalogue record for this book is available from the British Library

Library of Congress Cataloging in Publication Data
A catalog record for this book has been requested

ISBN 0-415-27648-9

Printed and bound by CPI Antony Rowe, Eastbourne

Contents

Illustrations

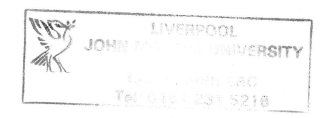

Foreword

Few issues are so important but so elusive as sustainable development and there can be very few such issues indeed where the role of learning is so crucially important to our future. To many people, sustainable development is a difficult and nebulous concept and yet its main themes are fundamental to the daily lives of everybody on our planet. People from all walks of life, whether they be politicians, business leaders, journalists, educators, working people, students, parents or people in retirement, readily appreciate and often have strong views about the main components of sustainable development. How we generate enough wealth to enjoy a good quality of life; how we organise our society so that this quality of life is available to all; how we do so in a way that protects our wonderfully rich but fragile natural world are all things that to greater or lesser degrees are understood to be important. But learning about sustainable development is more than learning about economic development, about social policy or environmental protection. It is a question of learning about how these three fundamental areas are intimately related. It is a question of learning about the perspective of time.

There are hard issues to tackle. The resources of our natural world help us to create the wealth that, if wisely used, will enable people to enjoy a good standard of living. Yet we must not use such resources in a way that compromises the ability of future generations to create good standards of living for themselves in turn. In particular, we must not allow our pursuit of wealth generation in the short term to mutilate or destroy our natural environment, for not only can this undermine the important cultural and aesthetic contribution that the environment makes to our lives, but can imperil the very survival of countless people.

Sustainable development presents a complex and challenging learning agenda and raises many questions. What skills are needed to learn effectively across all of the many components of sustainable development? How can learning experiences best be designed for all of the many stakeholders for whom such learning is, or should be, essential? How does one create learning programmes suited respectively to governments, to the world of work, to the formal education sector and to lifelong learners? How do we measure the effectiveness of different vehicles for learning about sustainable development? And how do we measure the effectiveness, or otherwise, of the outcomes in the field of sustainable development itself?

It is this crucial interface between sustainable development and learning that is explored in the two books. In *Sustainable Development and Learning: framing the issues*, William Scott and Stephen Gough set out an authoritative and searching analysis of the concepts underpinning sustainable development. They explore policy, then range across many important areas including learning theory and practice, evaluation and future challenges. The companion volume *Key Issues in Sustainable Development and Learning: a critical review*, edited by Scott and Gough, adopts the same framework but draws upon key readings from the literature, each of which is accompanied by concise critical appraisals by leading authorities in the field of learning and sustainable development.

The World Summit on Sustainable Development in 2002 in Johannesburg showed us the overwhelming need for effective learning in relation to sustainable development. These two books are therefore exceedingly timely and will be invaluable to all, whether they be professionals in the field, those undertaking academic programmes of study and research, or readers from a wide variety of other backgrounds, who need to explore further this vitally important field.

Sir Neil Chalmers
The Natural History Museum

Acknowledgements

In writing this book and its companion volume *Key Issues in Sustainable Development and Learning: a critical review*, we have attempted to draw on a wide range of research, literature and practice from worldwide and deliberately contrasting contexts. We have also drawn on our own work and those of interested colleagues from across the world. The debt of gratitude we owe to many people and institutions is obvious to us but to attempt to identify everyone runs the risk of inexplicable and unforgivable omission. However, it is very clear that the following networks and organisations need a special mention and a big on-going 'thank you':

- Our close colleagues in the *Centre for Research in Education and the Environment* at Bath with whom it is a privilege to work
- The wider network of colleagues in the Department of Education and the University's *International Centre for the Environment* who are a constant source of stimulus and opportunity
- Colleagues working in nearby universities, NGOs and local government, whose work 'on the ground' is of continued interest and hope
- Members of the UK's *FERN* research network whose friendly stimulus and penetrating challenge to each other is an excellent example of effective collegiality
- The director and staff of the UK's *Council for Environmental Education* whose keen interest in these issues is matched only by a dedicated professionalism which greatly benefits the field
- Editors within *Taylor and Francis* who not only put so much into this book and the companion reader, but who provide continuing world class support for the development of *Environmental Education Research* and cognate academic journals as vehicles for exploring the important ideas we are discussing here
- Colleagues within national and international NGOs and government ministries and agencies whose interest and stimulus are felt across sectors
- Colleagues who come together for regular international research development seminars which continue to prove so valuable in nurturing new researchers and stimulating co-operation
- Colleagues within the *North American Association of Environmental Education* who

bring long-established and well-honed expertise and interest but who are not afraid to think outside the box
- Colleagues within the special interest group on ecological and environmental education in the *American Educational Research Association* whose annual meetings helpfully continue to provoke and inform in equal measure
- Colleagues within the *Worldwide Fund for Nature* for the continuing invaluable stimulus to our thinking, and the Director of Education and her colleagues within the USA's *World Wildlife Fund* for the highest quality of partnership one could desire.

And finally (but in truth, firstly and uniquely), there are Pam, Jean, Jim, Ruth, Alex and Jonathan to whom this book is dedicated with love and gratitude.

Stephen Gough and William Scott
Bath, 2003

Authors' introduction

These two companion books, *Sustainable Development and Learning: framing the issues* and *Key Issues in Sustainable Development and Learning: a critical review*, explore in complementary ways the relationships between learning and sustainable development. This book, *Sustainable Development and Learning: framing the issues*, provides an analytical overview of the central issues within the field. Its companion volume uses the same chapter headings to present seminal readings from existing literature set alongside specially commissioned, critical vignettes from leading practitioners in order to explore differing perspectives.

The central thesis of the books is that there is a need to bring about constructive engagement between the diverse perspectives on both learning and sustainable development, and to explore their inter-relationship. In order to do this, the books set out to communicate both the essentials and the complexities of a wide range of inter-related issues, raising important topics for discussion, reflection and on-going consideration by readers. These books are written for all those with an interest in sustainable development and learning and for those who, irrespective of background and discipline, are seeking support for professional activities, and/or undertaking academic programmes of study.

A matter of definition

Definition is, of course, crucial, and a major purpose of the books is to help readers to develop understandings of both sustainable development and learning.

There exists considerable confusion in the popular usage of the phrases 'sustainable development' and 'sustainability', and often the terms are used interchangeably. The literature, however, shows a clear distinction in meanings with sustainable development as a process, and sustainability as a goal. The Brundtland Commission (WCED, 1987) saw sustainable development as a process of change with the future in mind:

> a process where the exploitation, the orientation of technological development and institutional change, are made consistent with future as well as present needs.

For Hamm and Mutagi (1998) the goal of sustainability is:

> a capacity of human beings to continuously adapt to their non-human environments by means of social organisation.

The notion of sustainable development that informs both books is that of a process through which we shall need to learn to live more in tune with the environment. But it is not enough to say that sustainable development and learning need to go hand in hand. Rather, we need to recognise that there will be no sustainable development where learning is not happening. Thus, sustainable development is, for us, inherently a learning process through which we can, if we choose, learn to build capacity to live more sustainably.

Emphasising learning

The emphasis on *learning* here (rather than on teaching, instruction, training or other input processes) is deliberate for two reasons; firstly, the learning that will need to be done transcends schools, colleges and universities; it will be learning in, by and between institutions, organisations and communities – where most of our learning goes on anyway. Thus, we begin with a view of learning which is as *inclusive* as possible in order to draw in all the learning that a person does (lifelong) between birth and death, *including* all that done in formal education and training. The second reason is that, as we do not yet know what we shall need to learn in relation to sustainable development, it is hard to be definitive about what needs to be taught, except, perhaps that we need to be taught how to learn and how to be critical in order to build our collective capacity to live both sustainably and well.

Rationale

In relation to sustainable development, learning (or more precisely, lifelong learning) has been consistently seen by the United Nations and its agencies, national governments, the European Union and NGOs as a key component of innovation and development because it is acknowledged as a prime vector of social change. The argument goes: through schooling, further and higher education, professional training and development, and more informal awareness raising and capacity building, people can both be helped to begin to understand emerging ideas about the need for change, and be helped to engage in debate and critique of the issues, thus making meaning for themselves and developing personal and social action plans. In addition, it is now widely accepted by institutions of all kinds that there is a need for: (i) new ways of conceiving and operationalising learning with shifts in curriculum, pedagogy, and in institutional management practice; and (ii) novel approaches to the professional development of teachers, trainers and non-formal educators across the field.

The case relating learning to environmental issues has been advanced by the conservation and environmental education movements for many decades now.

However, the *World Commission on Environment and Development* (1987) influentially introduced the terminology of sustainable development, and this became a powerful focus for further work, such as that of the IUCN which, in 1990, produced *Caring for the Earth: a strategy for sustainability*. These ideas were further developed through Chapter 36 of *Agenda 21* following the Rio Earth Summit (1992), the UNESCO conference in Thessaloniki on educating for a sustainable future (1997), the UNESCO/World Bank conference on environmentally and socially sustainable development and other United Nations and NGO initiatives since that time. Additionally, the concept of sustainable development is now subjected to searching scrutiny across the full range of academic disciplines.

Activity and development of these kinds which support the linkage of (lifelong) learning to the process of sustainable development can now be seen both nationally and internationally and are partly a result of United Nations and other treaty obligations. The effectiveness of developments thus far was an important consideration at the World Summit on Sustainable Development (Rio + 10) in Johannesburg in 2002. Many issues, of course, remain. Though sustainable development is now actively pursued in many quarters, there exists a range of not-necessarily-compatible views about what exactly it is, how it might best be pursued, and the nature of the changes which will most appropriately support such developments. Because of this, and other factors, progress is variable both in scale and scope from one place to another. It is, however, this very contentiousness which underlines the need for the sort of critical exploration of issues which these books set out to achieve as they explore and open up the issues for study. The main point, however, which is compatible with both the goals of learning and sustainable development, is to help people build personal and social capacity so that they, as learners and social actors, are enabled to grapple with the issues and relate them to their own lives and work, while at the same time appreciating and empathising with the perspectives of other individuals and institutions whose social context and the issues they face may well be quite different.

This book, together with its companion volume, will enable readers to explore both the practical and theoretical consequences of the idea of sustainable development for learning, and help readers develop their own understandings. The book will provide a means by which readers can explore the continuing development of their own and others' positions in relation to explicit and implicit theories of both learning and sustainable development, recognising that different approaches to practice are likely to be grounded in, and defended, on particular ideological grounds, and contested by others. The book will focus on the joint development of curriculum and management in order to meet the demands of learners and will critique programmes which have little or no regard for the management realities of effective curriculum and institutional development. Structural and pedagogical issues will be explored in relation to curriculum design. A range of assessment and evaluation approaches which have been used in practice will be critically appraised from a number of theoretical positions. Problems underlying the design and application of assessment and evaluation instruments will be explored in relation to practical questions to do with how we can know whether learning is taking place, how we can know that sustainable development has been enhanced, and what indicators can sensibly be used to gain such information. The concept of social capacity building for sustainable development will be explored. Readers will be encouraged to develop informed views of how learning might best link to other key elements in capacity building. The relationship between environmentally beneficial behaviour and economically beneficial behaviour will be explored. In particular, the book will examine reasons for apparent oppositions between these desired ends. Readers will be able to reflect on the implications for their own professional work of the insight that economics and ecology are inseparable and mutually interdependent. The book will examine how contemporary life can be characterised by two apparently contradictory trends: towards globalisation (of language, meanings, symbols, economic structures, communications etc.), and towards fragmentation (of nation states, belief systems, cultures, families etc.). The book will involve readers in an exploration of the prospects for learning for sustainable development as a global process, but one which is targeted at what people and institutions do, each in their own time and place.

The structure of the book

Each of the fourteen chapters has a distinctive focus.

1 Framing the issues: complexity, uncertainty, risk and necessity

The book begins by identifying and exploring the four core themes which underpin the issues raised by both books: that is, complexity, uncertainty, risk and necessity. This opening chapter considers the significance of these ideas in the light of economic, social and environmental issues and how these relate to emerging notions of both sustainable development and learning. It introduces a number of ideas which are to be developed in subsequent chapters.

2 The policy context

Chapter 2 provides an overview of worldwide policies on sustainable development and learning, as pursued by governments, NGOs and institutions. Drawing on practical examples, it provides an indicative summary of the promise of these polices and the generic problems of implementation that policy makers face in attempting to carry them out in the face of inertia and competing claims and demands.

3 Language and meaning

Chapter 3 critically examines the many different meanings which have been attached to the term sustainable development, and the different ways in which 'learning' and its importance may be understood. It explores the relationship between language and environmental reality, how this relates to change processes, and the possible meanings of the notion of 'environmental literacy'.

4 Learning and sustainable development: making the linkages

By reference to a cross-disciplinary literature, national and international policy documents, and international case studies, Chapter 4 demonstrates how learning is necessarily a core component in sustainable development. Through its analysis of these case studies it sets out to equip readers with the skills necessary to identify opportunities for, and threats to, approaches to learning which promote sustainable development. The chapter considers the implications for sustainable development of established approaches to education, training and further learning, and examines the problems that can accrue.

5 Humans and nature: tensions and interdependence

Chapter 5 explores the different ways in which the relationship between humans and non-human nature may be conceptualised. It examines, in particular, the view that this relationship may most usefully be regarded as 'co-evolutionary' and considers the implications of such a view for everyday ideas such as resource exploitation and living in harmony with nature.

6 Theory and practice: ideology and philosophy

Using real-world examples and case studies, Chapter 6 shows how theory, practice, ideology and philosophy are inter-related in the sort of learning that promotes sustainable development. It explores how these aspects are related to the issue of meaning, and provides a model by means of which readers can explore their own and others' positions.

7 Management of learning: issues in curriculum design

Chapter 7 argues that curriculum content and management structures need to be mutually responsive if sustainable development is to be promoted through learning. It illustrates this by reference to four examples.

8 Curriculum and pedagogy

Building on this, Chapter 8 argues that the content and the organisational context of learning are necessarily both key considerations in the selection of appropriate pedagogical approaches. It outlines a framework for choosing appropriate pedagogies in different settings and illustrates the use of this, inviting readers to consider critically its appropriateness in their own contexts.

9 Measuring learning: aspects of assessment

Chapter 9 explores how we can know whether learning (and what learning) is taking place. It argues for a view of assessment which places it integrally within learning processes, sets out a range of assessment procedures which have been used and invites readers to appraise these critically in terms of key points re-iterated from the preceding chapters.

10 *Measuring effectiveness: monitoring and evaluation*

Chapter 10 explores how we can know that sustainability is being promoted or enhanced. It argues for a view of monitoring and evaluation as integral to learning, and sets out a range of procedures which might be used. It invites readers to appraise these critically in terms of key points re-iterated from the preceding chapters.

11 *Building capacity, developing agency: evolving a theory of change*

Chapter 11 explores the concept of social capacity building for sustainable development and the place of learning within it. It examines the possible value of a notion such as a 'learning society' in the context of sustainable development and employs international case studies as illustration of the complexity of such issues. The chapter encourages readers to apply to these the principles of assessment and evaluation established in the previous two chapters.

12 *Economic behaviour: value and values*

Chapter 12 examines the triangular relationship between environmental value, economic value and human values, and further explores the linkages between this set of relationships and the wants and interests which individuals and organisations have and which are expressed through economic behaviour. It offers readers structured opportunities to reflect on the possible role of learning in this context, drawing iteratively on key ideas within the book.

13 *Globalisation and fragmentation: science and self*

Chapter 13 draws together the threads of complexity, uncertainty, risk and necessity which have run through the book and examines some of the literature which describes and evaluates trends in contemporary life. It enables readers to explore the prospects for learning which promotes sustainable development globally, but which is targeted at what individuals and institutions do, each in their own time and place.

14 *What happens next?*

Chapter 14 returns to the policy context outlined in Chapter 2 and argues both that there must be many possibilities for progress to be made and that good policy will tolerate and promote a wide range of approaches to sustainable development. It argues that good learning will ensue to the extent that the advocates of different approaches constructively engage with each other.

1 Framing the issues
Complexity, uncertainty, risk and necessity

Introduction

The conjoining of the terms *learning* and *sustainable development* in the title of this book and its companion reader *Key Issues in Sustainable Development and Learning: a critical review* may seem quite natural to some readers but very much less so to others. It is certainly possible to be employed as a sustainable development professional, conducting environmental impact assessments for example, without having any interest in learning beyond the personal need to acquire information and skills. It is also possible to be a learning professional, organising vocational courses for unemployed adults perhaps, without ever having given much thought to sustainable development, either personally or professionally. It is our intention to argue that, nevertheless, learning and sustainable development are inextricably entwined. At the same time we hope to lay bare the issues surrounding this claim, and so enable readers to judge its worth for themselves.

Immediate difficulties concern the question of definition. Both terms have been defined in a number of different ways at the theoretical level, for practical purposes by policy makers, and by professionals in everyday usage. Dobson (1996), for example, has recorded over 300 definitions of sustainable development. Both terms also relate to and/or overlap with other terms (for example, lifelong learning, adult education, human resource development, training, sustainability, conservation, environmental management) in ways that are often ambiguous, unclear, and/or contested.

Definition is, of course, important. However, because a major purpose of this book is to seek to further develop definitions of both (lifelong) learning and sustainable development, each by reference to the other, we see definition as a core process of the book as well as a provisional starting point. It seems most appropriate, therefore, to set precision aside and begin with working definitions which are as *inclusive* as possible. Thus, for the time being we shall take *learning* to include all the learning that a person does between birth and death. One important consequence of this is that schooling is not excluded, and neither, therefore, are any consequences that schooling may have for what is learned in adult life, or for our abilities to learn. A second consequence is that work by others which is based on narrower definitions of learning, or which while clearly concerned with it does not explicitly use the term, is not excluded from consideration. Hence ideas as diverse as those of OECD (1996), which sees lifelong learning primarily as a means to economic competitiveness, and of Lauder and Brown (2000), who argue for the fostering of 'collective intelligence', lie within our field of interest, and both these works are considered in the companion reader.

In a similar way sustainable development is treated here, at least initially, as a set of contested ideas rather than as a settled issue. This set incorporates many different, and indeed competing, definitions of both sustainable development and sustainability. The extent of contestation surrounding these terms is illustrated by, for example, the work of Sachs (1991) who sees the linking of environment and development as a 'dangerous liaison', and Hopkins *et al.* (1996), who see sustainable development education as the focus of an 'international consensus'. As with lifelong learning, extracts from both are examined in the companion reader.

Exploring linkages

(Lifelong) learning and sustainable development have a number of aspects in common.

First, both are policy objectives. It is clear from Hopkins *et al.* (1996), for example, that these authors see sustainable development as a desirable, and indeed necessary, *goal.* In taking this view they are being entirely consistent with the report of the World Commission on Environment and Development (WCED, 1987 – and see chapter 11 of the companion reader) – which first thrust the notion of sustainable development into the limelight, and which so powerfully influenced the development of Agenda 21 (UNCED, 1992). Promotion of lifelong learning, and its universalisation through the creation of a learning society, has been put forward as a necessary policy goal in response to the existence of a Risk Society (Beck, 1992; Adams, 1995; Rosa, 2000; Strain, 2000 – and chapters 1 and 4 of the companion reader).

As policy objectives, sustainable development and learning both respond to perceptions that:

- Scientific and technological advances have caused the human species to have more control over, and be less at the mercy of, its environment than ever before
- These same advances have increased actual risks to humans, habitats, ecosystems and some other species because of the ways in which our scientific and technological interventions are managed, mismanaged or abused, and from uncertainties about the environment's responses to them
- There is increased powerlessness in the face of risk's now seeming pervasiveness, although as both Redclift and Le Grange note (chapter 1 of the companion reader) this may be a phenomenon of more concern in developed economies
- Within the human species the once apparently solid elements from which individual and group identities were constructed – class, gender, seniority, ethnicity, nationality and so on – have become increasingly fluid and unreliable.

Second however, both lifelong learning and sustainable development have been promoted as policy *instruments*, typically for the end purpose of enhancing economic competitiveness at both national and corporate levels. For example, the UK's Sustainable Development Education Panel (2001) has justified its efforts as necessary to long-term national competitiveness and companies such as Shell (Jones, 1997) have claimed sustainability as central to their business strategies. The European Commission (1996), OECD (1996) and the Group of Eight Industrialised Nations (1999) have all placed lifelong learning at the centre of competition policy, and there is evidence (Hamilton, 2001) to suggest that there is growing corporate interest in the commercial value of being a 'learning organisation' (Senge, 1992; Argyris and Schön, 1996 – and see companion reader).

A third similarity between the two terms is that both have become slogans (Field, 2000; Redclift, 1987; Sachs, 1991; Stables, 1996; 2001a,b) which can sometimes be used to give an impression of substance or coherence where little exists. Thus, both may often be viewed as bandwagons, to which more or less unlikely causes can be hitched opportunistically. It is probably fair to say that even their staunchest advocates can sometimes appear confused about whether (lifelong) learning and sustainable development are means to ends or ends in themselves. They are not unique in this as such problems readily arise where, in the pursuit of narrow initiatives and intentions (eg, educational programmes of numeracy, literacy and ICT) one can lose sight of the point of the entire exercise (ie, the ultimate liberal purpose of an education). Of course, it may be that in some quarters such confusion is welcome, or at least found to be of some use. Nevertheless, the ends/means distinction is significant. As Sterling (2001:15–16) notes, the choice is about doing more of the same, or doing something radically and deeply different.

Fourth, both sustainable development and lifelong learning are widely conceived as being incapable of operationalisation solely through the actions of governments (Carley and Christie, 1992; Field, 2000). They necessarily involve participation by citizens, and probably by other groups such as businesses and voluntary organisations. Social inclusion, and the key role of individuals, tends to be theorised as at the heart of both. Ehrenfeld (1995: 183) notes:

> The ultimate success of all our attempts to stop ruining nature will depend on a revision of the way we use the world in our everyday living when we are not thinking about conservation. If we have to conserve the earth in spite of ourselves, we will not be able to do it.

and Martin writes:

> All the government, scientists, experts, organizations, laws, and treaties in the world will achieve nothing unless there are free-thinking and freely-operating individuals in a position to make their own decisions about the future of their natural environment.
>
> (WWF, 1996: 27)

However, we would argue that such similarities between two currently quite fashionable terms are symptomatic of a deep and problematic coherence between important and enduring aspects of the social and natural worlds. We set out to show through this book and its companion volume that exploring this underlying reality has potential to add value in practical ways to society's ongoing efforts to sustain, learn, develop and live. One initial problem is that the ways in which language is used to bring clarity to some issues can often obscure others, and this is explored in detail in Chapter 3. In a similar way, in Chapter 2 we exemplify the linkage between sustainable development and learning showing congruence and inter-connectedness, and the issues this raises for each.

However, it seems important at the outset to explore the meanings of some of the key parameters of our discussion.

Society, nature, environment

Munasinghe and Shearer (1995) use the term 'biogeophysical' to describe the non-human natural world. It is important, however, to realise that, for all the social construction of reality, the laws which govern such biogeophysical processes are not negotiable by humans. They are 'natural' and, in this sense of the word, *Nature* itself is beyond human threat. If the Earth is one day devastated then the processes of physical destruction and recovery will follow such natural laws, both those known by humans and those not, regardless of whether the destructive agency is a random collision with a comet or asteroid, or the planned lunacy of a tyrant. In this context 'conserving Nature' makes little if any sense.

Of course, when we use the word 'Nature', we tend to be thinking of the ecology of the planet rather than the blind calculus of biogeophysical processes. Because of this, we imbue Nature, understood broadly like this, with meaning and sometimes, as in the case of 'Gaia' (Lovelock, 1979) or the 'Earth Mother' and the related ideas of some ecofeminists (Spretnak, 1990; Mies and Shiva, 1993; Merchant, 1990; Gough, 1997), with human characteristics. In fact, as Ross (1994 – and companion reader) has shown, it has been common in Western societies to attribute two contradictory sets of characteristics to Nature, seeing it on the one hand as a tooth and claw battle for the survival of the fittest, and on the other as an intricate self-sustaining, collaborative web. This dissonance is deeply rooted in popular culture and will be familiar to devotees of, for example, *The Lion King*, an animated film in which the interests of 'The Great Circle of Life' are served by lions eating antelope but not, apparently, by hyenas eating lion cubs. Nor should the attribution of meaning to Nature be necessarily despised, since it may have useful social consequences; but that is to stray too quickly into the realm of value, values and value judgements, which are discussed in detail in Chapter 12.

The important point for our discussion here is that biogeophysical laws describe the environment of Mars just as well as the environment of Earth: they describe *an environment*. Only by adding in the meanings we attach to our surroundings do we come to a description of *the* environment – that is, ours, the one we live in. It should be noted that meanings here refer not only to sentiments (fondness for a particular landscape, place or species, for example) but also to apparently robust concepts such as *resource*. Whether an object qualifies as a 'natural resource' depends on two things: whether we *can* do something with it, and whether we *want* to – and both of these are crucially properties of the human subject not the environmental object.

Natural laws, then, are givens: but the given-ness of *the* environment can and should be questioned. For example, the jungles of Borneo are a hostile and threatening environment for an ill-prepared European, but reassuringly familiar and nurturing for the Penan people. In time, the European might learn the indigenous population's skills of survival and come to a different view; or might import technologies to transform trees into furniture. The Penan might come to prefer a lifestyle in towns with libraries, restaurants and television – or not.

What emerges from this discussion, however, is a point of central importance in understanding our topic: that there is a distinction to be made between what society, nature and the environment *physically are* on the one hand, and *how we think about them* on the other. Figure 1.1 shows a set of possible ways of thinking about the relationship between society and the environment.

How the relationship between society and the environment is perceived depends on responses to two inter-related questions. These are:

- How far is the environment determined by human behaviour?
- How far is human behaviour determined by the environment?

Human behaviour is determined by . . .				
Biogeophysical factors	**A process of biogeophysical and social co-evolution**	**Social factors**		
Combination 1 **A possible combination**	**Combination 2** *Not possible*	**Combination 3** **A possible combination**	**Biogeophysical processes**	**The environment is produced through . . .**
Combination 4 *Not possible*	**Combination 5** **A possible combination**	**Combination 6** *Not possible*	**A process of biogeophysical and social co-evolution**	
Combination 7 *Not possible*	**Combination 8** *Not possible*	**Combination 9** **A possible combination**	**Social construction**	

Figure 1.1 Possible combinations of views of the relationship between society and the environment.

It is possible to offer a number of pairs of logically consistent answers to these, while other pairs of responses are logically impossible. Such is the flexibility of the term 'sustainable development' that it can be pressed into service by adherents of any of the logically possible combinations. These different combinations also have different implications for the role of learning.

In Figure 1.1, the pair of views (*Combination 1*):

- Human behaviour is determined by biogeophysical factors
- The environment is produced through biogeophysical processes

seems consistent with the sociobiological view that all social behaviour has a biological basis (Wilson, 1975). However, this position has been critiqued on a variety of grounds. For example, Redclift (1987) argues that it is reductionist, commits the naturalistic fallacy of supposing an identity between what is 'natural' and what is 'good', claims universal characteristics for human behaviour while ignoring the diversity of human cultures and ideologies, and has unpalatable implications for theories of development (sustainable or not) because of its distinct whiff of eugenics. Sociobiology also appears to place limits on what we can hope for from learning, since so much is ruled in or ruled out by immutable biological factors. Such notions of immutability are, however, heavily circumscribed by selectivity theory (Edelman, 1987) which holds that whatever personal genetic inheritance we humans might claim (or environmental nurturing influences we might suspect), 'neurons form random connections by random growth during (foetal/infant) development. Those connections that are reinforced from external inputs during neural development are stabilised, while the others decay and disappear.' (Lewontin, 2000: 38). This structuring and restructuring in the developing and maturing brain dramatically affects, in non-deterministic ways, who we are, and might yet become.

For deep ecologists such as Devall and Sessions (1985: 74) – and Chapter 5 of the companion reader, the reality would seem to be one of socially determined human behaviour disrupting or sustaining biogeophysically determined environmental processes (*Combination 3*). For them a key question is: 'What kind of a society would be best for maintaining a particular ecosystem?', and much emphasis is placed on achieving spiritual harmony with nature. Tyler Miller Jnr. (1990: 613) writes:

> Somehow we must tune our senses to the beat of existence, sensing in nature fundamental rhythms we can trust even though we will never fully understand them.

Views of this kind have been critiqued by Luke (1988) as little more than a modern myth of humanity's fall. They also take a purposively one-sided view of what constitutes harmony, which is a state of being that, for example, gazelles and lions would surely never agree on, even if they could. They are also open to critique on the grounds that they are based on an outdated view of ecological succession (Holling, 1995). As Cronon (1990: 1128) also notes:

We can no longer assume the existence of a static and benign climax community in nature that contrasts with dynamic, but destructive, human change.

For the deep ecologist sustainable development must mean personal and spiritual change if it is to mean anything at all. There is a clear role for learning but perhaps only a questionable one for training or instruction (the distinction between these terms is touched on in Chapter 4). For example, Orr (1992) believes all education to be environmental education, and that the achievement of sustainability depends on the social replication of the structure and function of natural systems. He argues (Orr, 2001: 7–9) that 'We must build authentic and vibrant communities that sustain us ecologically and spiritually (and find) a new understanding of ourselves and our place in nature and time.' It is interesting however that, nevertheless, deep ecology has found a degree of theoretical applicability in the field of corporate environmental management (Bhargava and Welford, 1996).

Also interesting is that such assumptions of socially determined human behaviour 🦗 and a biogeophysically determined environment are shared by positivist researchers in environmental education. Here, the declared purpose is to change human behaviour in order to develop an environmentally responsible citizenry capable of initiating environmental action on the basis of appropriate, scientifically discoverable knowledge (see, for example, Hungerford and Volk, 1990; Roth, 1970).

A number of ecofeminist writers have also sought to maintain an element of deep ecology in their work, while at the same time insisting that the environment is essentially a social, rather than a biogeophysical phenomenon. For them, in the terms of Figure 1.1, human behaviour is socially determined and the environment is a social construct (*Combination 9*). For example, Greenall Gough (1993 – and chapter 12 of the companion reader) and Merchant (1990) both express regret at what they see as the social reconstruction during the sixteenth and seventeenth centuries of the image of the cosmos from an essentially female and organic entity into a male controlled machine. Emphasis on the social origins of human behaviour and the social construction of the environment is also found in socially critical theories of environmental education, as is a claim to ecocentricity (Fien, 1993), although this is arguably based on a mis-reading of O'Riordan's ideas (O'Riordan, 1981; 1989; 1990; Gough *et al.*, 2000). One problem here is that, if what is important about the environment is its social-constructedness, and if, as Shiva (1989: 28) writes:

> There is nothing like a neutral fact about nature independent of the value determined by human cognitive and economic activity

it seems difficult to substantiate the claim to ecocentricity, and therefore to any attachment to deep ecology. As Ross (1994) puts it, it is important not to confuse wisdom about nature for the wisdom *of* nature. That this is a theoretical problem is clear from Huckle's (1983: 104) revealing concern that liberal and Gaianist ideologies can lead to 'a rather naïve respect for both children and the environment'. It would seem that in this socially critical discourse the key concern is not ultimately with the spirituality of the individual, nor with nature, but with a broad-brush social project of a particular kind. This focus on achieving social change of a pre-specified sort is something held in common with the economic growth-focused approaches to lifelong learning mentioned earlier, a point made powerfully over time by Bowers (1993, 1995; 2001 – and chapter 11 of the companion reader).

To argue both for the biogeophysical determination of human behaviour *and* the social construction of the environment seems impossibly circular (*Combination 7*). This leaves only one coherent position remaining (*Combination 5*) in Figure 1.1, since co-evolution of human behaviour and the environment would seem to require that *both* are able to *initiate* change as well as be changed by the other, thus ruling out *Combinations 2/4/6/8*.

A co-evolutionary view of society and environment

The idea of the co-evolution of ecological and social systems has been theorised in the context of agricultural development by Norgaard (1984) (and see companion reader) who identifies the origins of co-evolutionary thinking in the (otherwise dramatically disparate) works of Alfred Marshall and Karl Marx, and acknowledges the influences of Boserup (1965), Wilkinson (1973) and Simon (1977) on its development.

For Norgaard, human activities:

> modify the ecosystem, while the ecosystem's responses provide cause for individual action and social organization.
>
> (Norgaard 1984: 528)

Such co-evolution is not necessarily beneficial to humans and does not necessarily result in 'development' or 'progress'. Humans are able to influence ecosystems (i.e., the environment) through their social institutions, including those which promote learning, but in a complex, non-linear, feedback-modified fashion which is unlikely to result in precisely the outcomes initially planned, and is capable in principle of inducing catastrophe. This is mirrored in education where learners rarely learn precisely what teachers set out to teach (Stables, 2002; Stables and Scott, 2001). Similarly, while ecosystem trends may threaten or promote human life, they should be extrapolated with caution, since human institutions can be expected to adapt and, in adapting, influence the process of ecosystem change itself. An example of this would be where unexpected coastal erosion arises from attempts to ameliorate damage by flooding caused by spring tides.

To accept the idea of co-evolution has a number of important implications. First, learning is central to the relationship between society and nature. People learn, organisations learn and, in a sense, the environment learns as nature responds to the results of human learning and activity. Second, authors as diverse as Sterling (1993) and North (1995) are surely correct when they argue that any dichotomy between 'economy' and 'environment' is false. Humans do not face a choice between benefiting the economy or benefiting the environment, but rather between different compatible combinations of the two. Third, as experience shows (see also Lomborg,

2001: 29) linear predictions of environmental catastrophe such as *The Limits to Growth* (Meadows *et al.*, 1972) should be treated with extreme caution. Fourth, we cannot model the future on our understanding of the past. Whether associated with the Earth Goddess (Spretnak, 1990), 'primal peoples' (Devall and Sessions, 1985), or something else, there was, save in creation myths, no 'golden age' of the environment to which we can seek to return. A co-evolutionary approach would see these and all other times past as points on a continuum of change, and not as natural equilibrium positions capable of restoration by one means or another. Fifth, any *management* of co-evolutionary development, for example through policy or educational interventions designed to make it 'sustainable', will necessarily require a sophisticated theory of change to guide it. Finally, however, it *is* important to note that, *within* a co-evolutionary understanding, scope remains for debate about the degree of *independent* influence over social and natural processes which humans can have. Figure 1.2 models some of the relationships that emerge from this discussion.

Human society exists in a dynamic context of social and natural reality which it is possible to know (for the present at least) only imperfectly, and which is constructed and given meaning in different ways by different people and organisations. As this context changes, learning takes place, both planned and unplanned, giving rise to further, often competing theories, of nature, of society and of change itself.

One powerful analytical method which has been used to try to understand this complex situation makes use of the interests that different people and groups have. This approach has been particularly associated with socially critical theory. The work of John Huckle (1983; 1991; 1996) provides a powerful example in relation to learning and the environment. However, it was noted earlier that those aspects of social structure which have in the past been most closely associated with the identification of interests have become increasingly unreliable as predictors in modern times. To put it quite brutally, a meaningful distinction can usefully be made between the interests social scientists *say* people have, the interests people *themselves* say they have, and the interests which appear to be expressed through what people *actually do*. Thus, we can ask: how do people come to think that they have the interests which are reflected in their actions in particular settings and at particular

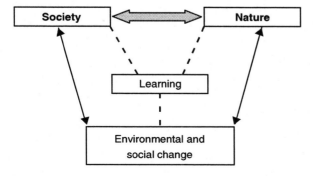

Figure 1.2 Relationships between society, nature, learning and change.

times? One approach which has tried to shed light on this process is that of cultural theory (Thompson, Ellis, and Wildavsky, 1990). Cultural theory has been influential in the fields of risk and environmental management (Adams, 1995; Thompson, 1990; James and Thompson, 1989; Thompson, 1997; Schwarz and Thompson, 1990 – and chapter 1 of the companion reader). However, its value and applicability are contested (Sjöberg, 1997). It is not our purpose here to seek to settle these debates, but rather to suggest that there is, within cultural theory, a useful, if possibly incomplete, set of categories which have value in analysing particular situations in relation to sustainable development and learning.

Cultural theory and the co-evolutionary view

An approach from cultural theory starts from the observation that human knowledge, both of the natural environment and of human interactions with it, is imperfect and characterised by uncertainty and risk. In the face of this uncertainty and risk, social actors construct their interpretations of environmental reality. Such interpretations, it is theorised, may lie within a range bounded by four archetypal interpretations: the fatalistic; the hierarchical; the individualistic; and the egalitarian.

These archetypes, in turn, represent possible combinations across two dimensions of social organisation which have been presented in a variety of ways. The one we shall prefer for the present is equality/inequality, and competition/no competition, as proposed by James and Thompson, 1989.

1   *The fatalist* (competition/inequality)
   - nature seen as capricious
   - trust to luck
   - what will be will be

2   *The hierarchist* (no competition/inequality)
   - nature seen as tolerant if properly managed – but otherwise perverse
   - trust established organizations
   - institutions should regulate behaviour in relation to the environment by making social rules

3   *The individualist* (competition/equality)
   - nature seen as benign
   - trust successful individuals
   - markets should regulate behaviour in relation to the environment

4   *The egalitarian* (no competition/equality)
   - nature seen as fragile and ephemeral
   - trust local participatory organisations
   - considerations of equity and justice should regulate behaviour in relation to the environment

Thus, the fatalist visualises the natural world as competitive and unequal, but for the individualist it is competitive and equal; and while the expectations of the hierarchist are built upon assumptions of inequality and uncompetitiveness, those of the egalitarian assume uncompetitiveness with equality.

Each archetype is further associated with a 'myth of nature'. For the fatalist, nature is capricious; for the individualist, it is benign. Hierarchists suppose nature to be benign within certain limits, but perverse if those limits are exceeded. Finally, egalitarians view nature as ephemeral; a delicate equilibrium which may be easily and irretrievably destroyed. Which interpretation or myth of nature an individual is likely to favour is a result of social influences or 'solidarities' (Thompson, 1997: 142) and is not immutable. Indeed, solidarities, and therefore interpretations, may shift repeatedly over time and in response to changes of social context such as that from, say, family home to workplace, and depending on the roles adopted from time to time within contexts, as noted by Adams (1995: 201) and commented on by Redclift in chapter 1 of the companion reader.

This approach is broadly consistent with the co-evolutionary analysis outlined above in its approach to issues of nature and society. Thompson (1997: 142) notes that, 'humans are both a part of nature and apart from nature.' He continues:

> The different forms of social solidarity of which we are the vital parts result in our knowing in several different ways, and it is this plurality of knowledges – often contradictory knowledges – that has to be addressed if we are to have effective policies.

It may be helpful at this point to summarise the main points made in this first chapter. These are that:

- Human relationships with nature are dynamic, complex and mutually influencing
- People form a constituent part of an environment which they comprehend in part, but have no foreseeable prospect of understanding completely. Learning, however, is possible
- Change is not only possible, but unavoidable, and may also lead to learning. However, such change will often take place in a hit-and-miss, surprise-prone fashion. It is subject to, and limited by, the responses of the ecosystem itself
- There are *at least* four distinct ways in which individuals and organisations make sense of complexity, cope with uncertainty, perceive risk and determine what is necessary in particular contexts and at particular times.

These issues are explored in the remainder of this book and in the companion reader.

2　The policy context

Introduction: policy origins of sustainable development and the crucial role of learning

In Chapter 1 it was noted that sustainable development and learning are both, separately, of considerable interest to policy makers. However, what is really of 'interest' in particular cases may vary a great deal. This is sometimes, but not always, reflected in the language used. For example, there are those who use the word 'sustainability' as a preferred alternative to 'sustainable development', thus perhaps avoiding perceived connotations of the word 'development' (for example, Huckle, 1996). Also, 'lifelong learning' may be used in such a way as to be distinct from 'education'. Further, both these terms are also often tacitly seen as essentially public-sector concerns, whereas 'training' may be much more a corporate-sector responsibility.

The history of sustainable development policy probably begins with the 1972 Stockholm Conference on the Human Environment. This led to the Stockholm Declaration, and established the issue of environmental management on the global policy agenda. Subsequently, the United Nations Environment Programme (UNEP) was set up. The origin of the use of the term 'sustainable development' is often considered to be in the report of the World Commission on Environment and Development (WCED) – or 'Brundtland Report' – of 1987 (see chapter 11 of the companion reader) though according to Rao (2000) the term had earlier appeared around 1980 in the literature of the World Conservation Union, the IUCN.

In 1992, following a UN resolution in 1989, the UN Conference on Environment and Development (UNCED) was held in Rio de Janeiro. This produced the 'work plan' known as Agenda 21, which has 40 chapters. Chapter 36 of this document (see chapter 2 of the companion reader) specifically concerns 'promoting education, public awareness and training'. It is extremely broad in scope, but identifies three 'programme areas' for learning, in addition to the prerequisite necessity to achieve universal access to education. These programme areas are: (i) reorienting education to sustainable development; (ii) increasing public awareness; and, (iii) promoting training. Other particularly significant consequences of UNCED were the setting up of a UN Commission on Sustainable Development (UNCSD), and impetus towards the signing of the Convention on Biological Diversity (1993), and the Framework Convention on Climate Change (1994).

In subsequent years a number of further meetings took place relating to sustainable development, including conferences on population (1994, Cairo), women (1995, Beijing), climate (1995, Berlin), and food (1996, Rome). UNCSD reviewed progress on Chapter 36 in 1996, producing an updated 'work programme' (Hopkins *et al.*, 1996, and chapter 11 of the companion reader) with the following priorities:

- Develop a broad international alliance, taking into account past experience and promoting networks
- Integrate implementation of recommendations concerning education, public awareness and training in the action plans of the major UN conventions and conferences
- Advise on how education and training can be integrated into national educational policies
- Refine the concept and key messages of education for sustainable development
- Advance education and training at national level
- Provide financial and technical support
- Develop new partnership arrangements among different sectors of society. Exploit new communications technologies. Take into account cultural diversity
- Work in partnership with youth
- Analyse current investments in education
- Take the preliminary results of the work programme on Chapter 36 into account in the 1997 review
- Make relevant linkages with the UNCSD programme of work on changing production and consumption patterns.

In 1997, the Earth Summit Plus Five review of progress was held, described by Rao (2000: 16) as 'rather unimpressive, and . . . much less eventful than the original summit'. However, steps to promote Chapter 36 did continue, for example the UNESCO 'Teaching and Learning for a Sustainable Future' multimedia teacher education programme (see Chapter 7). This particular initiative is interesting, because through its use of state-of-the-art electronic technology it provides a substantive response to a UNCSD 'priority' – that of 'exploiting new communications technologies' – which, by itself, seems hopelessly vague.

In August 2002 the UN Rio plus Ten World Summit on Sustainable Development was held in Johannesburg. As we shall see, it is far from clear that this meeting even maintained interest in education and learning at its previous, post-Rio level. However, and perhaps paradoxically, this is not to say that it gave no impetus to particular learning interventions at the time (see Chapter 10 and Chapter 14 – and chapter 14 of the companion reader).

Examples of sustainable development learning initiatives

A number of initiatives in countries around the world have sought to combine sustainable development and learning in various ways. Table 2.1 provides some examples of these.

Table 2.1 Some examples of sustainable development learning initiatives.

International	National	Local/regional
1 Mainstreaming environmental education into programmes (Department for International Development)	4 Developing environmental/ development skills: the empowerment of women in Pakistan (World Wildlife Fund)	7 Local Biodiversity Action Planning (Department for Environment, Food and Rural Affairs)
2 Ecoregion Conservation (World Wildlife Fund)	5 A Greener School and Village: livelihood and conservation. The production of vegetable charcoal in Tanzania (Tanzania Environmental Education Programme)	8 Solid waste management and education on the Caribbean island of St Lucia
3 Teaching and Learning for a Sustainable Future (UNESCO)	6 Learning to Last (Learning and Skills Development Agency)	9 Environmental learning* at Kampong Ayer, Brunei Darussalam

The examples shown are not intended to be representative, but they are interesting in their own right, and illustrate a number of frequently occurring tensions and paradoxes which are discussed later in this chapter. Many other projects and programmes both relate to learning, and appear to contribute implicitly to sustainable development, without actually using these terms.

Example 1: Mainstreaming environmental education into programmes

In 2000 the Field Studies Council, an environmental NGO, was asked by the UK government's Department for International Development (DFID) to undertake a project to research and write an *Issues Paper* on the mainstreaming of environmental education in DFID's programmes.

To deliver the project the FSC entered into a consortium with the Department of Education at the University of Bath and the International Education Unit of the School of Education at King's College, London. This team was supported by a consultative group of experts and a wider network of environmental educators. The team undertook a study of the linkages between environmental education and poverty eradication in developing countries and countries in transition, including a

---

* Environmental learning is defined purposefully broadly here as learning which accrues or is derived from an engagement with the environment or environmental ideas and thus can be the outcome from formal or non-formal educational programmes in schools, and/or communities, from designated 'environmental education' or 'education for sustainable development' interventions or from personal or incidental learning where no teacher or instructor was involved.

review of the global literature, and field studies in Pakistan and the Caribbean region. The study examined the institutional, legislative, policy and economic factors bearing on learning, the environment, and development, and provided advice and recommendations (Hindson *et al.*, 2001).

Example 2: Ecoregion conservation

An ecoregion is a relatively large segment of the earth's surface which contains a characteristic set of species, communities, dynamics and environmental conditions. WWF has identified more than 200 such ecoregions globally. Ecoregions are biological coherent, and this makes it possible to set strategic conservation goals which focus on those sites, populations, ecological processes and threats that are most important. They also provide an appropriate scale for assessing ecological viability, taking account of networks of key sites, migration corridors and large scale ecological dynamics. However, biological coherence does not necessarily imply social coherence, and ecoregions often cross political and administrative boundaries. For example, the Bering Sea ecoregion lies partly within the United States and partly within the Russian Federation. Learning is seen as being important within processes of ecoregion conservation at two levels. First, there is a need for learning to occur by the various stakeholders within ecoregions. Second, there is a recognised need for learning to occur within WWF itself, between those with different regional and/or disciplinary specialisms.

Example 3: UNESCO's 'Teaching and Learning for a Sustainable Future'

This programme is a free multimedia teacher education programme (see also Chapter 7). It contains 100 hours of professional development for use in pre-service teacher courses as well as in the in-service education of teachers, curriculum developers, education policy makers, and authors of educational materials. The stated objectives of the programme are:

- To develop an appreciation of the scope and purpose of educating for a sustainable future
- To clarify concepts and themes related to sustainable development and how they can be integrated in all subject areas across the school curriculum
- To enhance skills for integrating issues of sustainability into a range of school subjects and classroom topics
- To enhance skills for using a wide range of interactive and learner-centred teaching and learning strategies that underpin the knowledge, critical thinking, values and citizenship objectives implicit in reorienting education towards sustainable development
- To encourage wider awareness of Information and Communication Technologies (ICTs), the potential of multimedia-based approaches to education and the potential of the Internet as a rich source of educational materials
- To enhance skills in computer literacy and multimedia education.

Example 4: Developing environmental/development skills

The community development programme of WWF Pakistan has facilitated the empowerment of women by assisting a local community NGO in the suburbs of Lahore to shift the emphasis within project activity from awareness-raising to action-orientation with a view to bringing about change. The project focused on women as catalysts of change. It set up a 20-strong women's group which, over a period of 18 months, obtained significant resources from the local authority, instigated practical community-based projects such as vegetable and nursery gardens, and secured useful local political leverage. The programme's success has led to other community-based initiatives in Pakistan with workshops educating local women in practical environmental/development skills (Sterling, 1998).

Example 5: A greener school and village: livelihood and conservation

Primary school teachers from Kiroka, who attended the initial Tanzania Environmental Education Programme (TEEP)* workshops in 1992 on greening the school and the community, have been key catalysts in improving the local environment. They translated the workshop's conservation message into action working with fellow teachers, pupils and adult learners, and with school inspectors who had also attended the workshops.

At Kiroka, the bare areas surrounding the school buildings were bounded by stones and planted with grass and trees, simple soil erosion control measures were undertaken on erosion gullies, tree seeds were obtained from a local Women's Forestry Group, and a variety of trees were planted in the school farm. Fish ponds were dug and stocked to meet pupils' nutritional needs, and an agroforestry project started. Surpluses are sold with the proceeds going to the school fund.

Yohana Komba, one of the teachers behind the Kiroka initiative, went on to invent a vegetable charcoal which is now used by the community as an alternative to the conventional charcoal, thus reducing the use of scarce wood, and addressing severe local deforestation, one of the most pressing problems in the area. Yohana has won several international awards for this discovery and is now teaching other villages how to create and use this alternative energy source. (Sterling, 1998; WWF, 1999b).

Example 6: 'Learning to Last'

The book *Learning to Last: skills, sustainability and strategy* (Cohen *et al.*, 2002) was launched by the UK's Learning and Skills Development Agency (LSDA) in September 2002 at the Natural History Museum in London. A press release identified the context of the launch as that of the 2002 World Summit on Sustainable Development in Johannesburg, which, in particular, 'has drawn attention to the alarming gap between rich and poor, the continued abuse of the earth's resources and the need for

---

* NB: TEEP was funded by WWF and by the UK's Department for International Development (DfID).

a culture change amongst the world's wealthiest nations if the goals of a sustainable future are to be met'. *Learning to Last* explores the role of learning in shaping attitudes and action, and bringing about sustainable development. Its main purpose is to inform policy and strategic development of appropriate learning and skills. Launching the book, Lord Whitty, Minister for Food, Farming and Sustainable Energy at the Department for Environment, Food and Rural Affairs (DEFRA) said:

> *Learning to Last* is a product of the LSDA's dedication to fulfilling their sustainable development remit and I hope it becomes essential reading for everyone with an interest in promoting sustainable development. As citizens we all have a responsibility to consider sustainability and education plays a vital role in building sustainable practice into everyday life.

Example 7: Local biodiversity action planning

Another DEFRA initiative, Local Biodiversity Action Plans (LBAPs) are seen as integral to the implementation of Agenda 21 at the local level. Within the overall objective of involving communities in working towards sustainable development, conserving biodiversity is considered to be both a goal and an opportunity. In conjunction with the Council for Environmental Education (CEE), a DEFRA 'Guidance Note' was produced to support local level learning initiatives which promote biodiversity conservation within the sustainable development agenda. A national meeting of LBAP co-ordinators was held in 2002 to provide networking opportunities, and inputs from specialists and policy makers. The 'Guidance Note' comments that: 'True learning develops through applying concepts to real situations. Involvement in the LBAP process . . . can increase understanding of biodiversity and inspire participants to take action in their personal and professional lives'.

Example 8: Solid waste management and education on the Caribbean island of St Lucia

In St Lucia, solid waste management both drives and reacts to development. Building on a project of the Organisation of East Caribbean States, and with support form DFID, the St Lucia Solid Waste Management Authority (SWMA) has developed a revolutionary approach to solid waste disposal. Waste collection has been privatised and is operated as a competitive industry under SWMA regulation. This has helped to re-invigorate local economies while improving the service. It is linked to a strong programme of learning targeted across the community. Targeted groups include heads of households, waste contractors, retailers, fishermen, farmers, shipping and tour agents, building contractors and teachers. According to Carleen Jules and Michael Cowling of SWMA (1999: 6):

> The core philosophy behind public awareness and education strategies is that popular support for any issue can be greatly increased if the relevant public is

informed about it adequately and comprehensively. This is particularly true for issues where non-cooperation from the public will lead to negative effects on themselves, particularly their health.

Example 9: Environmental learning at Kampong Ayer, Brunei Darussalam

In 1994 the Ministry of Development of the south-east Asian country of Brunei Darussalam undertook a public awareness campaign to support the introduction of a new solid waste disposal technology in the Brunei River settlement of Kampong Ayer. This site is important not only because of its high population density, but also because of its status within the country's cultural and environmental heritage, and its potential as a resource for tourism. In addition to an exhibition, posters, leaflets and a series of Malay-language TV commercials, the project produced a set of resources for primary schools which were free of charge, locally focused and reproducible in both Malay and in English. Teachers and head teachers were involved in the development of these materials, which were designed to be usable in the context of a number of different school subjects.

Tensions and paradoxes

All of the above examples have much to recommend them as policy initiatives in themselves. However, juxtaposing them in this way raises a number of issues.

Change versus continuity

As noted in Chapter 1, both our focal terms make it possible to appeal (ingenuously or otherwise!) to two quite different constituencies. On the one hand, both seem to offer a radical response to what can be perceived as a new and substantial set of problems facing society – amounting, in the view of many, to a crisis. From this perspective, learning and sustainable development are all about change: about recognising that society cannot continue as it is; about questioning whether we should *want* society to continue as it is; and about responding in imaginative and adaptive ways. Timothy O'Riordan offers an insightful analysis from this perspective in Chapter 2 of the companion reader.

On the other hand, both learning and sustainable development can be pressed into service as technocratic and/or social fixes. From this perspective, by contrast, society-as-it-is needs conserving in the face of new problems, and these are the policies to achieve that goal. Change is still seen as essential, but it is change of a different, less fundamental order. As we noted in Chapter 1, Sterling (2001: 15/16) sees the choice as between change in terms of doing something radically and deeply different, and change within current frameworks: essentially doing more of the same. A tension for policy makers, and everyone else alike, is that of wondering whether short-term policy fixes to address the immediate problems will actually get in the way of, or delay, the longer-term change deemed (by some at least) ultimately necessary. Debates round the world about curriculum, about health care provision, and about pension reform all exemplify the difficulties inherent here. Example 8 above illustrates this well, since the SWMA is simultaneously (and ingeniously) fixing an environmental management problem and developing transferable skills in market-driven behaviour. In the example from Brunei also, there is an acute tension between *preserving* the past and *engaging with* the future.

Empowerment versus prescription

As was also noted in Chapter 1, both lifelong learning and sustainable development tend to be discourses of empowerment, at least in the minimal sense of requiring participation and appropriate, self-initiated action by individuals and their families. It is hard to see how either could simply be mandated by governments with any enduring success. However, people who are 'empowered' in the hope that they will do one thing have a stubborn way of doing another: particularly so, perhaps, when the transfer of power is not accompanied by any parallel transfer of real resources, but rather treated as an opportunity to effect savings at the centre. This may go some way to explain the phenomenon that, in relation to international educational aid policy, as the emphasis on learning and skills has tended to increase, so budgets have often tended to be cut (Müller, 1997). A further point is that empowerment of some people will often imply disempowerment of others, and those with power may be inclined to resist its removal. Power relations, and the ideologies which sustain or challenge them, will therefore be an influence on research in the field, whether explicitly or implicitly (Fien, 2002). So, for example, in relation both to ecoregion conservation and local biodiversity action planning, there may well be tension between using resources in ways which seem to be the most empowering of the most people, and using resources in ways which have the greatest impact in terms of environmental conservation. We return to this issue in Chapter 8.

'Me' versus 'we'

An important reason why empowered citizens do not always do as policy makers would wish is that the interests of society-at-large (with which policy makers tend, quite properly, to concern themselves) and the interests of particular groups or individuals may not coincide. This is well understood in the field of risk-communication, for example, where research evidence is clear that factors which are immediate, certain and personal in their effects are likely to carry more weight in individual decision making than those which are prospective, uncertain and collective (Krause, 1996). Any case for participation in lifelong learning and/or for the adoption of sustainable lifestyles is likely to have only limited public appeal to the extent that it promises potential future benefits for society as a whole, but involves short-term costs for individuals. Hence, even where teachers are sympathetic to the analysis offered by the UNESCO 'Teaching and Learning for a Sustainable Future' project, they may well find that, at the margin, they wish to give priority to immediate concerns such as meeting curriculum requirements, satisfying parent or business stakeholders, or maintaining classroom order.

Present generations versus future generations

This point is really a special case of the preceding one. However, it seems sufficiently important to merit separate treatment. Learning to support sustainable development necessarily has a focus on the interests of future generations and on skills of participation in inclusive decision-making processes. Agenda 21 (47) states that it: 'addresses the pressing problems of today but also aims at preparing the world for the challenges of the next century'. These are fine words, but they remain problematic as a guide for the use of scarce resources in situations where the present generation of young people are hungry and/or participation in civil society is constrained (Bak, 1995; Hindson *et al.*, 2001).

This is also a problem where global sustainable development may involve (real or apparent) present losses to future generations in some settings. For example, the 'Learning to Last' initiative highlights a tension between local sustainability initiatives in rich countries, which may tend to support traditional rural communities, and global sustainability imperatives, in terms of which these communities simply *are* unsustainable. This is because the inequality they embody is, and can be, maintained only by subsidies. However, rich-country farmers may not themselves feel very rich, and may not see why they should bear the cost of caring for rather vaguely defined 'future generations'.

Humans versus nature

This can also be seen as a special case of 'me' versus 'we'. The tensions are revealed in Chapter 5 which explores the different ways in which the relationship between humans and non-human nature may be conceptualised, and in the vignettes from Richard D. North and Tim Luke in chapter 5 of the companion reader. There was concern from some environmental NGOs going into the 2002 UN World Summit on Sustainable Development in Johannesburg that the Summit's emphasis on poverty eradication, and on bringing clean water and adequate sanitation to those without it (no matter how important that remains) was diverting attention from environmental issues: biodiversity loss, climate change, air pollution and so on. Environmental NGOs had two concerns: first, and near universally, that attention was being diverted in absolute terms from important environmental issues; second, but less universally, that the focus of the Summit on economic development in order to achieve Millennium goals of reducing illiteracy, infant mortality and poverty could only make matters worse. This is relevant in the Chihuahuan Desert ecoregion, for example, where poverty eradication on both sides of the US/Mexico border may appear to depend, in the short-to-medium-term at least, on increased use of environmental resources of all kinds (see also Chapter 13).

Local versus global

With regard to lifelong learning and sustainable development it is possible for what is locally appropriate to be globally (or nationally, or regionally) inappropriate. That learning which best serves the immediate or medium-term sustainability interests of individual learners and their communities may run counter to identified learning requirements for sustainable development at wider geographical and social scales. Conversely, learning aims proposed for the promotion of long-term global sustainable development may run counter to the imperatives of local-level, short-to-medium-term survival. Questions which ultimately hang over local level initiatives such as those described in Pakistan and Tanzania are: 'what happens when and if these enterprises begin to produce a surplus over immediate needs?' and 'what happens when and if local production is undercut by the produce of even poorer people?'. We might also ask whether the successful entrepreneurs in these cases should be entitled (in the interests of equality perhaps) to a wider – and therefore more widely marketable – business education.

Rich, poor and very poor

Much of the literature of sustainable development emphasises the essentially participatory nature of the concept. However, it does not necessarily follow from this that the *route* to sustainability will everywhere and always be participatory in the first instance. An interesting idea which emerged during a joint Russian/British conference on environmental education for sustainable development held at Moscow State University in 2002 follows from the notion that there might exist a special form of 'environmental Kuznets curve' (Levinson, 2000; Ekins, 1997), in this case relating the propensity of the population in a given country to care for nature to that country's level of economic development. This would suggest that the very poor tend to care greatly about the *local* natural environment because it is often directly implicated in their survival. The relatively rich tend to care too, because they are secure enough in the medium term to perceive and react to long-term threats, inconveniences or opportunities for outdoor recreation. Between these extremes, daily survival is separated from the *immediate* environmental context and environmental resources are likely to be seen as a means of self-advancement. We might think of the basis of such a model in terms of Maslow's (1943) 'hierarchy of needs', according to which as one kind of need is satisfied another kind arises. For the very poor the natural environment is essential for the satisfaction of survival needs. For the rich it becomes a means to feelings of self-expression and accomplishment. However, its perceived significance to those whose needs lie between these extremes, and are focused on the achievement of safety, social status or ego-gratification, may be low. If at all correct, the implication of this idea is that participatory approaches to learning and sustainable development might be expected to enjoy some success in poor countries (e.g. Pakistan, Tanzania), and in the richest countries (e.g. the UK). However, in countries which lie between these extremes and are undergoing rapid economic development things may be much more problematic. The view of the Russian delegation to the Moscow meeting was strongly that top-down direction of learning would be necessary in the short-term if sustainable development was to be achieved. Other evidence from the Russian Federation tends to support this view (Kasimov *et al.*, 2002).

Disconnected lumps of joined-up thinking

Both learning and sustainable development each contain within them a wide range of complex sub-issues. The intersection of the two ideas is even more complex and correspondingly difficult to manage – a point made with some force by Stephen Sterling in chapter 4 of the companion reader. One result of this is a proliferation of initiatives, committees and other bodies, each at least partly concerned with some aspect of the problem and often, equally, quite unconcerned with other aspects. A review of UK policy has recently argued (Reid *et al.*, 2002: 253) that:

> there is now a priority need for integrated and integrative leadership, within and across sectors, which synthesises existing knowledge and best practice, and makes them available to ongoing initiatives . . . Government, its ministries and agencies have a crucial role in stimulating such leadership . . . (and) an equally important role in encouraging all stakeholders not to wait for a lead from others, but to take their own initiatives.

By way of illustration we might note that, even in a small country such as St Lucia, in 2001 the following official bodies had a direct interest in environmental learning, *in addition to* the SWMA: the Ministry of Planning, Development, Environment and Housing; the Ministry of Agriculture, Forestry and Fisheries; the Ministry of Education; the National Conservation Authority.

The place of policy making

The implications of our discussion for policy making are a thread that runs throughout this book. Some of the issues raised above receive special attention in particular chapters. A number of these links have been pointed out in the preceding sections. As we move forward with our discussion the following are all points which should be borne in mind.

First, policy making is as much a result of what happens as it is a cause. Second, in relation to the natural environment, policy is often made under circumstances of complexity and uncertainty according to perceptions of risk and necessity. The 'best available' evidence may not, in fact, be much help. Third, how 'good' policy on sustainable development and learning turns out to be is likely to be a function of the geographical and temporal scales (as well as the social-interest vantage point) against which it is judged. Good short-term policy often has long-term costs and vice versa. Similarly, local gain may mean wider pain, and the reverse. Fourth, the 'customers' of learning policy and development policy respectively are likely to consider themselves to have needs and rights unrelated to sustainable development. Policy makers cannot ignore this. Fifth, policy on sustainable development and learning must compete for resources with other policy areas; presently it does not enjoy the highest priority in many cases. Finally, local and national policy making takes place in an international context in which the contested concept of 'globalisation' (see Chapter 13) appears to play at least some role.

3 Language and meaning

Introduction

Two distinct but related issues are discussed in this chapter. The first is how our use of language is implicated in our understanding of both sustainable development and learning as ideas. The second is how language is further implicated in our choice of actions in relation to sustainable development and learning as practice. We shall argue that a degree of insight into these matters is indispensable for any degree of practical planning in relation to our topic if it is to be effective. This is so even if some of the concepts involved initially may seem, to some at least, rather slippery, somewhat arcane or intellectually quite narcissistic.

To begin, two caveats are in order. First, we should be wary of assuming that the ways in which any given individual makes sense of the notion of sustainable development will be consistent with the way that same person makes sense of the idea of learning. Although there is a wide literature across a number of disciplines which assumes, for example, that people have attitudes and values which determine their behaviour in some predictable way, this view is not only the subject of much empirical critique (Hines, 1985; Hungerford *et al.*, 2000; Marcinkowski, 2001; Rogers, 1995; Rickinson, 2001; Stern, 2000), it is also quite contrary to common sense and much day-to-day experience. People (and organisations) are frequently inconsistent. One finds, for example, environmentalists who drive cars with poor fuel economy or smoke cigarettes; developers who campaign near where they live for conservation of biodiversity; and pop-stars who campaign for equality and social justice whilst enjoying extravagant parties and bouts of expensive cosmetic surgery. To explain all this simply as hypocrisy is possible but not very helpful, though it is consistent with an intellectual view, discussed briefly in Chapter 1, which sees people as having self-evident interests which guide their choices. However, the point was made at least as long ago as the *New Testament* (Matthew 23: 23) that hypocrisy is effectively a universal human condition and now, as also suggested in Chapter 1, human perceptions of self-interest appear to be more fluid than ever before. We should not assume, therefore, as the argument of this book develops, that any particular view of sustainable development can be inferred from a person's stated approach to learning, or *vice versa*.

Second, it is not our intention here to explore in great depth the extensive literature which exists in relation to, variously, the philosophy of language and learning, post-modernism, post-structuralism and so on. This is not at all because we believe these ideas to be unimportant. Indeed, readers will find these perspectives well represented in the companion reader. However, in setting out a co-evolutionary view of the relationship between society and nature in Chapter 1 we argued there that scope remained for debate about the degree of independent influence over social and natural processes which humans can have. We are focusing our treatment of issues of language and meaning, therefore, on the extent to which it can contribute to that debate.

Language and understanding; language and action

A 'scientific' or, rather more accurately, a 'positivistic' view of the biogeophysical world is characterised by (at least) two fundamental assumptions. The first is that 'truth' about the world can be established in an objective way, independent of the personal characteristics of any individual or group of investigators. This proposition depends upon a second assumption, which is that language is capable of conveying unique meanings which correspond to aspects of external reality in a transparent and unambiguous way.

That there are certain difficulties with the first of these assumptions became clear through the seminal work of Thomas Kuhn (1996). For the purpose of this discussion we might summarise the crucial finding of Kuhn's historical examination of the practice of science as being that, in all but the most exceptional times, scientists work not to establish truth but to complete and extend a particular discourse (a 'paradigm') to which they have an allegiance. Kuhn (1996: 126) writes:

> But is sensory experience fixed and neutral? Are theories simply man-made interpretations of given data? The epistemological viewpoint that has most often guided Western philosophy for three centuries dictates an immediate and unequivocal, Yes! In the absence of a developed alternative, I find it impossible to relinquish entirely that viewpoint. Yet it no longer functions effectively, and the attempts to make it do so through the introduction of a neutral language of observations now seem to me hopeless.

Thus, positivist research is purposive. It should be noted, however, that Kuhn himself does not advocate abandonment of the goal of objectivity. That goal, after all, underpins his own labours. What he does say is:

1   that the hypothesis of scientific progress based on a cumulative process of hypothesis-falsification does not itself bear empirical scrutiny;
2   that there are therefore problems of mismatch between that particular hypothesis and the available evidence about it; and,
3   that these problems merit further critical examination by practitioners.

If, however, the second positivist assumption, that language can unproblematically convey meaning about reality in an unambiguous way is abandoned, then *all* claims about an objectively-knowable reality are at once open to question, including the more limited, post-positivist notion that objective reality can serve as a 'regulatory ideal' (Connell, 1997). Edwards (1997; 6) describes the consequences as follows:

> Discourse therefore displaces knowledge as the object of study as problems and inequalities surrounding the universality of knowledge come to the fore. This can be illustrated in the practices of lifelong learning in a shift from a focus on teaching, as the transmission of the (usually) university-generated canon of disciplinary knowledge, to learning, in which greater weight is given to, for instance, the experience of learners and practitioner-generated knowledge.

This quote is interesting for two reasons. First, it makes an admirable job of linking an apparently abstruse point about epistemology to a concrete issue of professional practice which anyone professionally engaged in the fields of health care, education or social services, for example, would be likely to recognise immediately. Second, however, its first sentence links a change in the substantive focus of academic enquiry ('Discourse . . . displaces knowledge . . .') to a particular kind of ethical concern ('. . . inequalities . . .') in a way which appears to suggest that such a link is inevitable.

It should be said here, of course, that Edwards is absolutely correct in saying that issues of inequality (and power) have, *in fact*, tended to predominate wherever study has focused not on 'facts' but on 'narratives'. An excellent, and very scholarly, example will be found in the paper by Greenall Gough (1993) which appears in chapter 12 of the companion reader. Edwards (1997: 8) himself goes on to illustrate his point by reference to the work of Foucault (1981) for whom power and knowledge cannot be separated. However, whether such issues *necessarily* 'come to the fore' under these circumstances is open to question. It is at least credible, and arguably more consistent with the logic of these post-modern approaches themselves, to argue as follows:

- A case is being made here that value-free objectivity in academic study is a pretence which can no longer be maintained
- If this case is accepted, then researchers themselves become a legitimate part of the object of study, because of the inevitable value-content of the narratives they espouse and bring to bear (Greenall Gough makes this point very persuasively)
- In the work of those researchers who accept the above we would expect to find an ethical focus in keeping with their own self-narratives
- Such researchers tend to be those whose professional self-narratives valorise egalitarian discourses
- Why this is the case is open to question, but it clearly *cannot* be because those discourses are capable of empirical validation.

This is to say that what has 'come to the fore' through work of this sort needs, *by virtue of the logic of the approach itself*, to be explained in terms of the interests which particular researchers believe themselves to have at various times. Edwards (1997) goes some way to revealing the potential complexity of the situation, by following Gore (1993) in noting that, for example, critical and feminist pedagogies can be exclusive and oppressive of some persons even as they argue for the emancipation of others. Similarly, one can think without difficulty of social researchers who have accumulated a great deal of personal social and financial capital through consistently making the case for equality. To say this is to say no more than that, first, if an academic observer is wholly part of the picture rather than wholly detached from it, then that goes for all academic observers; and, second, that as we have noted in this chapter already, human perceptions of self-interest are arguably more fluid than ever before and cannot now be assumed to be consistent across time or context.

From anything resembling a positivist perspective, understanding sustainable development requires processes of definition and quantification. Assumptions will need to be made about what it means to 'sustain' something and what that 'something' might be. Well known discussions of this kind revolve around, for example, the delineation of different kinds of sustainability, such as 'weak', 'very weak', 'strong' and 'very strong', and the related issue of the acceptable rate of replacement of natural with human-made capital (Kerry Turner, 1993). Potential funders of research may well be attracted by the possibility of concrete research outcomes in terms of understanding sustainable development, and the presumed linear process through definition and quantification leading in turn to prediction and control and thus to desired change. An interesting example in this respect is the recent EU-funded project which set out to define marine-ecotourism (Garrod, 2003), seeing this as a step towards, as EU documents tend to put it, the 'operationalising' of sustainable development. Also from this perspective, to understand learning requires similar processes of definition and measurement. Learning styles can be identified and then targeted to bring about change. Characteristics of effective or improving schools and checklists of adult employability skills can be enumerated and similarly targeted and then measured.

Once the power of language reliably and consistently to describe an independently existing reality is in question, however, all of the above seems problematic. From any perspective towards the post-modern or post-structuralist end of the spectrum, the question of understanding sustainable development and related learning revolves not around *how* to sustain things, but about *whose* things it is proposed to sustain, *what* is to be developed in *whose* interest, and *who* is to be encouraged to learn *what*. Thus, 'sustainable development' becomes one strategic device in an arena of power-relations, and 'learning' another. Sachs (1991, and chapter 3 of the companion reader) provides a helpful example of a sophisticated analysis of this general kind.

Making a difference

Incompatible as the two general positions outlined above appear to be, both seem to have enjoyed some practical success, not only in enabling people to make effective conscious efforts to influence their relationship with their environment in a constructive way, but in establishing a degree of consensus in the process. For example, positivistic science has succeeded, in spite of the clear linguistic difficulties it faces, in demonstrating a relationship between atmospheric ozone depletion and the release of CFCs and halons which is now generally undisputed. This has led to policy and behaviour changes in what appears to be a quite linear way, particularly through the workings of the Montreal Protocol. Whether the process of ozone depletion proves to be straightforwardly reversible, or whether instead feedback from nature, in what is now clearly an entirely unprecedented set of circumstances, turns out to feature some surprises remains to be seen. However, whatever sustainable development comes to mean such processes can only be steps towards it.

At the same time, the notion that expert scientific knowledge can be applied unproblematically in all circumstances finds fewer and fewer supporters. Firms such as Shell (Jones, 1997) have developed well publicised procedures for consulting stakeholders in relation to the potential environmental impacts of projects, while the most reputable research-funding bodies in both natural and social sciences increasingly call for multi-disciplinary approaches and the involvement at all stages of end users and stakeholders. Elsewhere, experts in risk analysis and management have come to accept that purely expert calculations of risk are likely to miss the point in terms of policy and risk-management because there is, in fact, likely to be no single correct perception of risk (Löfstedt and Frewer, 1998; Falconer *et al.*, 1999). The rhetoric of 'multiple perspectives' and even 'multiple knowledges' is now widespread.

A similar situation prevails in relation to learning. On the one hand the (perhaps extreme) notion that formal learning takes place inside a professional 'black box', through the mysterious processes of which only the teacher or instructor can judge the (necessarily) qualitative value, has been effectively laid to rest by standard techniques of value added measurement, quality assurance, inspection and evaluation. On the other hand, widespread recognition of the need both to provide equal opportunities to learners while engaging with their varied social and cultural backgrounds – engaging, that is, with the experience and knowledge they themselves bring to the learning process – has led to ongoing mainstream debate about the design and operationalisation of what has been called an 'expansive' (Hlebowitsch, 1999; Westbury, 1999) or 'connective' (Young, 1998) curriculum for learners (see companion reader).

However, a problem remains in spite of these successes. It is that there appears to be no general rule capable of explaining or predicting them. When will one kind of approach succeed? When an other?

This difficulty arises from two separate, if related sources. First, there is the need, embedded in Western ways of thinking since Aristotle, to view any proposition as necessarily either true or not true. This issue has been explored interestingly, and in quite different contexts by, for example Haste (2000) and Falconer (1998), but the central point for the present discussion is quite straightforward. It is that the answer to questions such as, 'Can we learn anything useful about sustainable development and learning through positivistic science?' or 'Is learning from indigenous peoples valuable in achieving sustainable development?', can in both cases be either 'Yes', 'No', 'Maybe' or 'Sometimes'.

To put this another way, the notion that there are different ways of knowing (Greenall Gough, 1993) implies equally that there are different ways of *not knowing*. Multiple knowledges or rationalities (Thompson, 1997; James and Thompson, 1989) imply also multiple *ignorances* and blind spots (Gough, 2002). For example, scientific and technological prowess has been developed to its present level only by systematically excluding other ways of thinking. As noted in Chapter 1, this prowess has increased human control over the environment while creating risks and problems of its own: no one wants to have an operation without carefully managed anaesthesia or to be denied access to routine antibiotics, but neither do we want to develop skin cancer through over-exposure to ultra-violet radiation or have our children lose fertility through hormone-mimicking plasticisers. Some indigenous peoples have maintained traditional lifestyles by avoiding scientific rationality and are noticeably free of what Beck terms the manufactured risks of the modern world: on the other hand, some indigenous peoples who have similarly maintained traditional lifestyles are noticeably at the remorseless mercy of their environments, or are locked into rebarbative cultural practices about which the best one can say is that they make no obvious contribution to sustainable development. Maintaining traditional practices has to be a poor reason to starve through lack of technology, underdeveloped risk management skills or limited access to markets; indigenous tradition is no better justification for violence against women than unemployment or executive stress; and no stressed marketing executive could fail to be impressed by the Penan headman who, asked by one of the authors for his views on the West replied simply, 'You have nothing we want'.

The second source of difficulty is the existence of uncertainty and the acute problems we have in dealing with it. In Chapter 1 we outlined the cultural theory view that in the absence of certainty people try to create it through the application of particular rationalities. This gives rise to particular views of what is wrong, and what should be done about it. Thompson (1990) advocates what he terms a 'clumsy' approach under these circumstances, that is, one which entertains competing definitions of problems at the same time. Of course, such an approach can be difficult for policy makers to explain or justify to their various stakeholder groups, who are likely not only to expect the appearance of clarity of purpose, but also to wish to promote their own particular rationality with its corresponding problem definitions. However it is important to be clear that though this view is saying that many problems related to, for example, sustainable development are likely to continue to be characterised by uncertainty, it is possible to chip away at this uncertainty. It *is* possible to know things: but it is important to be absolutely honest about when we *really* know something, and when we just wish we did. There is nothing in the least bit scientifically rigorous about assuming values for unknown variables and then building these into policy prescriptions behind a screen of fine words and/or abstruse mathematics.

Literacies: the environment as text

Although many who write about environmental literacy (e.g. Disinger and Roth, 1992), are not necessarily aware of it, there is a real case to be made to the effect that we all 'read' and 'write' our environments – that is, that our very experience of living is a process of semiotic engagement with our surroundings, making sense and order of the environment through a process of naming, classification and patterning. As structuralists and post-structuralists have pointed out, one way of looking at the world is to say that *everything* is a text (Stables 1996; 1997; 1998; and Stables and Bishop 2001). This not a new idea; as the evidence of history suggests, ancient peoples read the movements of the stars, the clouds and weather, as signs. To be environmentally literate, properly understood, therefore, is and always has been purposefully to read, and write, the world. There can, however, be no single way of learning about reading and/or writing the world and thus effecting sustainable development. There are different cultural and disciplinary traditions, often with no logical link between them. For example, there are no obvious connections between learning about the production of urban photo-chemical smogs, and learning about the tendency in art and literature to ascribe human emotions and sympathies to nature (pathetic fallacy). Each stems from distinctive perspectives, yet both are clearly relevant to understanding aspects of the human-environment relationship. This, and the difficulty of arriving at absolute understandings of how different cultures view the world, has important consequences. For example, quite different assumptions about the human–environment relationship are possible. Science will likely continue to argue that its models of the workings of the natural world are getting nearer to some kinds of truth about reality, whilst social science will stress the relationships of social and environmental conditions, and tend to see issues in terms of equity, and in terms of social and environmental justice.

To the positivist, biogeophysical reality is one thing and language is another. To the philosopher of language, language and reality may be seen as necessarily complementary terms, like 'dark' and 'light' (Andrew Stables, 2002, pers. comm.). If both views can lead to successful interventions then, in the presence of uncertainty, we need the insights of both and the perspectives in between. But this begs the question, 'given these radically different epistemological perspectives, what would it mean to know anything, that is, for uncertainty to be absent'? Here too we must accept competing standards. The positivist will be confident when armed with hard facts; the post-structuralist will be calmed by a convergence of narratives. Where, as appears to be the case for the issue of ozone-depletion through CFC use, both facts and convergent narratives are present, we should stop worrying about uncertainty.

To illustrate the above, consider the example of a (hypothetical) stretch of tropical coastline that has hitherto been little visited by outsiders and supports a small local population. This place, considered as a text, will be 'read' quite differently by, say, an economist, a biologist, an engineer, a Western travel writer and a local poet and songwriter. The first three mentioned, at least, will have been trained to read environments in particular ways. Each will have a particular 'literacy' and will be influenced in the form of their reading by their organisational context (see Chapter 6): for example, the precise approach taken by the economist may depend on whether she is employed by a private firm or a government department. The readings of these different individuals may be in conflict. Which of them subsequently influences events the most, and so has the greatest input into the rewriting of the environment, is likely to be decided in the end not only by the force of their respective arguments but by extent and power of their institutional support. However, it is their different arguments, and different *forms* of argument, which are likely to seem the proper focus for any sort of learning intervention associated with environmental change.

If, say, the economist's cost-benefit analysis is decisive in a decision to build a tourist hotel complex, this will constitute a major re-writing of the environment. However, the resulting 'text' will be different from that envisaged in any plan. This is because a degree of uncertainty will surely be present, and the environment will change in some ways that have not been fully predicted by anyone. These changes will themselves then be read by each of our five actors in ways which, once more, reflect the particular literacy they bring to bear in conjunction with their institutional affiliations. As before, none of them will be 'wrong'. As before, they may see things very differently. However, in the subsequent event of an oil spill off the coast, it is perfectly conceivable that facts and narratives may converge, and that the Western and local writers might collaborate, for instance, to write a critical piece in which they quote separate evidence from the economist, the biologist and the engineer in describing the threats from the oil and the costs of remediation. We return to the important place of literacies in our argument in Chapter 6.

The significance of language

As we noted at the beginning of this chapter, there is an extensive literature on language and epistemology around which we propose to skirt. Our concluding thought here is provided by Stables (2001, 127):

> Whatever our broader philosophical assumptions – whether we see ourselves as scientific realists, critical realists, post-foundationalists, or even relativists – language permeates our lives as environmental educators. 'Sustainability' is a word. Like all words, it relates to something outside itself, but, like all words, its precise meaning is always dependent on the context in which it is used. Given the possibility that we might eventually fail to sustain life on this planet, or, at least, diminish its richness, then there seems little of more importance than pursuing the debate about what we mean by this term, what we might mean, and what the adoption of such a meaning might lead us to do.

'Pursuing the debate', in this sense, would clearly itself be a process of learning.

4 Learning and sustainable development

Making the linkages

Introduction: literacies and learning

At the beginning of Chapter 1 we noted that it is perfectly possible in practice to have a central concern with sustainable development without paying any attention at all to what anyone learns at any stage of their lives. Even if, perhaps among our more education-minded readers, there are those who were initially surprised by this then they may be less so now. Our observation in Chapter 3, that there exists a range of different literacies by means of which people 'read' their environment, offers a clear explanation why this may be so. For the trained educator, whilst lack of learning is likely to feature prominently in definitions of environmental problems, and learning itself is likely to be seen as integral to many solutions, much will depend, in this view, on how people think. For the economist, on the other hand, how people think is normally taken as given, consistent and expressed through the choices they make. For the conservation biologist, however, how people think may not merit much, or any, attention if it is held that there is an externally determined rational standard which enables judgements to be made about *what* they should think, particularly in relation to conservation. Note how fundamental these differences really are, depending ultimately on whether 'environmental problems' are seen as something people have, or something ecosystems have. This means that even if there is agreement about, say, the need to protect biodiversity in a particular area of wetland, which has economic value to local people and is also potentially attractive to tourists, there is unlikely to be agreement about whether it is best to achieve this by, for example:

- Engaging stakeholders in a mediated learning process through which the value of the wetland and the alternatives for its management are explored and internalised
- Controlling economic activity through the use of traded permits, supported by incentives in favour of particular alternatives
- Banning access and perhaps building a perimeter fence.

Of course, these are not the only possible literacies which might be brought to bear and therefore not the only possible solutions that might be offered. However, taking an overview of this very simple hypothetical example enables us to make the following propositions about it:

First, management of wetland biodiversity is an inherently interdisciplinary issue. It is also typically characterised by a good deal of uncertainty. This uncertainty cannot be eliminated, at least not for now. It may be made manageable by scoping assumptions which, for example, limit the geographical and/or temporal scales under consideration, or set out a particular methodological approach. However, such assumptions will always have the effect of concealing some things, even as they reveal others.

Second, interdisciplinary working is difficult because individuals accustomed to working within a particular literacy find it difficult to listen and talk to those who use another. Third, given uncertainty, it seems reasonable to assume that more than one literacy will normally be useful in understanding any particular sustainable development problem. Finally, the facilitation of collaborative working across literacies *is itself inherently a question of learning*. This is to say that learning specialists have a potential input at two levels:

• As co-contributors, with specialists from other disciplines, to the promotion of sustainable development
• As mediators of inter-disciplinary working and collaborative learning.

We are arguing here that there are more constructive and urgent roles for 'educators' within conservation organisations and that their role cannot simply be to teach somebody something *about* conservation. Having set out this position in the abstract it may now be useful to consider a real world example.

A Caribbean example

In many Caribbean countries the issue of sustainable development looms large. This is in no small part because of the large role the tourism industry plays in their economies. There is an extensive literature on tourism, development and, of particular relevance to our discussion here, the notion of ecotourism (see, for example, Fennell, 1999). However, the crucial issue in all of this is the tendency of any kind of tourism to consume its resource base (Cater and Goodall, 1992).

The environmental management of tourism requires inputs of knowledge from many different literacies. Some of these are associated with specific academic disciplines, for example marine biology, economics, engineering and ecology. Other relevant literacies are associated with professional expertise such as hotel management, law or forestry. Still others are significant across many parts of the region (such as cruise-shipping management) or within particular parts of it (such as Barbadian oil and water-colour painting; Guyanese forest culture; oral traditions of medicinal plant-use in Trinidad).

The interactions of these different literacies are mediated through institutions and through markets. Both are multi-layered. There are among Caribbean institutions active representatives of international bodies (e.g. UNDP), regional organisations (e.g. the Organisation of East Caribbean States), national bodies, often competing for limited resources (e.g. St.Lucia had in 2001 a Ministry of Planning, Development,

Environment and Housing; a Solid Waste Management Authority; and a Ministry of Agriculture, Forestry and Fisheries), influential sub-national bodies, including local NGOs (e.g. the Point-à-Pierre Wildfowl Trust in Trinidad), external bodies operating within local ones (e.g. the US Peace Corps), and in-country organisations sponsored by international organisations (e.g. the Iwokrama Rainforest Reserve in Guyana). Relevant markets are similarly complex and nested, ranging from the international (beach-resort tourism) to the highly locally specific (sea-moss production in Antigua) and including some with the apparent potential to span this divide (sustainable forest products from Guyana). How these interactions play out in practice depends, at least in part, upon the literacies which the individuals involved at particular times and in particular places bring to bear and their degree of receptiveness to the thinking of others. And when all this has been said perhaps the one general fact which should be wholly uncontroversial is that no one knows with any certainty what sustainable tourism development for the Caribbean actually means, or whether, ultimately, it is possible at all.

Coming to terms with this complexity also involves making assumptions about the scope of the problem: but this issue proves slippery. What is the relevant time-scale over which to assess sustainable development in these countries? What is the relevant geographical scale on which to focus – which countries should be included, for example? Only those which actually border the Caribbean? Barbados and Guyana hardly do, while Venezuela does. Those which share a 'Caribbean culture'? If so, does that exclude the hinterland of Guyana? Or Martinique? We could include all regions of the world which bear on the environmental integrity and social development of Caribbean countries but that would introduce into our calculations parts of the United States and Western Europe. Of course, some limiting assumptions *will* need to be made if any useful work is to be done. The point is, however, that as these make some insights accessible they will necessarily tend to obscure others. Multiple approaches using different conceptual frameworks therefore seem essential if sense and progress are to be made.

We have suggested that learning can and should make a contribution at two levels. The first of these is as one of many contributory disciplines to sustainable development. So, for example, useful learning at a variety of levels which is consistent with other sustainable development initiatives has been reported:

- In a number of Caribbean countries through the use of radio phone-in programmes. These present non-formal opportunities for both environmental learning and the development of skills of participation in civil society
- Also in a number of countries, the Darwin Initiative's *Coral Reef Biodiversity in the Caribbean* programme is a good example of building capacity in both the formal education sector (through the creation of resources for schools) and beyond (through its international collaborative structure and emphasis on training for evaluation)
- In Antigua, where an NGO, The Environmental Awareness Group, has built strong links with Ministries, teachers and the public to promote conservation through education

- In Guyana, where both the NGO, Conservation International, and the million-acre Iwokrama International Centre for Rainforest Conservation and Development, have a range of learning initiatives including training to enable the sustainable production and marketing of forest products
- In St Lucia, where the Solid Waste Management Authority has linked education to innovative reform of its own work, and where the Fisheries Department has supported its attempts to reform local fishery practices through learning initiatives at a number of levels.

The second level at which learning can make a contribution is that of facilitating understanding across organisations. We shall call this *environmental meta-learning*. An example of such an attempt to promote environmental meta-learning is a report arising from a subset of research commissioned by the UK Government's Department for International Development (DFID) (Hindson *et al.*, 2001; see also Chapter 2) which focused on issues of learning and sustainable development in five Caribbean countries. This aimed (with at least some reported success) to facilitate mutual understanding between stakeholders by organising its findings in way calculated to promote reflection and a disposition to future action. The simple structure employed is shown as Figure 4.1.

Meta-learning, learning organisations, learning societies

The term 'meta-learning' necessarily carries echoes of the discourses of the learning organisation and the learning society. These discourses have generated an extensive

	Environmental education *outcomes*	*Processes* of environmental education	*Context* of environmental education
Strengths for mainstreaming			
Weaknesses for mainstreaming			
Opportunities for mainstreaming			
Threats to mainstreaming			

Figure 4.1 Mainstreaming environmental education: reporting findings to promote learning.

literature and are represented in chapter 4 of the companion reader in the work of Elliott (1998) and Argyris and Schön (1996), and from slightly different initial focuses in chapters 1, 3 and 7 in the work of Beck (1992), Lauder and Brown (2000) and Young (1998).

Such discourses are not without their critics. Hughes and Tight (1995) describe the learning society as a 'contemporary myth' which is comprised in turn of four sub-myths: the productivity myth; the change myth; the lifelong learning myth; and the learning organisation myth. Their point in doing so, as Lelliott *et al.* (2000) note, which is consistent with the developing argument of this chapter, is not to deny the *power* of these ideas but to draw attention to their parallel capacity to obscure our understandings. Illustration of what this might mean in practical terms comes from Field (2000), who, writing about one of these 'sub-myths', lifelong learning, makes a number of points relevant to our discussion:

- It is only reasonable to expect some mismatch between what policy makers say and what actually happens, since a range of mediating institutions lie between the one and the other
- Lifelong learning is one of a number of contemporary policy concerns (Field cites enhancing public health and racial tolerance, and tackling crime and environmental issues, as other examples) which require citizenship action; that is, they cannot be expected to be achieved by government action alone
- Policy delivery has in practice focused on a very limited area, primarily relating to vocational skills training, the extension of HE to 50 per cent of the cohort and an emphasis on basic skills (literacy, numeracy, ICT) in formal education. Instances of 'walking the talk' seem few and far between
- There is a tension between learning as a matter of public policy concern on the one hand, and learning as a commodity subject to consumer choice on the other. To put it as bluntly as possible, sustainable development is one fashionable policy slogan and expansion of consumer choice is another, and there seems no particular reason why the two should support each other. This issue cuts very deep, and raises again some of the questions of Chapter 3, most particularly that of the 'radical difference between the modern view of the reflexive, yet transcendental self, for whom the finding of a stable identity is a normative goal, and the postmodern perspective of the self subject to images, through which there is a disturbingly pleasurable construction of multiple identities' (Edwards, 1997: 44)
- Government department internal discipline tends to require monitoring and evaluation against output measures which militate against the very nature of the reforms originally proposed. In particular, the pricing of investments and returns is done according to models which cannot accommodate concepts such as capacity building or cultural change.

Given all this, a useful framework for thinking about the role of learning in society, and about policies designed to promote it, has been offered by Young (1998). It is centred upon the identification of four possible models for a learning society. Young sees each of these models as being underpinned by different interests, and by different visions of the future.

First is the *schooling model.* Young (142) writes of this that it, 'stresses high participation in post-compulsory schooling as a way of ensuring that a maximum proportion of the population reach as far beyond a minimum level of education as possible'. It has been popular in a strong form in some Nordic and South East Asian countries. Young identifies the creation of a 'learning culture' as a strength of this model. There are also a number of weaknesses, of which those most pertinent to the present discussion are that it 'front-loads' the emphasis on and funding of learning into the early years of a person's life, and that it tends to insulate schooling from other forms and stages of learning.

Second, there is the *credentialist model*, which, 'gives priority to ensuring that the vast majority of the population has qualifications or certified skills and knowledge and that the qualifications people achieve are related to their future employment . . . it allows for the possibility that qualifications may be achieved in other ways than through full-time study, although in practice this is rarely possible for qualifications that give entry to high status occupations' (Young, 1998: 144). European countries following the German tradition are good examples of this model in practice. The most telling difficulty with this model is that it delineates specific qualifications as end-points and subjects disciplines as routes to them. It therefore militates against both learning as a continuous process and learning across disciplines. On the other hand, a strength may be that it creates and distributes social capital in standard units of which the value is, or should be, consistent and transparent across the society.

Third, the *access model*, 'represents a vision of a society of the future in which learning after the phase of compulsory schooling is increasingly freed from its ties with specialized educational institutions such as schools, colleges and universities. It is a vision of a learning society in which people will learn, if free to do so, in any context they find themselves in, by developing skills and knowledge as their needs change at different times of their lives' (Young, 1998: 146). Clear strengths include a tendency to break down barriers which many people continue to find obstructing their access to learning, and, significantly, the support of Internet and software companies in search of a market. Important weaknesses are the difficulty of linking adult learning to schooling in a coherent way through this model and, to return to a point made earlier, the difficult question of how consumers of learning can be helped to make wise choices about what to learn in a learning marketplace characterised by: (i) providers with products to sell; and, (ii) endemic uncertainty about what learning is likely to provide the best individual (or social) returns.

Young goes on to propose a fourth, *connective model*. This, he writes, 'implies a change in the internal relationships of organizations so that schools and colleges themselves begin to develop their research and human resource strategies, and in the external relationships between educational and other institutions as they identify shared purposes and explore new forms of partnership' (Young, 1998: 151). What is being argued for here, as Young makes clear, is an emphasis on what Engestrom (1994) has termed 'expanded learning', in which the learner is not content to learn what is necessary to solve a particular problem, but also learns through an investigation of the *origins* of that problem.

It is clear that Young's connective model represents a proposal which is very appropriate to addressing the issues of complexity, uncertainty and risk which were identified in Chapter 1 and which are implicit in the notion of sustainable development. Or, to put this the other way around, sustainable development is a response to issues of complexity, uncertainty and risk which would appear necessarily to entail learning across society (and between societies), of the kind envisaged by Young. Such learning would entail many individual, context specific instances of environmental meta-learning. However, two important caveats are in order.

First, as Schwab pointed out as long ago as 1978, it is impossible to persuade people of the merits of new ways of thinking when they are only equipped with old ways of understanding. The *schooling*, *credentialist* and *access* models of learning do have advocates, and indeed strengths, which those advocates can marshal in defence of the models. What is needed, therefore, is not only the development of a new model, but a process of meta-learning which engages stakeholders in the various alternative models with each other. Without this it is difficult to see how, for example, practitioners in Caribbean countries, who may be disposed to credentialism by virtue of their own experience and training, might be moved to a more 'connective' view. Further, such practitioners are likely to be worth listening to. For one thing they will have culturally specific experience and insights; more importantly, *not everything* is unknown, uncertain or contingent. There are plenty of problems of sustainable development, in poorer countries in particular perhaps, to which the answers are known and can be made available through schooling, the creation of a cadre of individuals with appropriate credentials or the provision of access opportunities. All this is to argue that instances of 'connective' or 'expanded' learning should be carefully and appropriately *focused*.

Towards a sustainable development learning model

Figure 4.2 proposes a model for thinking about the role of learning in sustainable development. In particular, it suggests a way of thinking about the appropriate focusing of learning interventions in different contexts, so as to maximise their effectiveness.

It is a commonplace of management that any complex task can only be attempted if it has first been broken down into smaller components. The complex task of learning in society has traditionally been broken down into component parts which have themselves become what Reid (1999: 111) has called 'cultural institutions', that is, they have become integral to culture and to ways of thinking about society. Such cultural institutions include 'primary education'; 'vocational education'; 'training', 'lifelong learning'; 'non-formal education'; and so on. The origins (MacIntyre, 1981) and implications of this analysis are discussed in Chapter 6.

In Figure 4.2 the large box represents all the learning that takes place in society. Although only education and training are shown here for sake of clarity, it includes all the types of learning mentioned above, and their subdivisions (e.g. museum

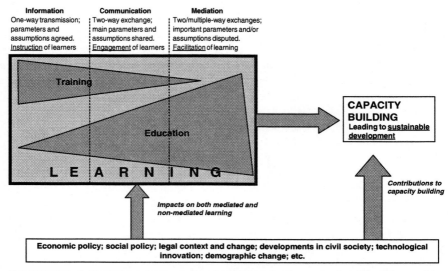

Figure 4.2 Information, communication, mediation: contributions to capacity building.

education, special education, assertiveness training, action learning), along with secondary education, informal education (including some advertising), social marketing, higher education, further education, e-learning, mentoring and the rest. It also includes forms of participation that may be of specific interest to the area of the environment, such as the education of parents by their children (Ballantyne *et al.*, 1998a; 1998b; Uzzell *et al.*, 1994; Uzzell, 1999). Most particularly, it also includes serendipitous and accidental learning, that is, it is primarily concerned with what learners learn, not with what teachers necessarily teach, and recognises that impacts of learning can be negative as well as positive (NCVO, 2002). Quite deliberately, the attempt here is to put the historically sub-divided notion of learning back together again in a new way which denies institutions, academic disciplines or policy makers the opportunity to assert territorial claims to authority over particular segments. This is not because institutions, academic disciplines or policy makers (and their activities) are necessarily the problem, or because established conceptual divisions of learning have no value, but because, consistent with the central argument of this book, we believe it can be useful to ask what complex problems look like from several entirely different viewpoints. It is important to note, however, that we exclude from the model all deliberate attempts to deceive, dominate or exploit.

Most of the traditional divisions of learning depend upon distinctions between either different types of learner (e.g. primary age children; people with special needs; students in higher education), different settings in which the learning takes place (e.g. museums; field study centres; the gym), different purposes of learning (e.g. assertiveness training; health education, professional practice), or some combination of these. It is interesting to note in passing that *environmental education* is a particularly elusive term at least in part because none of these established divisions captures it well. Our proposal through Figure 4.2 is to complement, not replace, these styles of division with another based on the *strategies* through which learning occurs. Broadly speaking there are three of these. We have called them *information, communication* and *mediation*, deriving these terms from past (WWF, 1999a) and ongoing work by the authors and others for the World Wildlife Fund in the United States. Which strategy is most appropriate for bringing about learning depends, we argue, upon the circumstances of the particular case.

Information: Learning by means of information provision occurs through a one-way process of instruction. The learner acquires a new piece of information which, internalised, becomes a personal, and possibly also a social, resource. In Chapter 1, speaking of natural resources, we noted that something becomes a resource when you, (i) can do something with it and, (ii) have a reason for wanting to. Much the same is true of personal resources acquired through learning. Both elements are important. Information, in the sense the term is used here, unproblematically becomes useful to the learner. There is no need for extensive negotiation of meanings or for complex, time-consuming or expensive pedagogies. So, for example, a carefully written leaflet explaining how to make a wildlife pond is all the aid-to-learning that is needed for people who already *want* to make one. There is a core of established, generalisable knowledge about garden pond construction which, whether it is seen as an accumulation of externally established facts (the positivist view – see Chapter 3), or as a time-limited convergence of all available narratives (the post-structuralist position), is effectively undisputed. Once the learner possesses this they will know what to do. The wildlife pond is one of many possible examples which range in scale from small and simple to large and complex. An example of a large-scale sustainable development issue for which much can be accomplished through information and subsequent action is that of toxic chemical or oil spillage.

Communication: Learning occurs by means of communication through a two-way process. There is more at stake than simply internalising externally provided information. This is because, at the margins, the knowledge itself may be open to question and dispute. Further, the *usefulness* of the knowledge may be debateable.

To continue our example, there may be those who are *interested* in the idea of making a wildlife pond, but who have doubts relating to effectiveness issues ('do wildlife ponds really work in attracting wildlife?'), construction issues ('don't all ponds leak?'), issues with wildlife itself ('frogs and butterflies are fine, what if the pond attracts mosquitoes or other pests?'), or general property issues ('won't a pond reduce the market price of my house?'). Whether or not the pond gets built will depend on a process of negotiation and engagement with the learner. A leaflet pushed through the door will almost certainly fail under these circumstances. A conveniently timed, and dialogue-focused, public event, radio phone-in, or school activity to which parents are invited might, however, succeed. Note also that major interventions, such as giving greater emphasis in school and lifelong learning curricula to knowledge about biological processes, while arguably a good thing in itself, has little bearing on most of the issues that actually make a difference in this case. A global issue amenable to communication approaches has been ozone depletion, on which progress has been possible even though the problem affects different countries to different degrees at different times, and at the margin potential long-term effects remain a subject of some debate. A potentially powerful tool for communication in relation to sustainable development is 'social marketing' which is an increasingly cited mechanism to help people adopt particular sustainable behaviours:

> The cornerstone of sustainability is delivering programs that are effective in changing people's behavior.
>
> McKenzie-Mohr and Smith (1999: 15)

> The transition to a sustainable future will require that the vast majority of people be persuaded to adopt different lifestyles.
>
> (ibid; 1999: 83)

In community-based social marketing people are not necessarily aware of the aims being pursued and the range of behaviours that might be affected is narrow. This raises at least three questions:

- How certain can we be as to what such different lifestyles will need to be?
- Will changing people's behaviours in the relatively narrow ways envisaged be enough, in and of itself, to contribute to sustainable development ?
- What ethical issues exist around such techniques to persuade the public to live differently?

However, it is clear that there is evidence to suggest that such social marketing *is* effective – albeit in its self-limited scope and vision and probably only over the short to medium term. But effective for whom? As it stands this is essentially about doing a small number of things differently (i.e., less of this; more of the other); it is *not* about doing different things in the way that Stephen Sterling (2001 – and chapter 4 of the companion reader) has cogently pictured the existential choices we now face.

Mediation: Our use of this term has its origins in the work of Laurillard (2002), who uses the term 'mediated learning', specifically in the context of higher education, to describe learning which enables the generalisation of insights from situated learning (Lave, 1988; Lave and Wenger, 1991; Fox, 2000) beyond the communities of practice which have generated them; but the notion that learning accrues from mediation processes is widespread in that the teacher role is to mediate children's experiences so that something can be learned. This is not to say, however, that teachers are necessarily needed for students to learn.

The issue here is that there are those who dispute, at both local and global scales, the significance of biodiversity loss. As with many of the most pressing questions relating to the environment and to human development, biodiversity loss is characterised by complexity and uncertainty, and these give rise to conflicting interpretations of risk and necessity. That different protagonists in debates about biodiversity loss and other sustainable development issues are able, with apparently equal facility, to marshal scientific evidence to support their contrary cases should not be seen as an indictment of science. Rather, it is clear evidence of the working of the scientific approach when confronted with uncertainty about the number and nature of parameters of a problem. This point is made powerfully by the former Assistant Director of the UK's Economic and Social Research Council's Global Environmental Change Programme (GECP), Alister Scott (2001: 136–7, original emphasis):

> The research evidence suggested that 'perhaps the greatest challenge of all is the need to open up the policy processes surrounding new technologies to far greater interaction with members of the public and their diverse values' (GECP, 1999: 4). Yet this solution was proposed not simply for reasons of democratic inclusion, nor even because such a way of proceeding might build a higher degree of legitimacy and therefore allow firm decisions to eventually be taken.
>
> Rather it was offered on the hard analytical grounds that such interactive policy processes are *more scientifically robust*. This is because in the presence of uncertainty and ignorance, judgements about risk are intrinsically subjective rather than objective. To pretend otherwise is likely to lead to an overly narrow focus of scientific enquiry and policy judgement.

It will be seen from Figure 4.2 that we suggest that these categories cut across and contribute to the more traditional ones of 'education' and 'training'. However, the figure also recognises that learning, and particularly deliberately sponsored learning, are far from being the whole story. Learning happens quite independently of the actions of teachers and policy makers, because of a whole range of external factors, including economic policy, social policy, the context of civil society and so on. These external factors also act directly, either positively or negatively, on sustainable development itself, and receive feedback, through learning, as non-human nature responds in predictable or unpredictable ways.

Under these circumstances, information or communication strategies are inadequate by themselves. This is because, first, in relation to those complex but important issues best suited to learning through mediation there exists insufficient undisputed content that can be conveyed. Second, however useful information or communication strategies may be in particular, time-and-place limited situations, they tend not to equip learners with skills which will enable them to continue to learn adaptively (or, to use Young's or Engestrom's terminology, *connectively*, or in an *expanded* style) in response to developing, feedback-modified circumstances. What is necessary instead is a process of exchange through which everyone involved may bring what they know to the table, and *everyone* involved should expect to learn. In terms of our earlier terminology, the implications are:

- Learning (and all other) specialists need to offer what they know to the sustainable development debate in the knowledge that insights from other disciplines will also be necessary for major progress to occur. Disciplinary chauvinism

(Lucas, 1980) will be as unhelpful from educationalists (see, for example, Fien and Trainer, 1993a; 1993b) as from any other quarter

• There is a particular role for learning through the even-handed mediation of the process through which different disciplinary specialists, and other stakeholders, engage with each other's insights: that is, for the facilitation of environmental meta-learning.

Third, people and institutions (learners and teachers) bring different value dispositions to the table which militate against the usefulness of information provision, and simple communications exercises which is why social marketing is effective only in contexts where there is no value dissonance between participants. It should not, perhaps, be surprising that, broadly speaking, the most difficult problems of sustainable development appear to call for the most complex solutions. We return to the question of the precise form which these different kinds of learning interventions might best take in Chapters 7 and 8.

The evidence

Any snapshot of a fast-moving inter-disciplinary field of study such as sustainable development is inevitably imperfect. Nevertheless, if one sets aside aspects of the specialist literature on environmental learning within which issues relating to sustainable development and learning feature, then it is hard to be optimistic about the potential not only for environmental meta-learning, but for the acceptance of any contribution from learning specialists at all. Pezzoli (1997), for example, divided knowledge about sustainable development into ten categories along broad disciplinary lines. All but two of these categories were then further subdivided. Works which were judged to be significant from more than one disciplinary viewpoint were included more than once in the resulting bibliography, which has a total of 521 entries. Section 2.2 is entitled, *Human Behaviour and Social Learning*. It has twelve entries. The word 'education' fairs worse than 'learning', and does not appear in the title of any category or sub-category.

More positive from the perspective of learning is Agenda 21 (see chapter 2 of the companion reader), which devotes Chapter 36 to issues of education and learning. However, it is as yet far from clear that this emphasis has been maintained following the Johannesburg 2002 World Summit on Sustainable Development. There is also evidence to suggest that some international environmental NGOs are increasingly focusing any resources they may have available for learning initiatives only using information and communication strategies. This is, of course, all very well if these are appropriately focused, but as we have suggested here, it will do little to address the most important and intractable issues in the way that it seemed, for example, that WWF's ecoregion conservation initiative might (see Chapter 7 for a critical commentary on this).

It is not all disappointing news, however. One recent initiative which seems promising is the UK Learning and Skills Development Agency's *Learning to Last* initiative (Cohen, James and Blewitt, 2002). Another, also in the United Kingdom, is the *National Biodiversity Strategy*, which identifies an important role for learning. In the United States of America there is also some cause for cautious hope in the approach of the National Science Foundation (Leinan, 2001), while a number of interesting cases can also be found in developing countries around the world. Again, we return to and expand on these examples during our discussion of curriculum in Chapters 7 and 8.

5 Humans and nature

Tensions and interdependence

Introduction: knowing what we need to know

In Chapter 1 we discussed in a preliminary way the interrelationship between human activity and the environment, discussed a number of possible competing ways of *thinking about* that interrelationship, and stated our own preference for a co-evolutionary view. We also noted a tendency, at least in Western societies, to inbue nature with two, contradictory, sets of characteristics. The reality is considerably more complex in both respects.

First, it is worth re-iterating that the society-environment relationship (on the one hand) and the relationship between *how we think about society* and *how we think about the environment* (on the other) are, to borrow a phrase from management literature, 'loosely coupled' (Weick, 1976). Figure 5.1 will be partly familiar from our earlier discussion.

The picture has been extended to suggest that learning can take place:

- By individuals, who may change their ideas about society, environment and change
- By society, as it adapts in planned and unplanned ways
- By the environment, in the sense that it too adapts in response to human activity.

Note that it is also possible for adaptations to occur in ways which entail no human learning, at least in the sense we developed that term in Chapter 4.

This is to say that the way we think about society, environment and change influences (and is in turn influenced by) environmental and social change as they occur. However, influence is one thing: linear causality is another. Since our knowledge is frequently imperfect (see Chapter 4), and is mediated through literacies, institutions and cultures (see Chapter 6), we should expect that there will be many instances in which what is really happening, and what we think is really happening, are quite different. Such instances are likely to be characterised by the existence of 'contradictory certainties' (Thompson, 1990). This is to suggest that, where we find competing social groups marshalling impressive but incompatible bodies of evidence to support entrenched views, the most rational response is not to try to adjudicate between claims, but rather to assume that all parties are likely to be both (a bit) right and (a bit) wrong.

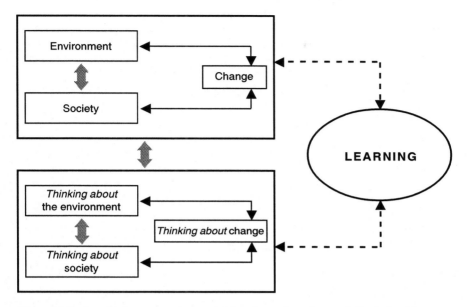

Figure 5.1 Society, environment, change and learning: a 'loosely coupled' relationship.

This provides (for Western thinking at least) an uncomfortable lack of closure to a problem. It is best explained not (or, at least, not only) in terms of the different interests which the protagonists to the dispute may have. Rather, we should admit the possibility that, not only do we not have enough knowledge to settle the matter, but we also do not know fully *what we would need to be knowledgeable about* in order to do so. In these circumstances, in which it is not necessarily possible to specify with confidence the variables which bear on a problem, science (for all its great value) can provide at best only provisional guidance (Scott, 2001). What is called for is not the kind of debate, critiqued in relation to public hearings by Kemmis (1990), at which no one listens to anyone else and everyone argues for the adoption of the position they themselves already hold. What is needed, rather, is learning across competing perspectives informed by a rather sophisticated theory of change (see Chapter 11).

An example which illustrates aspects of this argument is provided by Chalmers (2002), following Southgate (1997). This concerns the Senegal river basin where, from 1985 onwards, a series of dams were built in response to recurring droughts. Before building went ahead potential impacts were studied, taking account of environmental and social factors. One such factor was the serious tropical disease schistosomiasis, which is spread by a water-born parasite. The study found relatively low incidence of the disease and concluded that while it was difficult to predict the effects of dam-building in this respect, there was no apparent reason to expect negative consequences.

The dams were duly built. Subsequent monitoring revealed massive growth in infection from the parasite. Particularly spectacular was the infection rate from one particular form of the parasite which had previously been thought to be altogether absent from the Senegal river basin. With hindsight, it was possible to infer a number of reasons why this chain of events might have happened. Many expected benefits of the dam building project were, however, realised. Chalmers (2002: 98) draws two conclusions relating to learning:

> Scientists are not easily able to predict what will happen if things change . . . This degree of uncertainty, arising from the complexity of the overall situation, should perhaps have been better appreciated by decision-makers at the time. When scientists communicate with each other they have well-understood ways of expressing their degrees of uncertainty about their state of knowledge. When they are in dialogue with non-scientists, however, whether they be decision-makers or the general public, there is much less understanding about what is certain and what is not . . . scientific inputs into sustainable development projects must carry with them statements about certainty and risk . . .
>
> A second educational message . . . relates to human behaviour . . . Had the risk of schistosomiasis infection been assessed to be severe at the outset, the initial project costs might valuably have included those needed to finance public education programmes and improved sanitation.

However the reality, sadly, is that there are many instances of presumption either in favour of, or opposed to, dam-building and other engineering solutions to problems of development and environment almost *regardless* of context (e.g. Joseph and Mansell, 1996; Jansen, 1990). The actors come to the performance having learned a script which they are determined to deliver, even if the stage has been set for a quite different play.

A second source of additional complexity is that thinking about the environment-society relationship has been characterised by more than just one single pair of opposed assumptions. There are many others, some of which are discussed below.

Environment as scarcity: environment as bounty

In Chapter 1 (and also in chapter 12 of the companion reader) we have drawn on Richard Norgaard's 1984 paper on co-evolutionary agricultural development as a source of seminal thinking. Here we continue to draw largely on that paper, but before doing so we should make two points. First, Norgaard has continued his work on coevolution and readers will find a large body of work to explore. Examples of some considerable interest in relation to the argument of this book include Norgaard (1994), and Lele and Norgaard (1995). Second, Norgaard (1984: 535–7) himself is at some pains to acknowledge the many formative influences upon his work, noting with a wry humility which we feel is even more appropriate to our own present endeavours that:

In the early stages of discovering and honing a new theoretical construct, one feels considerable creative pride. As the product develops, however, one begins to notice with equal chagrin that others have discovered the idea and honed other edges before.

Norgaard's purpose in developing his co-evolutionary approach is to create a linkage between ecological and economic ways of thinking. In tracing the historical divergence between economics and the natural sciences he identifies a number of exceptions and special cases, but these do not detract from an overall pattern in which the classical models of Malthus and Ricardo, with their emphasis on resource scarcity, were successfully adapted by the natural sciences (for example through the work of Darwin and Wallace) but ultimately cast aside by economists. This divergence was well illustrated subsequently by the differing responses to the publication of *The Limits to Growth* (Meadows *et al.*, 1972). It was well received among natural scientists while, Norgaard claims in a footnote, the *only* economist to accept unequivocally at the time the inherent unsustainability of exponential expansion of resource-use was Daly (1973). Thus, at the extremes of a spectrum consisting entirely of rational, scientific approaches, we find on the one hand the view that resource scarcity threatens human survival (Ehrlich, 1968), and on the other the proposition that human development can be encouraged by resource constraints when they lead to social and economic adaptation (Boserup, 1965): natural scarcity in one case; natural bounty in the other.

An important aspect of the co-evolutionary case is its treatment of entropy and entropy change. Ultimately, by virtue of the laws of thermodynamics, resources *are* limited. However, from the particular perspective of the human species, and over what are rather long periods of time in human terms, negative entropy change is perfectly possible providing appropriate and appropriately focused inputs of energy are available. Norgaard (1984: 531–2) writes:

> The oxygen we breathe, the plant and animal life we eat, and the hydrocarbons we tap to fuel our industry all arise from biological processes. Even the ordering of minerals has improved for man over eons by various physical processes stemming from solar energy and the gradual cooling of the earth. From a perspective limited to man and the earth, the evolution of life has been a negentropic process.

> This seemingly optimistic view, however, must be tempered with three severe caveats. First, evolution and man's position therein have been largely a process of chance . . . Second, though no available data are adequate, many scientists are persuaded that man is currently exploiting the accumulated low entropy of his environment, through both extraction and pollution, to the detriment of future generations far faster than he is coevolving with nature to the benefit of future generations …most of the technologies we associate with development may simply allow us to use low-entropy stocks faster. Third, too little of our current

knowledge and research efforts are directly applicable to the immense task of influencing coevolution to our benefit.

This analysis does not resolve issues of complexity, uncertainty, risk and necessity but it does help us to frame them more clearly.

Ecocentrism: technocentrism

An approach which parallels some aspects of the above analysis in developing a set of categories relating to perspectives on environmentalism is that of O'Riordan (1989). This has proved to be a most influential perspective, not least in its impact on the field of environmental education, where it has to a significant degree underpinned the development of an influential 'red-green' strand of thought (Huckle, 1993; 1996; 1998). Advocates of this position argue that synergistic collaboration is possible between ecocentric and ecosocialist approaches to environmental education, based upon a number of characteristics which, it is argued, they have in common.

This supposed overlap may be inferred from O'Riordan's (1989) formulation, which drew on a range of ideas and developed his own previous (1981) thinking. Through it, O'Riordan notes that conceptions of environmentalism represent a:

> constructive tension between two major worldviews . . . a distinction between on the one side a conservative and nurturing view of society-nature relationships, where nature provides a metaphor for morality (how to behave) and a guide to rules of conduct (why we must behave so), and on the other side a radical or manipulative perspective in which human ingenuity and the spirit of competition dictate the terms of morality and conduct.
>
> (O' Riordan, 1989: 82)

O'Riordan (1989: 85) pictured ideas on environmentalism as lying along an *Ecocentrism – Technocentrism* spectrum.

Ecocentrism was characterised as a 'demand for redistribution of power towards a decentralised, federated economy with more emphasis on informal economic and social transactions and the pursuit of participatory justice', whereas O'Riordan saw *Technocentrism* as a 'belief in the retention of the status quo in the existing structure of political power, but a demand for more responsiveness and accountability in political, regulatory, planning, and educational institutions.'

O'Riordan gave *Ecocentrism* two perspectives: *Gaianism and Communalism* where Gaianism represented 'faith in the rights of nature and of the essential need for co-evolution of human and natural ethics', and Communalism represented 'faith in the co-operative capabilities of societies to establish self-reliant communities based on renewable resource use and appropriate technologies'.

Technocentrism was also given two perspectives: *Accommodation* and *Intervention*, where Accommodation represented 'faith in the adaptability of institutions and approaches to assessment and evaluation to accommodate environmental demands', and Intervention represented 'faith in the application of science, market forces, and managerial ingenuity'.

This conceptualisation has been developed further by O'Riordan himself (for example, 1990), and by others including Sterling (1993), who has sought to add an explicitly educational dimension to the analysis. Nevertheless it remains a powerful influence, and this is our reason for including it here in its original form, as well as using it a basis to problematise two issues.

First, we may ask whether the red-green, perspective of 'radical socialists' (O'Riordan, 1989: 82–4) should really be associated with a nurturing rather than a manipulative worldview. As noted in Chapter 1, this perspective tends to be associated with a particular egalitarian social project in which superior social knowledge – which dismisses contrary opinion as either selfishness or false-consciousness – coupled with socialist managerial ingenuity, will create a collectivist utopia. For O'Riordan's 'interventionists' the position is, at least, somewhat similar: superior scientific knowledge, coupled with (non-socialist) managerial ingenuity will deliver progress and improvement. One might wonder whether ecocentrism really has anything to offer socialists except a bandwagon of convenience, particularly given Edwards' (1997: 45) characterisation of the key notion of false-consciousness (Fien, 1993; Fay, 1987) as: 'a deeply embedded but patronising position which some radicals share with conservative critics of the contemporary world'.

The goal of critical research, and of the critical theories which inform and underpin it, is to promote a particular politics, i.e. one devoted to what Braybrooke (1987: 68) describes as the: 'emancipation . . . of social classes from oppression or contempt; emancipation of people throughout society, from ideas that inhibit rationality'. Thus, there is a contradiction built into socially critical theorising about environmental education: namely that, if research or development has to be underpinned by specific and specified values, and if these are to be taught (and learned), how can practitioners have autonomy, and learners be free to evolve their own value positions? Hart and Nolan (1999: 22) report, without comment, Robottom's contention that a socially critical education is a central notion of environmental education, although this seems to be a good example of 'western goals and evaluative criteria (being) applied globally', a process which they understandably deplore. Whatever the problem, the solution from critical theory is a priori always of the same form and thus the theory finds it difficult to provide solutions to complex and diverse (environmental) educational problems.

Second, it is important to probe the limits within which it is possible to be 'ecocentric' at all. Drawing on work relating to the notion of natural capital (Holland, 1994) and ecocriticism (Buell, 1995), Andrew Stables has argued that only a partially ecocentric viewpoint is possible (Gough *et al*, 2000; Stables, 2001a). Such a viewpoint would be one for which, as a minimum, human history was implicated in natural history; human interest was understood not to be the only interest; there was a sense of ethical accountability to the environment; and, the environment was conceived as a process rather than a given entity. Beyond this one is foiled by the inescapability of using human language to define, let alone valorise or patronise, the non-human.

Finally, we should note that like Norgaard, O'Riordan (1989: 102) sees strength, not weakness, in diversity. He writes: 'For environmentalism to survive, it must always experience an internal as well as an external struggle'.

Paradigms and worldviews: emerging and otherwise

Mary Clark (1989: 235) writes: 'In Western history there have been but two major periods of conscious social change, when societies deliberately critiqued themselves and created new worldviews': during the Golden Age of Greece and during the European Enlightenment. In both periods, philosophers who deliberately critiqued the societal worldview were esteemed by society. A considerable literature exists to advance the case that human society is now either: (i) undergoing a 'paradigm shift', or (ii) needing to undergo such a shift. This case is often linked to another: that particular academic disciplines also need, or are in fact undergoing, corresponding paradigm adjustment (Skolimowski, 1982; Robottom and Hart, 1993; Fien, 1993; Sterling, 1993; 2001). Finally, there is sometimes an attempt to link the notion of a new social paradigm in the West to the rediscovery of Eastern or indigenous wisdom, though it should be noted both that the case for such rediscovery can be made quite well without invoking the rhetoric of paradigms (e.g. Bowers, 2002), and that Said (1985) warns us forcibly that to present the history of the non-Western world merely as the context in which Western ideas have failed is no less patronising than to present it as the context of Western success.

As noted already, the use of the word 'paradigm' in these formulations has its origins, explicitly or otherwise, and more or less loosely, in the work of Thomas Kuhn (1996). We should therefore note in passing that Kuhn himself was writing predominantly about the history of the natural sciences, and that he did not see the emergence of scientific paradigms as a matter of choice or planning. Further, we may say that the social sciences continue to exhibit what Kuhn saw as possibly evidence of pre-paradigmatic immaturity in academic disciplines, rather than imminent paradigm shift. He writes:

> Both during pre-paradigm periods and during the crises which lead to large scale changes of paradigm, scientists usually develop many speculative and unarticulated theories.
>
> (Kuhn, 1996: 61)

On the subject of paradigms operating at the level of society as a whole, Kuhn has nothing to say.

Figure 5.2 lists, on the left, some of the characteristics often associated in these discourses with 'new' or 'emerging' paradigms and, on the right, the elements of the old paradigm which they purport to replace, or to be replacing. How far, at the present time, this has in fact happened in each case is an open, and as it stands rather vague, empirical question for consideration by historians.

Whether any degree of social paradigm shift has actually happened is one question, whether it is further possible to identify any sort of continuing trend is another. Finally, we may ask whether there is any good reason to believe that the items in Column A really cohere in any meaningful way which sets them in opposition to those in Column B. In thinking about this we should note the following:

- We remarked in Chapter 3 that binary thinking in terms of which entities are expected to exhibit either a given characteristic (say, decentralisation) or its opposite (centralisation) but not both, has been embedded in the Western mind since Aristotle. This is only a way of thinking, however, not a necessary property of an entity as complex and multi-faceted as 'society'

- In Chapter 1, we discussed cultural theory and its notion of competing rationalities (James and Thompson, 1989; Schwarz and Thompson, 1990; and chapter 1 of the companion reader). This provides an example of a possible non-binary way of reorganising at least some of the characteristics listed in Figure 5.2 under the headings of the four types of rationality which, as Thompson (1990) notes, are mutually constitutive: that is, each defines itself in relation to the others and so needs them if it is to make sense itself. This would mean that, rather than there being a process of replacement of one characteristic by another over time, we would expect to find evidence of both sets of characteristics at all stages of human history. This does not seem unreasonable here in a number of cases. Once again, for example, centralisation/ decentralisation offers a possible example

- From a rather different perspective, Foucault (1981: 7) warns us that, 'discourses are not once and for all subservient to power or raised up against it, any more than silences are . . . there can exist different and even contradictory discourses within the same strategy; they can, on the contrary, circulate without changing their form from one strategy to another, opposing strategy'. We should therefore perhaps not expect the different discourses enumerated in Figure 5.2 to be fixed in relation to each other for all time.

This has been a necessarily brief discussion of the case for emerging paradigms, but it does not seem to be going too far to say that no case for learning specifically targeted to promote any particular paradigm of social organisation has been convincingly made. More consistent with our wider argument would be an attempt to encourage dialogue between paradigms, when and if these seem to be in

Column A	Column B
Ecocentric	Anthropocentric
Postmodernist	Modernist
Decentralist	Centralist
Libertarian	Authoritarian
Feminist	Patriarchal
Co-operative	Competitive
Participatory	Managerial
Egalitarian	Hierarchical
Holistic	Reductionist
Protective	Exploitative
Nurturing	Manipulative
Seeking stability	Seeking progress
Environment is a social construct	Environment is a given

Figure 5.2 Possible opposed orientations to the environment.

opposition. This is not in itself entirely inconsistent with the views of at least some who have written more extensively in relation to this question. For example, Robottom and Hart (1993: 16) comment:

> If we can agree that educational enquiry is multiparadigmatic there is no need to fuse, no reason or need to find compromise, but there is a need to value different perspectives, assuming that knowledge is a social construction of communities of inquirers operating from various paradigmatic perspectives.

Behaviour or empowerment: mechanism or organism

Two competing strands of thinking in relation to learning, change, environment and society focus on, respectively, changing human behaviour and human empowerment. Both continue to be influential. In the fields of environmental education and environmental management training, for example, empirical work which aimed to establish and operationalise clear goals for learning (Hungerford *et al*, 1980; Hungerford *et al*, 1983; Hungerford and Volk, 1984; Hungerford *et al*, 1988; Hungerford and Volk, 1990; Linke, 1976; Roth, 1970) had established a dominant intellectual position by the end of the 1980s. The focus of this work was behaviour change and this continues to be central to many approaches to learning and the environment (e.g. Tanner, 1998; McKenzie-Mohr and Smith, 1999; Wehrmeyer, 1996). The anticipated result of learning in this view is the development of an environmentally knowledgeable and responsible citizenry (or workforce). Once given this, it is considered that the democratic structures of Western society, or the enlightened managerial approaches of the contemporary workplace, are adequate to act as a vector for change. This position was initially challenged primarily from the perspective of socially critical theory, which argued that behaviourist approaches were an attempt at a technocentric quick-fix to environmental and educational problems which was based in a naïve view of science, a mechanistic metaphor for nature, and a simplistic view of power relations and political realities (Robottom, 1987a, 1987b; Greenall Gough, 1993; Huckle, 1983a, 1983b, 1993). From an educational point of view this approach owed a substantial debt to the work of Friere (1971) which argues for an emancipatory role for education. This Frierean approach has also been, and continues to be, influential in fields such as environmental management (Sharp, 1992) and lifelong learning. Similarly, the claim that science is not ultimately value-free but has values implicit within it has attracted support across a number of fields (e.g. Lele and Norgaard, 1995; Tesh, 1988). However, and as we have already noted, the particular claim of socially critical theorists to have adopted an ecological or organic, rather than a mechanistic metaphor for society has been critiqued, particularly by Bowers (1993; 1995; 2001 and chapter 11 of the companion reader).

A North American example: NAAEE

The annual conference of the North American Association for Environmental Education is *the* gathering for people who are interested in the environment and learning. Those attending in any year include school and college teachers, university researchers, graduate students, NGO staff, private sector representatives and officers from Federal, State and local government agencies. It is a meeting at which many of the oppositions identified in this chapter are in evidence, and at which thinking about issues of society, environment and learning goes on from a number of perspectives.

Some of those who attend are primarily interested in the study of the processes of nature in order to understand them. Others see nature as a metaphor for a preferred social order, which may be 'competitive' or 'co-operative' according to their world-view. Table 5.1 is based on observations at NAAEE conferences over a number of years. In it are set out nine *categories of interest* which capture, albeit in a rather tentative way, a range of the different focuses and objectives of those who espouse and promote environmental learning.

The disposition towards sustainable development across the various categories of interest varies markedly. Many of those who would call themselves environmental educators welcome a focus on sustainable development because it provides the opportunity to raise issues of social justice, while others use it strategically to promote particular social change.

Of course, any such categorisation has to be a simplification as these categories are not necessarily fully discrete and any given individual might be involved in two or more of them, but it does allow us to consider how those interested in environmental learning can have widely differing assumptions about both purpose and process. For example:

- From point 1 to point 8, interest in nature, *per se*, decreases markedly, along with a shift from a realist view of nature to a metaphorical one. There is also a shift from interest in the individual learner to the social context
- From points 3 to 7 the environment (natural and otherwise) is viewed mainly heuristically, i.e. as a means of exploring issues and achieving particular goals
- point 8 sees the natural world as providing a coherent and liveable philosophy that explains our social and ecological obligations. Some of those we have placed in this category may have very little else in common
- point 9 is a mix of those interested primarily in social/environmental issues and those whose focus is on educational issues. It can usefully be further subdivided along lines of preferred educational research methodology.

All the perspectives represented by these categories of interest are both legitimate and valuable in that they all have something to contribute to learning about the human condition and our relationship with nature under conditions of complexity, uncertainty, risk and necessity. These perspectives are not evenly distributed on national lines however. In North America and the United Kingdom, representation from points 1, 2, 3, 4, 5 and 9 would be strong. In South Africa and Australia, representation of point 6 would be likely to be more marked. Danish work on action competence (Jensen and Schnack, 1997; Jensen, 2002; and chapter 9 of the companion reader) represents the most successfully developed example of point 7 across the world.

Table 5.1 Categories of interest in environmental learning.

Categories of interest . . .	Focus and outcomes	Exemplified by . . .
1. those **interested in sharing the joy and fulfilment derived from nature**, in order to bring about significant life-enhancing and life-changing experience for learners	**Nature** *values and feelings*	**non-formal educators** and **interpreters** seeking attitudinal and/ or value change; possibly seeking to introduce and extend particular philosophies of living
2. those **interested in the study of the processes of nature** in order to understand, or to teach about them	**Nature** *understanding*	**teachers** of ecology, (physical) geography, the earth sciences and rural studies; **researchers** in these (and other) areas
3. those **using nature as an heuristic** to foster the development of knowledge, understanding, skills and character which, although situated, are transferable to other contexts and through time	**Nature** *skills*	**teachers**, **environmental interpreters** and **field studies officers** seeking to develop students' cognitive/conative/affective/ psychomotor skills related to environmental work
4. those **using the natural and/or built environments as heuristics** to achieve conservation and/or sustainability goals	**Conservation** *understanding*	**conservation/heritage scientists** (and others) working for government or NGOs bringing communication and education strategies to bear on conservation and sustainability issues
5. those **advocating/promoting individual behaviour changes** in order to achieve conservation/ sustainability goals	**Conservation** *behaviours*	**environmental activists** and **teachers** who have clear views on what the problems are, and on their solutions
6. those **advocating/promoting particular modes of social change** in order to achieve environmental/ conservation/sustainability goals	**Social change** *social justice*	**environmental activists** and **teachers** with clear views on the form of social organisation needed to achieve sustainability
7. those **using environmental, conservation and/or sustainability issues as contexts** for the development of skills and knowledge related to the exercise of democratic social change	**Social change** *democratic citizenship skills*	**teachers** and others interested in helping (young) people acquire democratic and citizenship skills which will enable them to participate in open-ended social change relating to human–environment relationships
8. those **promoting nature as a metaphor for a preferred social order** – which may be 'co-operative' or 'competitive', according to worldview	**Social change** *values*	**sociobiologists, deep-ecologists, social Darwinists, Gaianists** who engage in communication and informal education in relation to the relationship between humans and nature
9. those **interested in the study of environmental learning** (and environmental education) itself	**Learning** *learning about learning*	**educational researchers** interested in various aspects of learning and teaching related to environmental and sustainability issues

If all the perspectives represented by these nine categories of interest are each both legitimate and valuable, it follows that, individually, none of them has the full picture in relation to learning and sustainable development. This offers a positive way forward. Individuals can select distinctive perspectives for learning in keeping with their own particular priorities and/or responsibilities in the knowledge that doing so does not render other perspectives illegitimate. What is crucial, however, is that environmental meta-learning (see Chapter 4) occurs over time between those taking different approaches.

6 Theory and practice
Ideology and philosophy

Introduction

We have identified a complex relationship between, on the one hand, society, environment and change and, on the other hand, between the ways in which we think about these (Figure 5.1, p. 45). We have suggested that these two sets of relationships are 'loosely-coupled', that is:

- They are ultimately connected by processes of cause and effect
- Those processes tend to be unpredictable both in relation to their direction, and according to context and time-span.

To put this simply, what we think makes a difference to what really happens in our environment, but it does so in ways which are very hard to predict. Long-term consequences are swamped by short-term variations in the many parameters involved, and by other, sometimes unexpected, long-term effects.

Situations of this kind are not unusual in the social sciences. Economists, for example, cannot predict exchange rates, though this would seem on the face of it to be a relatively simple matter when compared to the task of predicting medium-to long-term environmental change and its impacts. However, the experience of economists should be seen as encouraging rather than the reverse. First, though prediction necessarily remains elusive this has not meant that systematic study of the problem has been useless. Second, economists have developed a theoretical tool, the notion of purchasing power parity, which enables useful predictions to be made about the pattern of exchange rates we *would* see if it was not, as it always actually is, distorted by interference from many other factors. Similarly, writers on educational change have made great strides through *recognising* the inherent complexity and unpredictability of their area of study. Michael Fullan (2001: 95–6), for example, has written:

> For the growing number of people who have attempted to bring about educational change, 'intractability' is becoming a household word. Being ungovernable, however, is not the same as being impervious to influence. And the inability to change *all* situations we would ideally like to reform does not lead to the conclusion that *no* situation can be changed . . . Understanding why

most attempts at educational reform fail goes far beyond the identification of specific technical problems such as lack of good materials, ineffective professional development, or minimal administrative support. In more fundamental terms, educational change fails partly because of the assumptions of planners, and partly because solving substantial problems is an inherently complex business.

(original emphasis)

In this chapter we attempt to make some modest, systematic progress towards understanding in practical terms the complex relationship between human beings, the societies and environments in which they live and learning processes by and through which change occurs. Our particular focus is on social artefacts: on the theories, practices, ideologies and philosophies which accumulate at the boundary between our external reality and our internal sense-making in relation to it. Readers will note that this maintains a consistent theme of our approach, that of asking not only, 'what interests do particular individuals and groups have?', but also, 'how do such individuals and groups come to believe themselves to have such interests at particular places and times?'.

An analytic model: practices, institutions and literacies

The importance of distinguishing *practices* from *institutions* is a point made by MacIntyre (1981). This distinction, together with our earlier, preliminary discussion of literacies, provides the basis of the model shown in Figure 6.1.

Teaching is a practice. So are management (of all kinds), parenting, construction work, retailing, policy making and so on. The existence of a practice further implies the existence of practitioners, who will have a set of beliefs or theories which constitute their own view of their practice. For example, teachers' beliefs are likely to

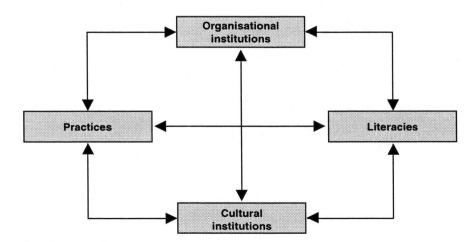

Figure 6.1 A model of categories of social influences on sustainable development and learning.

include particular views about how students learn, effective pedagogy, professional development, school and classroom management, curriculum and, more generally, the purposes of education (Gough *et al.,* 2001). In the context of schools, Walker (1997) has drawn attention to the inadequacy of approaches to change which ignore the theories of practitioners. A point to note is that practitioners' 'espoused' beliefs – those which they say, and perhaps believe, they have – may diverge markedly from their 'theories in use' (Argyris and Schön, 1978) , that is, those which appear to guide what they actually do. We noted in Chapter 3 that hypocrisy was not always a useful term in relation to inconsistent environmental behaviours. The foregoing provides a more analytical and less judgemental way of thinking about such discrepancies.

The practice of teaching and the theories which teacher-practitioners have of it, are particularly well studied and provide a number of interesting insights. First, it is notable that practices may possess considerable inertia; that is, practitioners may be resistant to changing the way they go about things even when under very considerable pressure from policy makers and others to do so. This inertia may persist over very long periods of time and as Lundgren (1991: 45) notes, over such periods, 'the closer we come to the teaching situation, the more stable are the processes of education'. For example, didactic teaching methods have been around for (at least) hundreds of years and the ways in which we organise schools seem remarkably stable.

Second, however, there is evidence that changes in the theories of one group of practitioners can have a real effect on the theories of another group. One case is that of work by school effectiveness and improvement researchers (see, for example, Gray *et al.,* 1999) which appears to be increasingly finding its way into the thinking of teachers through their participation in research and/or professional development programmes.

Third, both the espoused theories of teachers and/or trainers, and their theories-in-action, may vary between different organisational levels. What a teacher thinks appropriate for school systems as a whole, or for education in general, may vary markedly from what she or he considers suitable for the particular class he or she happens to be teaching. It is possible, in other words, for an individual teacher, or a school department, or even perhaps a whole school staff, to see their own practice as a justifiable exception to rules which they nevertheless believe should govern practice more generally.

It seems likely that the circumstances in which the promotion of sustainable development through learning might occur will be characterised by the presence of different practices and influenced, in turn, by the associated theories of practitioners. These theories will be multi-faceted and prone to change both over time and from one context to another. Work in the field of educational change has identified some of the potential influences on the theories of practitioners as a range of possible perspectives which may be dominant at particular times and places, and in relation to particular problems. Blenkin *et al.* (1997) identify five such perspectives in education:

- A *technological* perspective. In this view desired learning results can be achieved through efficient and effective instrumental action. One makes a clear plan, implements it, and evaluates the outcome (see Chapter 10), perhaps setting this whole linear sequence within a framework of specific quality requirements which have been set independently of context and identified in advance by external inspectors.

- A *cultural* perspective. This is characterised by a belief that learning can best be achieved where practitioners and others defer to cultural norms which are deep-rooted and, for the most part, intuitive and implicit. A very good example is provided by a study in the south-west of England (Drew, 2000) which used focus-groups to investigate the shared perceptions of primary school teachers, pupils and parents. Even though these groups were exposed to a rigorous, nationwide and highly instrumental regime of external inspection, and took this very seriously, they also exhibited strong attachment to a quite different, cultural interpretation of the purpose of education. This was that it should equip children with, and so perpetuate, the perceived special cultural characteristics of the school catchment area – a small rural town and its surrounding villages.

- A *micropolitical* perspective. Learning is considered to be contingent on the outcomes of micropolitical power struggles within, or outside of, the institution. Will specific vacancies be filled by staff sympathetic to sustainable development? Can the Principal be prevailed upon to make resources of one kind or another available in the face of competition from other curriculum areas? Will sustainable development be mentioned in the National Curriculum's latest version? Will its provision be inspected?

- A *biographical* perspective. Practitioners' views of learning depend on where they are in their careers and what is happening in the rest of their lives. It should be noted here that this does not necessarily mean that practitioners should be expected to be innovative (or pro-sustainable development) early in their careers and cynical as they near retirement. The reverse trajectory is perfectly possible, as is one which maintains enthusiasm (or cynicism) at a high level throughout.

- A *structural perspective*. Broad social trends influence practitioners' views of learning. Such trends may include, for example, changes over time in the credibility of particular ideologies, or changes in demography. A particular instance of relevance to our discussion here is that of the growing association of the notion of 'empowerment' of learners with increased consumer choice in the education marketplace. This, as Edwards (1997) notes, has created a conflict in the thinking of many educators. For many environmentalists, the notion of 'consumption' is an ill-fit with either 'learning' or 'sustainable development'.

A final point in relation to the theories of education, and practitioners concerns the emergence of global discourses (Payne, 1997). Practices of all kinds are increasingly characterised by global information exchange, both through electronic communication and other means. As this occurs there is inevitable pressure towards the creation of shared terms of reference which, at the extreme, can result in globalised assertions. The work of Townsend *et al*, (1999) and Townsend (1999), for example, makes claims about '3rd Millennium Schools' and 'The Global Classroom'. Whether approaches of this kind really have discovered the global educational lowest-common-denominator or are just further manifestations of a globalising Western culture of sound-bites and slick presentation, only time will tell. The point here, however, is that they seem likely to have a significant but as yet uncertain influence on the way practitioners involved in learning processes conceive and think about what they do.

Returning now to MacIntyre's (1981) distinction between practices and institutions, we can usefully further identify two broad kinds of institution. These are *organisational* institutions and, as noted in Chapter 4, *cultural* institutions. Schools, colleges, NGOs and charities, government departments, trades unions and private corporations are all organisational institutions. An important generic characteristic of these, as MacIntyre (1981, 181) himself points out, is that they are necessarily involved the pursuit of external goods to sustain themselves and the practices they promote. Potentially this has at least two important consequences. First, we may expect it sometimes to act as a brake on idealism and an influence on policy. So, for example, a political party which strongly favoured sustainable development in principle, and in general terms while out of power, may retreat rapidly from that position in practice, and in specific terms. This will be especially so if once in power, if faced with the best lobbying efforts of powerful and rich interest groups. Similarly, an environmental NGO which would really like to campaign for widespread changes in social and economic practices as a long-term approach to halting biodiversity loss, may instead find itself asking the public for money to conserve specific populations of large mammals because of its need to fund-raise to survive and because that is something it knows the public is likely to contribute to.

Second, the need organisational institutions have for resources means that individual institutions usually need to compete with others of the same type. So, a country's Ministry of Environment may compete with its Ministry of Education for allocations of tax-payers' money in circumstances where success for one means failure for the other; NGOs such as WWF and Conservation International compete to save species by attracting charitable donations which will not be made twice; at the local government level, adult education initiatives may compete for funding with recycling initiatives; schools and colleges compete for teachers and students; and corporations compete for customers.

The notion of a cultural institution was developed by Reid (1999: 111), who gives the example of age-related class enrolment.

> Once such things achieve social and cultural significance, they acquire a life of their own. They become institutionalized in a dual sense. They need institutions to preserve them, but they also *become* institutions in the more elusive sense of an idea that is integral to a culture and seen as significant by most of its members. Being in the third grade becomes an important defining characteristic of a person – as does being a third grade teacher.
>
> (original emphasis)

An example of a cultural institution in many countries is a National Curriculum. In our view, *sustainable* development has not yet become a cultural institution anywhere, however much some may wish it had. On the other hand, 'development', and' economic development' clearly have done so in many cases, along with other, more problematic formulations such as 'sustainable growth'. All this may be evidence of just how much sustainable development itself is what Sachs (1991, and chapter 3 of the companion reader) has called a 'dangerous liaison'.

Organisational institutions may enhance their standing and promote the practices they favour by successfully encouraging the establishment or acceptance of particular cultural institutions. This means that when, for example, a particular NGO decides to campaign on a platform of sustainable development there is more at stake than just ideas about development or environmental sustainability. The future of the NGO itself becomes coupled to the success of 'sustainable development' in capturing the attention of those who, through whatever means, control its flow of funds and other resources. If, at some point, that NGO (with others, perhaps) is so successful that sustainable development becomes a cultural institution – embedded across society as an accepted goal of taken-for-granted importance – the NGO's continued existence would be secure, or at least much more so than before. It is probably not going too far to suggest that debates about ideas of this kind are *always*, at another level, battles for institutional prestige, enhancement or survival.

If an organisational institution is successful in promoting a particular cultural institution, therefore, its access to resources will be enhanced. However, whether it can achieve such success will depend not only upon the quality of its arguments, but also upon the resources (tangible, financial and cultural) it is able to marshal in the meantime. It will obtain these through competition, through forming alliances and through distributing rewards effectively. This inescapably means that discussions about the forms of learning which either should or could contribute to sustainable development cannot be separated from discussions about how a rather wide range of organisational institutions are managed and interact. For instance, academic fields with names like 'curriculum studies', 'educational management', 'environmental management', 'environmental economics', 'conservation biology' and so on have become cultural institutions. They are sponsored by organisational institutions which create and manage knowledge relating to (among other things) sustainable development and learning, including universities and the faculties and departments within them. This is not to diminish any of these admirable disciplines. It is, rather, to suggest that there are those organisational institutions in whose quite legitimate interest it is to preserve the *distinctiveness* and *apartness* of academic fields, and of the different practices each represents or supports, even as they may simultaneously issue rhetorical statements about the need for 'inter-disciplinary approaches' and the like. From the point of view of any disciplinary specialist there are powerful reasons for wanting to see the achievement of inter-disciplinarily provided it is on one's own terms.

An approach which echoes much of the above is that of Kemmis and Fitzclarence (1986: 92–3) who identify three 'registers of social formation'. These find their expression through *organisations* (broadly equivalent to our 'organisational institutions'), *practices* and *language*. Learning and sustainable development, however defined, are clearly aspects of 'social formation'. We have identified 'practices' as a component of our own model and refined the concept of an 'organisation' within a wider notion of 'institutions'. Finally, in Chapter 3 we have already considered the significance of language in some detail, developing the idea of multiple 'literacies' for inclusion in our model. In the remainder of this chapter we now seek to illustrate the application of this model, firstly in a hypothetical way by revisiting an example we first developed in Chapter 3 and expanded in Chapter 4, and then by exploring two real contexts of learning and sustainable development, one in a developed country and the other in a region of fairly rapid economic development. In each case we set our own approach, which emphasises the relationship between *what is* and *what and how we think about what is*, against a recent and very comprehensive model of the substantive nature of sustainable development itself.

Example one: tourism and sustainable development

In Chapter 3 we briefly discussed the case of a tropical coastline which was under consideration for development. We did this to illustrate the existence of different literacies and the ways in which these led to:

- Different *readings* of the environmental 'text'
- Particular *re-writings* of the environment, as any particular literacy became dominant. We are now in a position to see that this dominance would occur as a result of competition between different organisational institutions, each of which would seek to promote particular literacies. Re-writings would occur through the particular practices which dominant organisations and literacies supported
- Subsequent new, but still probably quite different *re-readings* of the environment, from the perspective of each of the original range of literacies.

In the Chapter 3 example, an economics-based literacy supported by development-focused institutions was dominant, leading to tourism development taking place. Far from being hypothetical, the example describes, as we saw in relation to Caribbean countries in Chapter 4, a situation common to many developing countries, where tourism, whether being planned or already fully introduced, is often seen as *the* route to development because it:

- Depends upon resources which developing countries often have such as beaches, rainforest, or culture, or combinations of these
- Creates a range of often usefully geographically dispersed, employment opportunities
- Creates apparent synergies with other industries which developing countries often have, such as national airlines or construction companies
- Appears to have the potential to earn large amounts of foreign exchange
- Above all, is arguably the world's largest and fastest growing industry.

In Chapter 4 we indicated some of the organisational institutions implicated in tourism development in the Caribbean region. A fuller but still incomplete list would include the following: Ministries of Education; multiple Ministries concerned with aspects of environment and environmental management; regional organisations such as the Organisation of East Caribbean States, international bodies such as the UK's Department for International Development and The United Nations Development Program; Regional NGOs such as the Caribbean Conservation Association; local NGOs such as the Antiguan Environmental Awareness Group; local churches; local companies; international companies such as hotel chains, airlines and holiday operators.

Cultural institutions which have a bearing include: sense of national independence; sense of regional inter-dependence; land use and ownership arrangements; national school and college curricula; established views of the value of certain resources, such as reefs; and established approaches to parenting (Jemmott, 2002). Established practices include those of fisherfolk and farmers, teachers, parents, consumers (domestic and foreign), members of religious congregations and immigration officials, as well as those of economists, biologists, geographers, planners, managers, policy makers and engineers. All of the foregoing practices are supported by at least one literacy. Some practitioners, policy makers for example, may switch between literacies depending on context.

The above analysis will not correspond to that of those who are involved, or at least not much. Rather, those involved will explain their differences and agreements in terms of their understandings of theoretical and practical issues, or in terms of ideological or philosophical differences. The purpose of our analysis is therefore twofold. First, it seeks to provide a single format through which apparent (and actual) theoretical, practical, ideological and philosophical differences may be conceptualised and understood. Second, it aims to reveal in a preliminary way the potential of environmental meta-learning to promote sustainable development under conditions of complexity, uncertainty, risk and necessity. We return to the mechanics of this in Chapter 8. For now, however, we may say that all parties to the issue of sustainable tourism development are likely to have something useful to say (although none of them will know everything), *not* about what the *solutions* to problems of sustainable (tourism) development may be, but about what those problems *are*. It follows from this that there is no way forward without learning within and between institutions.

It should be said at once that this is not a view everyone would share. For example Goodland (2002) argues that there are in fact four different kinds of 'sustainability', distinguished briefly as follows:

- *Human sustainability*: This involves the maintenance of human capital, which includes health, education, skills, knowledge, leadership and access to services. Human capital is conceived as a private good of individuals.
- *Social sustainability*: Involves the maintenance of social capital, which includes, for example, community cohesion, tolerance, compassion, forbearance, fellowship, love, discipline, ethics and, most importantly, shared values.
- *Economic sustainability*: Involves maintaining the total stock of natural plus manufactured capital by consuming no more than the value-added through economic activity.

- *Environmental sustainability*: Involves maintaining natural capital as both a source of economic inputs and as a sink for wastes.

Goodland's argument is that while these four kinds of sustainability overlap to some extent they are fundamentally different and should be dealt with separately by different kinds of expert. For example, social scientists would contribute to our understanding of social sustainability, economists would take care of economic sustainability, and biophysical specialists would look after environmental sustainability. At first this may appear to be opening the door to multiple literacies and practices. In fact, it is no more than a (quite possibly unwitting) attempt to hegemonise a particular (in itself, immensely valuable) literacy and its associated practices. It supports, and is supported by, the position of a major global organisational institution (the World Bank) which has a powerful stake in one of the most potent of all global cultural institutions (economic development). In our example it would seem to point to clearly separated responsibilities for:

- Economic and environmental managers in specialist departments which control the bulk of economically valuable assets where experts can safely be left to get on with it
- Community and religious organisations, with additional inputs perhaps from education, in developing social capital, where everyone will then love their neighbour
- Training, education and the healthcare and utility industries in managing stocks of human capital where schools and colleges can train people to give good service to tourists, understand the ecology of their surroundings, make the most of their leadership potential, and complain effectively when they receive poor service from water or power suppliers, and where everyone will know their place.

Let us be clear about this. We are not against reductionist thinking or mechanical metaphors *per se*. We are not against the World Bank, or economic development, or economists or biologists, as we hope our developing argument has made clear. What we are against, on the grounds that it is, always has been and always will be entirely useless, is the attempt to insist that any single way of thinking about immense global issues involving complexity, uncertainty, risk and necessity will be adequate for their resolution. To illustrate, let us ask the following questions:

- *Given that there are plenty of biophysical scientists, why is environmental sustainability in doubt?* The answer is, of course, that the causes of environmental degradation are not to be found in the environment. They are to be found among humans in society, and (which amounts to saying the same thing) in economics.
- *Given that there are plenty of economists, why is economic sustainability in doubt?* Because not all economists say the same thing, and because humans in society, who anyway have different degrees of power, tend to listen to the economists whose message is closest to the one they want to hear. We might also add here that the

whole notion of 'natural' and 'manufactured' capital is problematic in the context of sustainable development since, as we have noted, what counts as a resource depends crucially on what you want to do with it and whether you can. Neither of these is necessarily given.

- *Given that there are plenty of social scientists, why are human and social sustainability in doubt?* In the first place, a cynic might say, no one pays much attention to social scientists. Like economists, they disagree a lot. More importantly, what happens to an individual's private degree of access to services, or level of skills and knowledge depends crucially on the economic and environmental resources to which they have access. Similarly, the presence or absence in society of love, connectedness, tolerance, compassion and so on depends in very large part upon the stock of available economic and environmental assets, the degree of competition for them, and the perceived justice of the arrangements under which that competition occurs.

Our own claim would be simply that it is worthwhile, as a meta-level goal, to promote learning through enhanced awareness across individual, social, economic and environmental perspectives. Such learning would encourage individuals and groups to challenge the theoretical, practical, ideological and philosophical foundations of their thinking, while at the same time provide opportunities for them to share that thinking with others and to influence and learn from them. Clearly, to achieve this goal will involve discovering approaches to learning which appear acceptable *in the first instance* to a very wide range of existing institutions, literacies and practitioners. It is no small challenge.

7 Management of learning

Issues in curriculum design

Introduction: four examples

This chapter focuses on four varied contemporary examples of curriculum design in relation to a consideration of sustainable development and reviews each in the light of the theoretical principles developed in the preceding chapters. The four examples are:

- The UNESCO 'Teaching and learning for a sustainable future' multimedia teacher education programme
- 'Biodiversity Basics', a part of the larger 'Windows on the Wild' project for conservation education developed in the United States by the World Wildlife Fund
- 'Learning for sustainable development: a curriculum toolkit' produced by the UK-based NGO, Forum for the Future. This focuses on higher education, and is linked to the Forum's 'Higher Education Partnership for Sustainability' (HEPS) initiative
- The 'Education for Sustainable Development' (ESD) toolkit developed by Rosalyn McKeown at the University of Tennessee. This work uses the word 'education' in the wide sense, and has the international perspective envisaged by Chapter 36 of Agenda 21.

These four examples have been chosen because they provide international coverage and focus on different constituencies of learners. All four bring to bear the benefits of considerable, but different, experiences in relation to learning and sustainable development over many years. All will be found useful by very many learners. It is not our intention in what follows to judge, or in some way rank, this work. Rather, we hope that through examining all four examples, in turn, within a similar framework it will possible to draw useful conclusions: not about what might have been done instead, but about what might best be done next, or as well.* In the following

---

* In the interests of intellectual honesty and transparency we need to record our slight interest in each of these projects. Both of us were reviewers for parts of the UNESCO programme, and have been involved as reviewers and evaluators for *Windows on the Wild*. We evaluated for Forum for the Future their HE21 initiative which preceded HEPS. We had no substantive input into the ESD toolkit, but have worked closely with Dr McKeown on related projects over a number of years.

sections a brief description is provided of each example. They are then discussed in the light of the developing argument of this book, and in particular in terms of:

- The sustainable development learning model illustrated by Figure 4.2 (p. 38)
- Figure 6.1 (p. 57), which sets out the context of sustainable development learning in terms of institutions, practices and literacies.

The UNESCO 'Teaching and learning for a sustainable future' multimedia teacher education programme

The focus of this programme is teacher professional development. It is available from UNESCO free of charge, both as a CD Rom and also via the Internet at www. unesco.org/education/tlsf/

The programme draws upon, and develops, previous work in this area in many countries around the world, particularly in the Asia-Pacific region and in South Africa. It takes as axiomatic that education is a potentially effective means through which society can confront its problems. A contribution from one of the authors, John Fien, will be found in chapter 6 of the companion reader.

The programme is technologically and pedagogically sophisticated and beautifully presented. It is organised into five main sections, these being: 'getting started'; 'curriculum rationale'; 'across the curriculum'; 'curriculum themes'; and 'teaching and learning'. The belief of the authors in the power of education is quickly in evidence, since the problems which are to be confronted through education could hardly be more all-embracing. There is, we are told in 'getting started', a global crisis of a fundamentally cultural nature facing humanity as a whole. The most serious aspects of this crisis are subsequently identified as: demographic trends; poverty; pressures on the natural environment; problems of lack of democracy, human rights abuses, conflict and violence; and difficulties surrounding the very concept of development. The change mechanism which is to link education to the resolution of this suite of issues is that of influencing learners on a global scale to think in terms of, and commit themselves to, the 'common good' as they participate in society and make decisions. Education can cope with issues of this scale because, it is noted, there are over sixty million teachers in the world.

The programme works with a 'four dimensional' model of sustainable development ('sustainability' is its preferred term as one might expect given the difficulties perceived with 'development'). These dimensions are: the natural; the economic; the social; and the political. Each is linked to a corresponding 'value-principle', respectively: conservation; appropriate development; peace, equality and human rights; and democracy.

'Teaching and learning for a sustainable future' is explicitly self-aware of the potential limitations of multimedia-based learning and makes good use of the available technologies of delivery in this mode. As the programme itself notes: it employs an interactive pedagogy and it makes best use of opportunities for experiential learning, and for learning through reflection in the learner's own context. It is made clear from the outset that thinking about pedagogy and curriculum are seen to be conceptually of a piece with thinking about the human environment, and the programme holds itself strictly to the difficult challenge of maintaining within its own educative process the high standards of conduct it asks learners to adopt and promote.

Finally, the programme places emphasis on both formal and non-formal learning of an interdisciplinary nature. Eight 'interdisciplinary curriculum themes' are identified: culture and religion for a sustainable future; indigenous knowledge and sustainability; women and sustainable development; population and development; understanding world hunger; sustainable agriculture; sustainable tourism; and sustainable communities. In each case information is provided (with detailed sources), ideas elaborated and activities for learning and teaching proposed. A range of pedagogic approaches are also presented in the 'teaching and learning strategies' section. No one could use this product without learning something, or without being impressed by its scholarship and presentation. Many teachers will use it, and their teaching will be the better for it.

Biodiversity Basics

Biodiversity Basics is a segment of the World Wildlife Fund (WWF)'s 'Windows on the Wild' (WOW) education initiative which is funded by the Eastman Kodak Company. WOW aims to promote discussion, critical thinking and informed decision making by people of all ages. It promotes partnership and interdisciplinary working and draws on WWF's very considerable scientific expertise, as well as on its energetic and experienced education staff. A contribution from the Director of the WOW development team, Judy Braus, will be found in the annotated reader. Biodiversity Basics is concerned to promote both formal and non-formal learning experiences, but is principally targeted at school-age, particularly middle-school-age, children. There is a 'Student Book' and an 'Educator's Guide'. These follow the same sequence, supporting each other through the introduction of a total of thirty-four activities organised around four main questions: what is biodiversity?; why is biodiversity important?; what's the status of biodiversity?; and, how can we protect biodiversity? There is also a guide to help facilitate community action projects.

Like 'Teaching and learning for a sustainable future', Biodiversity Basics (and WOW as a whole) sees its approach to the environment and its approach to learning as part of a coherent whole. Guidance is provided to teachers on how to link activities into units of study which deliver both progressive and iterative learning. There is clear commentary on the ways in which the activities are designed to be accessible to learners with different learning styles, to promote questioning and problem solving, to link to areas in the established curriculum, and to accommodate learners with different degrees of language proficiency. It is further made clear to teachers that the activities are underpinned by a range of experiential, reflective models of learning processes, and that there is an intention to encourage collaborative learning. The design of Biodiversity Basics draws on insights and experience from futures education and community-based learning. Finally, an explicit link is made to sustainable development, though, as before, it is the term sustainability which is used. On page 16 of the 'Educator's Guide' we read:

Thinking in terms of sustainability – and finding ways to balance economic issues, social equity and ecological integrity – also requires thinking beyond our immediate needs and interests. The activities in this module encourage students to consider the perspective of other individuals, communities and cultures, and to look forward to assess the way actions today will affect the lives of people and other species in the United States and around the globe in the future. These activities also challenge students' thinking about fairness, individual and community responsibility, and other concerns that are critical to our understanding of sustainability.

The care taken to ensure the quality of this product, both in presentation and content, is breathtaking. For example, no fewer than 81 expert reviewers were consulted and 29 educators involved in piloting.

An example of a Biodiversity Basics activity which illustrates the attempt to tackle an extremely complex curriculum issue in an innovative way is number 28, 'Dollars and Sense'. This begins by focusing on something close-at-hand, chewing gum, and asking why it costs what it does. The activity guides teachers, and provides materials for students, in exploring and understanding simple supply and demand issues (a very ambitious, but surely worthy curriculum goal in itself for this age group). The components of supply and demand are examined and, for older students, the notion of externalities is introduced in an accessible way. A link between chewing-gum production and biodiversity issues is made. Students are encouraged to establish and reflect on something small scale and familiar (the dollar price of a pack of chewing gum) and something large scale and remote (forest ecology). Not all the activities are this difficult, but they are all engaging, careful in the factual claims they make, and animated by equal concern for learners and for biodiversity.

See www.worldwildlife.org

Learning for sustainable development: a curriculum toolkit

As noted above, this toolkit is promoted by Forum for the Future in conjunction with its HEPS initiative. HEPS itself is a collaboration between the Forum and eighteen UK Higher Education Institutions (HEIs). It receives financial support from the Higher Education Funding Councils in the UK, that is, from taxpayers.

A number of theoretical conceptualisations underpin this work. These include:

- The notion that HEIs should be thought of as having three different roles in relation to three aspects of sustainable development. Specifically, they operate as places of learning and research, as businesses and as key community players, in each case in relation to the environment, to society and to the economy.
- A view that the 'triple bottom line' view of sustainable development as requiring simultaneous improvements in the environment, the economy and society, while useful up to a point, is over-simplistic. A more complex formulation expands these three aspects into five kinds of capital: natural; human; social; manufactured; and financial capital.

- The identification of twelve criteria (linked to the five kinds of capital) which, it is claimed, would define a sustainable society. These relate to: non-renewable resource extraction; manufacture and use of artificial substances; the integrity of the ecological system; human health; learning and social skills; employment, creativity and recreation; governance and justice; positive values and social cohesion; positive (for both environment and people) institutional change; safe and supportive living and working environments; resource-use efficiency and the promotion of human innovation; and, accurate valuation of all forms of capital.

- As with the preceding two examples, a concern is that to be compatible with the promotion of sustainable development, learning has to take place in a particular way. However, some of the characteristics of desirable approaches to learning identified in this case have a crisply instrumental flavour. Learning must, it is argued, be: learner-focused; 'holistic', drawing together economic, environmental and social strands; compatible both with the physical environment in which learning takes place and with the socio-economic characteristics of learners; applicable at a range of degrees of complexity so that use can be made of a variety of teaching opportunities; and, focused on identified learning outcomes.

The toolkit itself has been developed from work done by the Forum with the University of Antofagasta in Chile. It provides a methodology which is extremely ambitious in its scope, since it is intended to contribute to the design of learning activities of all kinds, from short courses through to whole degrees. It is also recommended by the Forum for use by organisations outside the higher education sector such as businesses or government departments.

The approach using this toolkit is systematic, involving seven stages. First, a 'learner profile' is drawn up. The purpose of this is to map the world from the learner's perspective as a series of concentric circles. The 'learner' here might be characterised as a particular type of professional or graduate. Those people and the organisations or environmental aspects or entities with which the learner interacts most strongly and/or frequently are placed near the centre. Those with which interaction is infrequent and/or weaker are placed further out. Second, prospective course content is identified by listing the knowledge and skills necessary to manage each identified relationship in a way that is consistent with sustainable development. The categories 'ecological', 'social', and 'economic' are used to organise these lists, but it is stressed that the most interesting entries are likely to be those which span categories. Third, the identified knowledge and skills are prioritised by awarding them quantitative scores in terms of their ability to contribute to the Forum's twelve criteria of a sustainable society. This enables, fourthly, the specification of desired learning outcomes and, fifthly, the design of delivery mechanisms. The sixth stage is a 'values audit', designed to check whether the course, as now designed, is compatible with the values of staff and students. Following this, a course guide can finally be prepared.

This approach combines and builds on both a range of academic studies and work conducted in-house by Forum for the Future. In particular, it promotes the importance of learning with a style likely to be found congenial by non-education and non-social science specialists. It recognises the significance of the contexts in which learning takes place. It is also a determined attempt to generate practical progress towards sustainable development, undaunted by difficulties of definition of terms or institutional inertia.

See www.forumforthefuture.org.uk and www.heps.org.uk

Education for Sustainable Development (ESD) Toolkit

The ESD Toolkit aims to help educators operationalise the thinking on learning and sustainable development which has emerged since sustainable development was first endorsed at the UN General Assembly in 1987 and, most particularly, since the appearance of Chapter 36 of Agenda 21 following the 1992 Earth Summit in Rio de Janeiro. The author began work on the project following her participation at the 1998 Commission on Sustainable Development's review of Chapter 36. The influence of this UN policy-stream is evident throughout, most fundamentally in the identification of four 'priorities' for ESD which mirror those identified in Chapter 36. These are: improving basic education; reorienting existing education to address sustainable development; developing public understanding and awareness; and training. Other acknowledged influences of this kind include the UN Global Conference on the Sustainable Development of Small Island Developing States (Barbados, 1993); the International Conference on Population and Development (Cairo, 1994); the World Summit for Social Development (Copenhagen, 1995); the Fourth World Conference on Women (Beijing, 1996); the Second UN Conference on Human Settlements (Istanbul, 1996); and the World Food Summit (Rome, 1996). The Toolkit is funded by the USA's Waste Management Research and Education Institution and can be downloaded in its entirety from www.esdtoolkit.org

Underpinning the ESD Toolkit is the notion of progress toward sustainable development through a mechanism in which community sustainable development goals on the one hand, and educational sustainable development practice on the other, develop simultaneously and interactively. That education is essential to the achievement of sustainable development is taken to be axiomatic. Further, the concept of 'education' which informs this thinking is strongly influenced by the literature of the academic field of study which calls itself environmental education. This is significant because this field, in fact, has relatively little to say about literacy and numeracy education, training or public awareness. Conversely, it would appear likely that there are many practitioners in these fields who are working in ways which seem wholly or partly consistent with sustainable development but are unaware of the environmental education literature (see, for example, Wehrmeyer, 1996, and much of the output of Greenleaf Publishing, Sheffield). Also we should note that the notion of sustainable development itself is far from uncontroversial in the literature of environmental education (Jickling, 1992 – and chapter 8 of the companion reader; Jickling and Spork, 1998; and Sauvé and Berryman, 2003). One aspect of the appeal to the literature of environmental education is the insistence that education should be for rather than about sustainable development, which has been a topic of interest in that field since the work of Lucas (1979). In justifying this view of education as an instrument of social policy the ESD Toolkit compares its own purposes to those of driver education or fire safety education.

The ESD Toolkit conceptualises the relationship between sustainable development and learning in terms of subdivisions of each, set out in a grid. So, on one axis, to represent sustainable development, we find the familiar components of environment, economy and society. On the other axis, to represent learning, we have the categories of knowledge, issues, skills, perspectives and values. A particular merit of the approach is that it is informative both for, say, a teacher who wants to focus on values education or skills training and for an economist who wants to identify a focus for the provision of educational materials. The toolkit is also realistic enough to acknowledge that many barriers exist to the operationalisation of what it proposes, and these are classified under twelve headings, drawing on the very considerable experience of the author and her advisors over many years. The toolkit provides many practical exercises which might be used with learners in a variety of settings. These are overwhelmingly participatory in nature.

An analysis

Let us begin this section by stressing, once again, that each of the four examples explored above makes available the fruits of hard work, experience and considerable thought in an accessible form. Each will be found valuable by practitioners. This is so even though they often use different conceptualisations of sustainable development and/or learning. We would like now to ask what can be learned from exploring themes which are common across some or all of them.

Inter-institutional competition

Returning to Figure 6.1 we might firstly ask, in each of our four examples, what institutions are involved.

Both the UNESCO 'Teaching and learning for a sustainable future' programme and the ESD Toolkit have a clear attachment to UN institutions and both the authority and claim to legitimacy these embody. This is particularly appropriate since both see their task as in some sense global. The UNESCO programme is globally accessible, while the ESD Toolkit appeals to a notion of 'global citizenship'. In many ways it is also true that these two curriculum innovations would tend to support each other in practice. Teachers trained through the UNESCO programme would be more likely to use the ESD Toolkit and to use it well. However, it is important to note that the focus of the two projects is subtly different in relation to the UN institutional sponsor. The UNESCO work is a product of many years of innovative work with teachers which has set out deliberately to strongly influence institutional agenda in line with a particular literacy or group of literacies based in a particular academic tradition (See Fien, 1993 and chapter 6 of the companion reader). Its purpose is to shape the potential cultural institution (sustainable development) to which UNESCO is attached. The ESD Toolkit is more predominantly an attempt to promote that cultural institution in the form in which successive UN resolutions and declarations have embodied it.

The Learning for Sustainable Development/HEPS Toolkit is far more focused on UK institutions, principally Forum for the Future, HEIs, and official and semi-official bodies into whose policies the Forum would wish to embed its own preferred cultural institutions. This is, of course, in no sense a criticism. It is, after all, what institutions do.

Forum for the Future has developed the cultural institutions it seeks to promote through a different suite of literacies than those which underpin, for example, the UNESCO teacher education work. In particular, more emphasis has been given by the Forum to thinking originating in economics and in natural science: its approach to learning is more managerialist and less emancipatory (See Huckle, 1993; Kemmis and Fitzclarence, 1986; and Bowers, 1993; 1995; 2001). This is evident in:

- the different chosen target population for learning, i.e. graduates and profes-sionals generally, rather than school children reached through school teachers
- the emphasis on measurable learning outcomes informed by the 'twelve features of a sustainable society' (a potential cultural institution), rather than a pedagogy of individual and collective self-discovery
- most fundamentally perhaps, a view of learning as instrumental to the achieve-ment of sustainable development, rather than a view of learning as being, of itself, a vital and substantial aspect of any ongoing process of sustainable development. For the Forum, sustainable development is ultimately about what happens to five kinds of capital. For the UNESCO 'Teaching and learning for a sustainable future' programme it is ultimately 'not so much about a destination as about the process of learning to make decisions that consider the long-term economy, ecology and equity of all communities'.

WWF is also an institution competing for resources and a hearing. It is also to some extent at least informed by literacies of education and economics. However, it is also very strongly influenced by other literacies, including those of advocacy, communication and, probably most importantly, that of conservation biology. It is not, as is UNESCO, fundamentally concerned with learning. It is not, as is Forum for the Future, fundamentally concerned with sustainable development. WWF is concerned with conservation. Whether it can work with particular educational institutions – either organisational institutions like UNESCO or cultural institutions like a curriculum – depends on how far WWF can influence these institutions to promote conservation. Further, the education section of WWF must, quite properly, account for its work on Biodiversity Basics to the sponsor, the Eastman Kodak Company. Finally, advocates of both education and sustainable development must compete for resources within WWF itself against those who advocate other, non-learning-related approaches to conservation.

It might be argued that, in relation to our over-arching topic of global sustainable development and learning, these are small differences. However, the point to bear in mind is that debates about sustainable development and/or learning are not determined solely by the quality of ideas, but by the degree of success organisational institutions have in competing for resources of all kinds. One way they compete is by promoting particular ideas or ways of organising, if possible creating cultural institutions in the process; and in human affairs, as we all know, small differences between neighbours are typically far more contentious than big differences between people who have little or no point of contact with each other.

Other institutions

We should note here that many other institutions, both organisational and cultural, have a bearing on the success or failure of each of these initiatives. To illustrate each in turn:

- UNESCO is very dependent on the willingness of other organisations, particularly at the national level, to support it. Its influence is also a function of its relationship with the United Nations as a whole, and of its present relatively lowly and marginalised status within that organisation. Field (2000: 251), for example, has described it as, 'a rather discredited body with a vague remit and a large and diffuse membership'. In terms of cultural institutions UNESCO promotes notions such as 'global citizenship' and the 'Earth Charter', which tend to appeal quite widely to constituencies of environmentalists and educationalists, but may cut little ice when competing for attention and resources against 'economic growth' and 'national development', to name but two other cultural institutions
- WWF is not only an internally complex institution, it fully recognises the complexity of its working context through, for example, its focus on ecoregions as a focus of conservation action (see Chapter 8). An example of an ecoregion – an ecologically coherent segment of the biosphere – is the Bering Sea. This ecoregion, like many others, spans more than one country, is home to multiple cultures, and experiences environmental impacts from itinerant industries (such as fishing and oil extraction) that are bent on resource exploitation, and driven by economic demand elsewhere
- HEIs have external responsibilities to business organisations and to Research Councils which are to a greater or lesser extent – but increasingly – mediated through market mechanisms. If a university's graduates cannot find work then new students will be less likely to come. If research grants are not won then the research effort will falter and funding for research will fall. Of course it is true that many businesses have some sort of policy relating to sustainable development, and may take account of it when recruiting staff. Similarly, research councils increasingly recognise environmental issues as a theme of research: but in both cases the relationship of sustainable development to learning may be poorly articulated and at the margin other things are quite likely to be deemed more important. HEIs have no choice but to respond to this ordering of priorities. They must also respond to the interests of internal stakeholder organisations such as their governing councils, which may or may not place

sustainable development high on their lists of priorities as far as the academic curriculum is concerned. However, the picture is more positive in relation to the management of HEIs' physical resources, where potential savings from sustainable resource procurement or energy saving measures are increasingly unlikely to be ignored, just as conforming to existing legislative frameworks in relation to pollutants will remain a priority. It is fair to say that the Learning for Sustainable Development curriculum toolkit recognises and seeks to address many of these difficulties. Note also however that well established cultural institutions such as 'academic freedom' are not necessarily helpful to the attempt to manage higher education learning to the benefit of any particular policy initiative

- The ESD toolkit is dependent not only on UNESCO's developing role, but also on the willingness and ability of its host institution, the University of Tennessee, to maintain it, as well as on multiple curriculum decisions across the United States about what teachers can and should teach. To the extent that the Toolkit is intended as an international resource, this depends, for example, on the willingness and ability of teachers in other countries to work within participatory pedagogies. There is evidence (Hindson *et al.*, 2001) to suggest that this is often not the case.

Practices

All these approaches to curriculum design seek to influence the practices of teachers, lecturers and/or other professionals. We would simply wish to draw attention to the inertia which practices may have, and in particular the many factors which may bear upon both the espoused theories and the theories in action of teachers (see Chapter 6).

Information, communication and mediation

In Chapter 4 we argued that the question of an appropriate pedagogical approach to learning in the context of sustainable development had no absolute answer. Rather, we suggested, an approach should be selected which matched the characteristics of the learning context.

On the face of it, all four of our exemplar curriculum initiatives make a similar claim. The UNESCO 'Teaching and learning for a sustainable future' multimedia programme identifies the necessary role of multiple cultures in shaping sustainable development to locally appropriate ends. Biodiversity Basics emphasises 'service learning' and 'community action'. The Forum for the Future 'Learning for Sustainable Development' curriculum toolkit begins by mapping the context of the learner and includes a values audit to keep course development on track. The ESD Toolkit provides materials which offer choice and adaptability to teachers in different contexts. However, at least three important issues remain, which are reflected in Figure 4.2 on page 38. These are:

- We can ask whether elaborate (and expensive) pedagogies are always necessary. Where learners want to act sustainably, but cannot do so because they lack knowledge or skills, simple information provision will often suffice. (Note however that the converse holds equally well – simple information provision will often not suffice, since on other occasions learners may initially be indifferent, or actively disinclined towards sustainable behaviour)

- Learners do not necessarily learn what teachers teach. Any strategy for social change needs to take account of learning which happens incidentally and independently

- The notion of capacity building for sustainable development (Fig. 4.2) suggests that learners bring important knowledge, values and skills to the learning process, and that these are productively supplemented through external inputs. The question is, how far to privilege the prior knowledge of the learner, how far that of the external expert and/or educator? We have already touched briefly on this issue in Chapter 3, where the notion of an 'expansive curriculum' was mooted. We return to it again in Chapters 11 and 12. For now, however, we note that all four of our examples set out a clear 'expert' element which is considered to be beyond the scope of negotiation. For example: the UNESCO multimedia programme sets out a number of 'global realities'; Biodiversity Basics sets out a case for the absolute importance of biodiversity and evidence that it is being lost rapidly; the Learning for Sustainable Development curriculum toolkit ranks knowledge, and sets learning objectives in relation to 'twelve features of a sustainable society'; and the ESD Toolkit points to '18 principles of sustainability'.

In Chapter 5 we noted O'Riordan's (1989) distinction between two world views, the one conservative and nurturing, the other radical and manipulative. All four of our examples, and most others we could have chosen, exhibit predominantly the former. In Chapter 1 we drew attention to cultural theory and its identification of four competing, but also mutually interdependent rationalities: the hierarchical; the egalitarian; the individualistic and the fatalistic. A glance at both the social ambitions and the pedagogies of our examples reveal that they are overwhelmingly inclined towards an egalitarian view, in which things make sense if they are fair and just. In many ways this does great credit to everyone involved in their design.

However, the following passage, focusing on the environmental management of land degradation, illustrates some of the difficulties at a practical, rather than a purely conceptual level.

> A reader ideologically inclined to the left may put forward the notion that under 'real' socialism, even if that could be defined and agreed upon, the necessary co-operation between producers themselves, and between them and a democratic and representative state, would be easier to obtain. However, in all societies there will continue to be conflicts between private and collective interests, between local and national priorities in land use and management.
>
> (Blaikie and Brookfield, 1987: 83)

The problem in our examples (which we chose because they are the best available in the English language) is that other world views and rationalities are missing or, at least, insufficiently explicit. A sustainable world will not only be a world of justice and collaboration because no such world is possible. For example, when the UNESCO multimedia programme says of 'sustainability' that 'it will be shaped at the local level by the mosaic of cultures that surround the globe and which contribute to the decisions that each country, community, household and individual makes', it overlooks the fact that the very essence of many cultures has been formed in opposition to others, and that good decisions at the level of a country, for example, may be bad ones for particular households or individuals. Similarly, when Forum for the Future's eighth 'feature of a sustainable society' requires that: 'The structures and institutions of society promote stewardship of natural resources and development of people', it is hard to see how this can be done without losers being created who are, whatever the curriculum tells them, unlikely to be pleased about it. Other than in our imagined Utopias (Berlin, 1990), these are issues which cannot be wished, legislated or educated away, no matter how some might want to.

Of course, this is not to dismiss our examples. They make a real contribution to sustainable development through learning but they are not complete. Whatever sustainable development ultimately looks like it will need to have room for human ingenuity and inventiveness in manipulating the environment, competition for environmental and economic assets, rule-making, rule-breaking and the self-interest of individuals and groups. It will even need to accommodate a disillusioned (and one would hope one day small) minority who think sustainable development is a plot, a trick or a bore; alongside generosity, justice and equity. If we could remove from the picture complexity, uncertainty, risk and necessity it might all be different but we cannot. The greatest irony here is that even institutions which unequivocally advocate egalitarian values and collaborative practices have no choice but to compete among themselves and with others.

In the next chapter we begin to consider how forms of learning might be developed to complement those examined here and to address the issues we have raised.

8 Curriculum and pedagogy

Introduction: themes for environmental meta-learning (TEMs)

In Chapter 4 we identified a need for *environmental meta-learning*, learning which occurs across the boundaries between different institutions, literacies and practices. In Chapter 7, we examined four different contemporary examples of approaches to curriculum design in sustainable development. We concluded that although each was in many respects excellent there was a need to go further: a need to create learning opportunities through *engagement* with worldviews and rationalities which primarily value, for example, hierarchy or competition, rather than through *opposition* to these.

In this chapter we consider two examples of recent applied research, one success-fully completed the other not, which explore the possibilities for learning of this kind. In both cases, the process of curriculum design made use of *themes for environmental meta-learning* (TEMS). Finally, we consider whether our analysis has implications for decision-making processes and ask what these might be.

Example 1: sustainable development and the training of managers in North Borneo

The research described here took place during 1996–8. It was, for the most part, carried out in the small Sultanate of Brunei. However, the designation 'North Borneo' is also used here as a wider descriptor to include the East Malaysian state of Sarawak, which surrounds Brunei and, in fact, divides it into two disconnected parts. This is done because:

- Some official policies which had a bearing on the research were conceived, at least in part, at this scale (e.g. tourism development)
- Some environmental impacts relevant to the research crossed international boundaries (e.g. forest fires and the smoke they produced)
- This wider setting of North Borneo was used in conceptualising the study (Gough, 1995).

From the point of view of sustainable development North Borneo has a number of interesting characteristics. It is located approximately 5°N of the Equator, has a hot, humid climate year-round, and was until as recently as the end of World War II entirely covered in tropical rainforest (Harrisson, 1959). Three main cultural forms are present: Muslim Malay, overseas Chinese and indigenous Dayak. Each of these categories is capable of further subdivision. The term 'Dayak' conceals a particularly wide range of diversity. Dayaks are united, however, by a moral and religious worldview know as *adat* or *adet*, which defines an individual's rights and duties (Hong, 1987).

The three cultures have interacted in this setting for a very long time. Trade between Dayaks and China may have begun in the second century BC, while political control by Malays may have been initiated in the sixth century AD (Colchester, 1992). There are records of the existence of Brunei's *Kampong Ayer*, or Water Village, as a large and thriving settlement in the sixteenth century, by which time government by the present line of Sultans was long established. There has also been influence from Western culture for a significant time. The first White Rajah, James Brooke, arrived in Sarawak in 1839.

These social arrangements are framed by a unique natural environment. Local flora and fauna are rich and diverse. Coastal waters are shallow and warm and conceal an abundance of both traditional and modern resources, in the forms of fish and oil respectively. Upland areas are notable for their traditionally cultivated Dayak (in this case Kelabit) rice-fields. Gunung Mulu National Park boasts (by far) the world's largest caves, an exotic array of troglodytic species, and some of the most rugged terrain anywhere on Earth. Close to the small town of Batu Niah, Niah Caves are home to a multitude of swiftlets and have long been a major commercial source of edible birds' nests. Belalong, in the remote Temburong district of Brunei, is the site of a major international centre for the study of the rainforest.

North Borneo provides a fascinating example of tensions between 'sustaining' the natural environment on the one hand and 'development' on the other. Economic growth is rapid; environmental degradation widespread but uneven. For instance, Brunei remains largely forested having, compared to Sarawak and Malaysia as a whole, greater oil and gas reserves to draw on relative to its size. Sarawak is heavily logged, with consequent silting-up of rivers being a problem. In addition, the region both exports and imports environmental impacts. At least one Sarawak-based company has been responsible for extensive logging in South America (Colchester, 1992). Smoke from forest fires, particularly in Indonesian Kalimantan, is a recurring environmental and health problem which reached disaster proportions in 1998.

The research differed from the examples discussed in Chapter 7 by beginning not with a focus on what learners should know, nor with a particular view of the state of the planet, nor again with a particular environment-related issue. Rather, it began by considering a form of education which was:

• In high demand
• Likely to influence learner behaviour in relation to sustainable development.

This was management education, which at the time was being introduced at post-16 level across the country. Courses were over-subscribed, no doubt in part because of the perceived need and opportunity for managers in a developing economy in which the number of public sector jobs had been effectively frozen and official messages stressed strongly and repeatedly the need for entrepreneurship and management skills.

Of course, demand for management education is high across most of the world. It exists at both an academic and a popular level. Evidence of the former may be found in the large number of MBA programmes which exist, and of the latter in the many popular titles about management found at airport bookshops and other outlets. These two market segments are not absolutely distinct however, and some authors, such as Tom Peters and Peter Drucker, have made a great deal of money from both. It seems clear that there is widespread believe that management education makes a difference to what managers actually do. As far as we know, no one has ever become rich by writing a book about sustainable development and, as we saw in Chapter 4, it is far from universally accepted that learning has much of a role in its achievement.

There is a simple but frequently overlooked truth here. Just because educators have identified given educational content as important, or even essential, it does not follow that learners will be willing to learn it. Wherever possible, 'what learners want' is likely to be a more effective starting point for curriculum design than 'what teachers are worried about'. This point has been confirmed quite spectacularly by the growth of private education in some countries where official education provision has been dictated by suppliers' interests (Bray, 1999).

Of course, there is no question that the actions of managers and entrepreneurs often impact in a major way on the environment. Corporate behaviour is an important concern of advocates of sustainable development, for example Christie and Warburton (2001: 38) write:

> Many steps can be taken to promote more sustainable and ethical business which will benefit companies as well as communities and the environment. But while some corporations are developing impressive policies for social and environmental responsibility, many are not.

It would seem, therefore, that management education offers opportunities for learning which might promote sustainable development. The most crucial test for any intervention of this kind, however, will not be how closely it conforms to one set of predetermined 'principles' of sustainable development or another, but simply whether it is perceived by learners to be good *management* education. If it is not they will conclude, rightly, that they have been expensively misled.

The core of the research consisted of three case studies conducted with two cohorts of approximately 150 young people ('the students') aged between 17 and 24 years. The ethnic distribution of this group approximated to that of wider Brunei society, with Dayaks under-represented. All the students had applied, and been accepted, to study management through an accredited programme. The research also focused on the lecturers (at different times between five and eight in number) teaching the programme, as well as educational administrators, local business people and officials in more than one government department. Note that *none* of these individuals was known to the researcher to have *any* interest in sustainable development. They were people who saw themselves as students or teachers of business management, or administrators of programmes which favoured dissemination of business management skills, or potential employers of graduates.

The themes for environmental meta-learning (TEM) employed with the first cohort during the first year of the study was *Quality*. Its use was repeated during the second year with the second cohort, who also yielded a separate data-set related to the TEM *Design*. The educational potential of the concept of quality had been suggested by a literature review and, indeed, specifically pointed out by Charter (1992). This potential lay in the fact that quality was an idea of recognised significance from the perspectives of business management, environmentalism and education. In the Brunei context, officials within government departments were at the time concerned with the adaptation and adoption of international quality standards for business and related standards for environmental management systems (Brunei Government, 1996). Quality is also a key issue according to a document (UNESCO UNEP, 1977) considered foundational by specialists in environmental education working at opposite ends of the paradigmatic spectrum (Hungerford and Volk, 1990: 8–9; Fien, 1993: 54–5). Entrepreneurs and managers in Brunei had particular reason to be concerned with quality management systems (Oakland, 1993; Rothery, 1993) as a result of the official promotion of these. This led to interest on the part of management educators and examiners. Of course, 'quality' meant different things to all these people, but that was seen to be its possible strength as an aid to learning.

Primary data were collected in predominantly written form during an intensive week-long period and at other times during the year as appropriate. All students were provided with a nine-page resource booklet by their regular lecturers who had approved and, at their own discretion, adapted and/or expanded, the contents. The booklets directed students to four group-based activities, making clear that the work was time-limited and would be integrated in normal assessment procedures. It was also announced that some students would have the opportunity to present their work at a seminar organised by the Ministry of Development.

The activities related to a fictional proposal by a local/foreign joint venture company called Progressive Plastics to establish an industrial plant for the manufacture of plastic bags. This facility was to be located at an industrial estate (which really existed) near the mouth of the Brunei River. Though fictional, such a proposal was entirely credible for that location given that plastic bags are manufactured from ethane gas, which is produced as a waste product by oil and gas refineries and was therefore potentially available as a raw material. Further, industrial chemical industries were officially favoured with 'pioneer industry' status and so subject to tax advantages. Each activity required students to engage with the proposed development from a different perspective. These perspectives were those of:

• A local manager hired by Progressive Plastics to report on the local policy situation with regard to quality and environment

- A Ministry of Development official charged with regulation and monitoring of the proposed plant
- A citizen responding to debate in the local paper, the *Borneo Bulletin*, about plastics and quality of life. This mirrored an actual debate in the *Bulletin* which weighed the visual pollution caused by plastic waste in the Brunei River and elsewhere against the convenience value of plastic containers
- A scenario-writer for the multi-national joint-venture partner of Progressive Plastics. This role was loosely modelled on a that of a real individual, employed by Shell.

The further themes for environmental meta-learning *Design* was identified not through literature review, as 'quality' had been, but through the process of coding the data collected during the first case study. It became the basis of a separate case study following a similar procedure. Once again, support from lecturers, administrators and government officials was considered to be a prerequisite. Students were provided with materials and activities to be completed in small groups. Specifically, they were required to prepare a detailed projection of the most appropriate use of the North Borneo coastline over the next five years and in the light of this to write a conventional ('product, price, promotion, place') marketing mix for the nascent Brunei tourism industry. It was announced that, in this case, the Ministry of Industry and Primary Resources wished students to present work at an official function. Once again, data were collected during an intensive week-long period, and at other times over a year.

Not all the findings of this research are of direct concern here and the reader will find fuller accounts elsewhere (Gough *et al.*, 1998; Gough and Scott, 2000; 2001). However, the following outcomes are of note for the present discussion:

- There was evidence of environmental learning by students against two separate (and competing) sets of criteria derived from the literature of environmental education
- It was felt by lecturers, and confirmed by analysis of students' work submitted for examination, that the interventions had enhanced students' business management learning
- Senior officials of the Ministry of Development and the Ministry of Industry and Primary Resources expressed themselves satisfied that the interventions had been helpful from their separate perspectives. The Ministry of Education, similarly, was satisfied with the work as an aspect of the introduction of top-quality business management education
- Not only students, but also local business people, college administrators and management lecturers were exposed to an environmental perspective on particular issues, perhaps in many cases for the first time. This happened particularly through the functions at which students presented their work
- In the case of the 'design' TEM in particular there was evidence of frequent enthusiasm and involvement on the part of students' family members.

Caution is in order in interpreting these results, but to claim that some degree of capacity for sustainable development was built (Figure 4.2, p. 38) does not seem unreasonable and that in a context in which there were present many external, and not necessarily helpful, influences on learning. To a degree, in fact, capacity was built by *engaging with* those influences. This means of course that ambitious educational goals of the kind envisaged by Fien and Trainer (1993a, b) or Trainer (1990), which involve the absolute, root-and-branch transformation of individuals and (thus) society from a bad (environmentally manipulative) state to a better (environmentally conservative or nurturing) one, were not addressed. But we can ask with some cause whether there is any evidence that this kind of Damascene salvationism provides a credible paradigm for any kind of educational effort. Learning, we would argue, takes place incrementally at the margins of who we already are and what we already know, not by giant leaps to imagined ideal states (see Lindblom, 1992 and chapter 11 of the companion reader for a discussion of this point in a slightly different context).

However, if our first example would seem to deliver a message of cautious optimism about the potential efficacy of environmental meta-learning, our second raises further doubts.

Example 2: Ecoregion conservation and World Wildlife Fund staff training

As noted in Chapter 7, an ecoregion is a biologically and ecologically coherent segment of the biosphere. Over 250 ecoregions have been identified by WWF, which has made them an organising focus of its conservation work. This involves, in turn, a great deal of staff training and development. In conjunction with WWF's 'College for Conservation Leadership' an e-learning programme was developed for WWF ecoregion staff in 2001, both to enhance this training effort and improve understanding of organisational learning as it might occur across WWF's many, multi-national, facets. A contribution from Bronwen Golder, one of the key staff at WWF involved in commissioning this work, will be found in chapter 11 of the companion reader.

One key difference between this example and the first is immediately apparent. In the case of the North Borneo innovation the environmental meta-learning which was promoted took place, predominantly across institutions, both organisational (a college, government departments, ministries, businesses) and cultural (management curriculum, international standards, generally accepted marketing concepts). In this second example, on the other hand, meta-learning was required within a single (if very diverse) institution across different literacies. The participants had been trained in a wide range of skills and were very varied in both their academic backgrounds and their professional experiences, but all worked for WWF. Box 8.1 sets out some of the initial information provided for students. Communication between students, and between students and facilitators, was electronic and spanned a wide range of time-zones.

Box 8.1 Ecoregion conservation: information for participants

It is likely that approximately 20 participants will be studying this module at the same time as you are. This group is called your <u>cohort</u>. The cohort will be divided into four or five smaller groups. These smaller groups are called <u>cells</u>. You will belong to only one cell. A cell is the equivalent of a small discussion group. So, just as face-to-face workshops often use the device of breaking a large group into smaller discussion groups, this module breaks a large group of on-line participants (the cohort) into a smaller number of on-line discussion groups (the cells). You will be allocated to a particular cell by the facilitators. The facilitators will try to create cells that are as heterogeneous as possible by mixing participants with different backgrounds within WWF. This is being done because an important aspect of this module is the need within ecoregion conservation to promote dialogue among those with different specialities and backgrounds. . . . You will be guided through a series of eight 'virtual workshops'. Each virtual workshop will contain a number of activities for you to complete. Each workshop is scheduled to last one week and to be undertaken by all participants in a cohort at the same time. . . . You will be asked to think about two overarching tasks during the period of the whole module and to address these specifically in Virtual Workshops 7 and 8. These overarching tasks involve a simulation in which you will be asked to use factual information (about the Chihuahuan Desert ecoregion and about WWF's policies and procedures developed for ecoregion conservation) to respond to a series of fictional situations.

Two themes for environmental meta-learning (TEM) were centrally implicated in the ecoregion conservation module, as this work was known. Interestingly, both were also identified in the North Borneo work. The first, *Vision*, is central to the WWF conservation approach. For each ecoregion, the first step is to set out long-term (i.e. 50-year) goals for conservation which identify key sites, populations and ecological processes. While it is accepted that the achievement of this vision may be a very long-term objective, it sets the biological ideal against which judgements are made and trades-off evaluated. The biodiversity vision thus provides a common denominator to which all literacies engaged in this specific work of ecoregion conservation must relate. Hence, therefore, one of the early activities required of each multi-skilled team (or cell) participating in the module was the development of a vision for the Chihuahuan Desert ecoregion from real data provided.

The second TEM was *Network*, with many exercises focusing on organisational learning, communication and building stakeholder alliances. The 'overarching tasks' required participants to think in terms of the best ways of presenting ecoregion conservation to two wider networks. One of these, the United Nations, was external. The other was WWF as a whole, reached through its executive Programme Committee in Switzerland.

Through a series of eight 'virtual workshops' the module encouraged participants to consider WWF's published strategy for ecoregion conservation both through short activities and in relation to the larger overarching tasks. Throughout, the Chihuahuan Desert ecoregion was used as an example. At a late stage in the participants' progression through the module a pre-planned but, to them, unheralded simulated emergency (rapid depletion of a key local environmental resource) was introduced to force each cell of learners to bring its collective skills to bear quickly and effectively.

Yet for all its careful preparation and innovative e-learning pedagogy the ecoregion conservation module was not a success. Although some excellent work was produced by some individuals and within some cells, participation and completion rates were less than satisfactory. No doubt some of the problems experienced were technical in nature. For example, some participants had inadequate access to the internet during the period the module was scheduled; many of the exercises proved to be more time-consuming than either the facilitators expected or the participants had allowed for; and some of the activities were clearly inadequately explained to participants. This may have been particularly so where, as in the case of exercises about communication or organisational learning, it may not have been apparent to many participants just *why* these were relevant to the (for them) everyday business of working to conserve biodiversity in an ecoregion. However, there is a need for a more far-reaching explanation than this.

Learning and decision making

A recent study by Ravenscroft *et al.* (2002) explores approaches to active citizenship through participation in public forums in relation to outdoor recreation in England and Wales. Such forums are required in certain circumstances under the provisions of the Countryside and Rights of Way Act of 2000 and represent, more broadly, an approach to the devolution of power to individuals at the expense of, particularly, local authorities. Ravenscroft *et al.*'s (2002: 729) conclusions include the following:

> Improving participation at the local level may not necessarily achieve the core emphasis of government policy, on improving people's experience of local government and their willingness and ability to engage in deliberative democracy . . . few studies have established an enduring link between the processes of participation and the generation of improved decision making . . . full political participation by local people may slow and confuse decision making, which is likely to prove unpopular among other members of the public . . . Experimentation with new methods of participation, such as citizen juries, can further slow decision making processes, as well as adding to the cost of local service provision.

Two points stand out. First, the kinds of forum which are under discussion here are examples of an attempt to bring about exchanges of views and information, debate and consensus building across different institutions, literacies and practices. To that extent, they appear very similar to the proposal made in this book for environmental meta-learning. Second however, we should note that learning is one thing and decision making another. In Chapter 4 we noted, in our discussion of 'mediation', the work of Laurillard (2002) who uses the term 'mediated learning' to describe learning which enables the generalisation of insights which have arisen in particular contexts so that they become valuable in other contexts. For this to occur, she notes, a degree of abstraction from the original context is necessary. Knowledge is in this way detached from the setting in which it was created, and made available to be usefully and adaptively re-attached to other settings. Learning, therefore, occurs at a level of abstraction which is necessarily one stage removed from application. It is appropriately assessed and evaluated in terms of *what has been learned*, not in terms of whatever consequences are seen to follow when that learning is applied by the learner in whatever the circumstances happen to be. Those consequences follow not from learning, but from subsequent decision making, and are discussed in more detail in Chapter 10 on Evaluation.

All four of the examples examined in Chapter 7 were concerned centrally with application, that is, with a perceived need for people to learn particular things so that particular decisions (about the characteristics of a sustainable society, about bio-diversity, or about teaching) could be operationalised. If there were no complexity, uncertainty, risk or necessity this would not matter: but as these things are often very much present there is a need, as we argued in that chapter, to find ways of engaging learners who do not accept what the curriculum designer has decided.

In the case of the ecoregion conservation module, agreement had been established among participants about the importance of biodiversity conservation: but complexity, uncertainty, risk and necessity continued to cause debate and confusion from the perspectives of different literacies. The problem, we believe, and only continuing work will bear this out or not, was that while the module itself maintained an adequate degree of abstraction from actual context-specific decision making processes, the participants themselves, throughout the period of study, were fully engaged in day to day ecoregion conservation activities in which firm and often complex choices needed to be made, and for which entertaining contrary, competing or confusing viewpoints was likely to create the same kinds of delays and costs identified by Ravenscroft *et al.* Only in the North Borneo work was the approach simultaneously realistic enough to make learning seem important and detached enough to make engaging with alternative perspectives seem an affordable luxury. This has severe implications for any attempt to engage learners who continue to work during the learning period.

Jensen and Schnack (1997 – see also chapter 11 of the companion reader) have noted that it is not and cannot be the function of education to solve society's problems. We might add that, ironically enough, education which sets out explicitly to solve social problems is doomed to fail, since it cannot hope to engage the very people it most wishes to convert. This is not to say that such initiatives contribute nothing, only that they cannot determine for themselves, and in advance, what it is they are contributing to. Environmental learning in the presence of complexity, uncertainty, risk and necessity, we argue, must be accepting of multiple perspectives supportive of meta-learning across perspectives, and detached from the making of decisions in its (and learners') own immediate contexts.

9 Measuring learning
Aspects of assessment

Introduction: assessment and evaluation

By 'assessment' we mean the process of establishing what has been learned, or more narrowly, the extent to which learners have learned what they were supposed to. A difficulty with the narrow view, which should be apparent at once from the discussions of the foregoing chapters, is that, in relation to complex sustainable development issues, it may be difficult to pre-specify with any precision and/or confidence what learners should learn. We shall return to this. First, however, it is necessary to distinguish 'assessment' from 'evaluation'.

In essence, if assessment has a learner–learning focus, evaluation has a course or programme focus and is concerned with the measurement of effectiveness or quality. This means that assessment outcomes should be expected to feature as part of evaluation reports. One indicator of the quality of any intervention intended to result in learning is how well the pupils, students or trainees did. However, it is clearly possible that, for example, a course in which every student obtains an A++ grade has been pitched too low. Similarly, if every student on a programme fails one might want to ask questions of the tutors before necessarily blaming the students themselves. Assessment is concerned with the learning that has taken place; evaluation is concerned with that too, and also with, for example, course design and delivery, instructional materials used, timetabling, record-keeping, quality and availability of facilities and a host of other factors, contextual and other.

Environmental learning, meta-learning and assessment by sector

We have distinguished environmental learning, which takes place within the frameworks provided by institutions, practices and literacies, from environmental meta-learning, which crosses such boundaries. In Western countries, as a general rule, meta-learning becomes less common and the influence of institutions, practices and literacies through subject disciplines more pronounced, as the learner advances through formal education, further and higher education and lifelong learning in the adult world.

Before exploring the implications of this statement we should say that it is very much only a *general* rule and is most applicable to developed countries. There are plenty of examples of poorer countries in which primary education, where it exists at all, is focused not on any sort of meta-learning but, perhaps quite properly, mainly on literacy and numeracy. However, in such settings traditional ways of living may be undermined and, for some societies at least, it is precisely these traditional institutions, practices and literacies that embody the benefits of various forms of environmental meta-learning. Assessment is implicated here because as Biggs (1996) points out, it is very well established that the nature of assessment is a major determinant of what is actually learned. Assessment regimes which focus on, for example, grammatical skills in English or context-free use of numbers, may marginalise traditional knowledge to the point at which it is lost.

This general point has been powerfully made by, among others, Bowers (1993; 1995; 2001). Based on a study in Tanzania, the following observation by Da Silva (1996: 122), captures the problem neatly as it relates to education:

> Education is alternately criticised and praised, first as the culprit responsible for the irreversible acculturation process that has been forced on Africa, and next as the panacea for ameliorating underdevelopment.

The underlying paradox here is that during the colonial period 'acculturation' was a consequence of the West's preoccupation with 'civilising' the rest of the world, in large part through education. Since this period acculturation has often been a consequence of the West's preoccupation with expiating its colonial past through discourses of development or globalisation (Said, 1985; Inayatullah, 1993), again often transmitted through education. Western interest in the way local people themselves see their circumstances and history has often been as minimal in the latter case as in the former. This indifference has transmitted itself to the ways in which education is assessed and assessment regimes have in turn influenced learners' views of what is important. To complete the irony, the value of the traditional has now been rediscovered by enlightened development donors. For example, as we saw in Chapter 4, the UK's Department for International Development (DFID) has recently commissioned research into how, among other things, an environmental focus for education, and particularly primary education, may improve the overall quality of that education. Box 9.1 is an extract from the Executive Summary of the report of that research (Hindson *et al.*, 2001) which carries clear implications that educational assessment in developing countries may need to explore learners' abilities to, for example, apply their learning appropriately at the level of local economic activity and political participation. To a cynic this may all seem like putting Humpty Dumpty back together again; he *is* broken, after all.

Box 9.1   Extract from report to the Department for International
             Development (Hindson *et al.* (2001))

The potential of mainstreamed environmental education to promote the goal of Universal Primary Education (UPE) is significant, but not necessarily obvious to all stakeholders. This potential consists in the following:

- Locally significant issues relating to the environment and its management provide a productive, relevant, development-oriented focus for literacy (and numeracy) teaching in schools. DFID's *Learning Opportunities for All* headlines the following quotation: 'Literacy in itself is not sufficient to empower people unless conscious and planned efforts are made to interweave it with a participatory and empowering development process'
- Such a focus can be shared with contiguous adult literacy programmes (and other non-formal educational interventions). As *Learning Opportunities for All* notes: 'effective adult literacy programmes contribute to effective UPE'
- Environmental education provides a possible approach to designing basic education programmes which are simultaneously 'top-down' and 'bottom-up', making possible a 'strategy which avoids prescriptive dictates', while adhering to 'global priorities that emerge from . . . the international education goals, and from the consensus that there must be an unrelenting focus on the quality of teaching and learning' (World Bank Education Sector Strategy). Literacy and numeracy may be top-down prescriptions. Community environmental concerns can provide bottom-up themes for learners which are also likely to stimulate the use of participatory pedagogies
- Where environmental education can be linked to the enhancement of economic opportunity it may increase the probability that children will attend school rather than go to work or perform tasks at home
- Environmental education offers the possibility of being both *relevant* to what learners already know and at the same time *expanding* their under-standings. 'The curriculum, whilst being meaningful to their environment, must also open up wider horizons for the learners' (UNESCO, 2001, *Improving Performance in Primary Education – A Challenge to Education for All Goals, International Workshop TOR*)
- Environmental education also offers a way of responding to the obser-vation that, 'Primary education is more than cognitive learning . . . values, attitudes, social and emotional problems, career concerns, and security at school are often not addressed, whereas they have repercussions on performance in education' (UNESCO, 2001, *Improving Performance in Primary Education – A Challenge to Education for All Goals, International Workshop TOR*).

Note Views expressed in this report are those of the research team, not necessarily those of the Department for International Development

Nevertheless it remains true that for many people in many countries it is only in the early stages of formal education that anything even approaching environmental meta-learning is likely to be encountered. Given teacher skill and school security, it seems uncontroversial for small children to bring to bear a whole range of subjects on their studies of a single topic. A river, a field or an old building, for example, may serve as excellent focuses for learning experiences which might otherwise be segregated into 'history', 'geography', 'maths', 'science', 'art', 'creative writing' and so on. In Chapter 7 we saw how, for slightly older children, WWF's 'Biodiversity Basics' provided a means to juxtapose different perspectives (ecology, economics) on particular aspects of students' own behaviour (chewing gum). Of course, even at this age children (or their teachers) may be subjected to assessment regimes which tend, through their 'backwash' onto what is taught, to narrow the curriculum. But, that aside, meta-learning may well be uncontroversial: the facts about what is being taught are likely to be clear, the consequent capacity of the children themselves to make far-reaching decisions slight, and the assessment regime catholic in the sense of recognising as valid a wide range of pupil achievements.

However, secondary schooling tends to bring with it specialisation and higher education tends to extend this. Uncontroversial facts may become more elusive, with one way of excluding conflicting or confusing evidence being to narrow one's intellectual focus; far-reaching decisions, of which this narrowing of focus is likely to be one, become inescapable; assessment becomes more subject-specific, with a back-wash effect on what is then studied. The Forum for the Future *Learning for Sustainable Development* curriculum toolkit, discussed in Chapter 7, is an example of a sophisticated attempt to address this problem of specialisation: but the problem still remains that someone can only be an engineer (or a forester, economist, project manager or any other kind of professional) with a cross-disciplinary concern for sustainable development if they are *first* an engineer, that is, they have met the assessment requirements within those accredited programmes considered fundamental for admission to that profession. Hence, any focus on sustainable development remains essentially secondary.

Specialisation is not about to go away. For sustainable development to be a primary factor in the identity of professionals (that is, both to their practices and their shared literacies) it must be fundamental to the assessment regimes which restrict admission to their professions. Progress has been made in this respect. For example, in many professions a concern with environmental health and safety is now normal and routine (Hedstrom, 1996). However, we return to the point we made in Chapter 8, that learners do not learn things just because educators think them important. So, for example, even if the achievement of 'trusted and accessible systems of governance and justice' is fundamental to sustainable development, as in its *Curriculum Toolkit* Forum for the Future tells us it is, then it is clearly *not* fundamental to being an engineer. Quite clearly, however, there are, as a matter of fact, large numbers of capable, experienced and respected engineers working in settings around the world whose views on governance and justice would not accord with those of the Forum. Indeed, one might argue that good governance is a prerequisite for socially and environmentally responsible engineering, rather than the other way round. The Forum recognises this issue and offers a number of processes to prioritise course content in Higher Education so that it reflects the values of students and institutions. However, the more it does this, the less it can challenge those values and, in particular, the less likely it is to bring about learning across and between practices, literacies and institutions. Is it possible, perhaps, that what we know about assessment offers any way out of this apparently intractable 'Catch-22'-type difficulty?

Approaches to assessment

Biggs (1996), developing the work of Cole (1990), has identified implications for assessment in two broad traditions of educational thinking: the quantitative and the qualitative. The quantitative tradition sees learning as a process of accumulation of knowledge. Learning, therefore, happens in one of two possible ways. The most common by far is that it is transmitted in manageable chunks (facts, lectures, papers, books) from somebody who has it to somebody who doesn't. However, at the extreme there will also be individuals who are concerned to extend the knowledge available. These people are usually called 'scientists', and rather than (or in addition to) *learning* knowledge they are also engaged in *discovering* it. This view implies an approach to assessment which measures the amount of knowledge accumulated by an individual. It is particularly associated with multiple-choice tests or scoring of open-ended work by enumeration of valid points or references made. It can be particularly useful for anyone who wants to create a rank-order of a particular group of individuals according to what they know or who wishes to aggregate to a cumulative mark for a given student across radically different elements of a course, or across different subjects. There are three points we should make here.

First, as Biggs (1996) points out, assumptions are made in this model which are incompatible with what we know from the (paradoxically) scientific study of human learning. Perhaps worse still, these assumptions are also incompatible with what we have learned from the (scientific) investigation of the workings of science (Kuhn, 1996). Application of the positivist scientific myth reveals positivist science to be a myth: it is an odd situation.

Second, the fact that this quantitative view of knowledge is *useful* for purposes such as ranking people is probably a more powerful factor in its continuing widespread adoption than any claims it may have to be (universally, at least) *true*. To put this bluntly, social institutions of many kinds have a need for such rankings and for 'truths' to justify them. Finally, so pervasive is this view of knowledge that many people do not realise that it *is* a view and so deserving of that critical challenge which, science itself tells us, mere opinion must always be subject to. Rather, such institutions see it as a self-evident fact, incapable of challenge.

The qualitative tradition sees learning very differently, as an iterative, reflexive process through which the individual progressively constructs meanings out of past and present experiences. Knowledge, in this view, is not an externally given reservoir of facts but artefact of human society, in the production of which learners (and scientists) are themselves inescapably implicated. Many aspects of this way of seeing things were touched upon in Chapter 3 and we would revisit them here only to say that a range of theoretical positions is possible in general, from those which see objectivity as a regulatory ideal to those which would abandon it entirely (Connell, 1997; Reid and Gough, 2000). In the present context, however, it is the implications that this qualitative view of learning and knowledge has for assessment that are of particular interest. According to Biggs (1996) these implications are that assessment should be either *developmental* or *ecological*.

Underpinning *developmental* models of assessment is the assumption of some sort of taxonomy of stages through which a learner will pass in the process of acquiring understanding or skills. Biggs himself refers to a number of such possible schematics and a further example is considered below. *Ecological* approaches to assessment, by contrast, seek to test what has been learned in an authentic, 'real-world' setting. Interestingly, Biggs links these different approaches to different kinds of knowledge, suggesting that developmental approaches are more appropriate for the assessment of *declarative* knowledge, that is, of ways of understanding the world: ecological assessment, on the other hand, is better matched to *procedural* knowledge about how to do things, in as much as these can ever be separated. In practice, as ever, such things are not neat and tidy. However, let us begin our exploration of the issues with the following provisional hypothesis: that the kind of assessment most intrinsically appropriate to learning which will promote sustainable development is itself developmental. On the face of it this seems reasonable. It is consistent with the many approaches to sustainable development which call for changes in 'worldview', or 'paradigm' (see Chapter 5) and also those which identify a need for something better than is presently available to fuel human aspirations. As Christie and Warburton (2001: 13) have put this, for example:

> In the West . . . the gap between the official story of prosperity and the reality of everyday living is not simply about the gulf between rich and poor, or between private consumption and under-investment in public services. It is also about the gap between the promise of affluence and its failure to deliver real satisfactions and a sense of worthwhile endeavour.

It is instructive to set this quotation directly against another, which comes from the literature of developmental assessment.

> . . . development to the fourth order . . . represents the capacity to balance and choose among possibly conflicting roles without feeling selfish and conflicted. The person at the fourth order of consciousness *has* roles and relationships; his or her identity and self-definition is greater than the sum of those parts. The person at the third order, however, is *had* by (defined by, subject to) his or her roles and relationships
>
> (Taylor and Marienau, 1997: 238, original emphasis)

A reasonable inference might be that progression to the 'fourth order' is a prerequisite before people can be expected to go in search of 'real satisfactions' rather than relative affluence.

Taylor and Marienau's analysis draws on a particular taxonomy of 'orders of consciousness' originally proposed by Kegan (1994). They also provide a useful overview of developmental thinking, dating its origins back to, at least, 1641. Most importantly for the present discussion, they point to the Mission Statements of many contemporary organisations in making the case that higher order learning goals, such as those embodied in many such Statements, are only likely to be realised if they are intrinsic to the curriculum and are assessed. It seems clear that sustainable development involves higher rather than lower order human development, in this or any other developmental taxonomy. We should also expect sustainable development to be an increasingly common aspect of the 'mission' of contemporary organisations and for this to be linked to learning. As the Chair of the UK Government's Sustainable Development Education Panel has recently noted:

> The businesses of Britain, key stakeholders of the education system, will increasingly demand staff with skills in sustainable development. They themselves must accept some responsibility for developing these skills themselves for their own staff.
>
> (Holland, 2002: 59)

If all the foregoing is so, then the case for institutionalised *developmental* assessment of learning seems beyond doubt. Taylor and Marienau favour student self-assessment techniques as a methodology through which this can be achieved. A case for one of these, the learning journal, has been made by O'Rourke (1998: 404) in terms which seem, in the light of the foregoing discussion, particularly apt:

> The learning journal uses reflective and analytic writing to record and comment on a course of study. It links that learning to other experiences and ideas beyond the course and allows the students insights into their own learning style . . . When the learning journal is an active, experiential self-study aid it can help students move from surface to deep learning both within and across modules.

At the beginning of this chapter we noted the apparent difficulty for assessment, in relation to learning and sustainable development, that one could not always pre-specify what should be learned. It should be clear that our discussion has now led us to identify both an overall approach and one specific form of assessment, which appear perfectly appropriate for such a circumstance. However, the working hypothesis that brought us to this point, that the kind of assessment most intrinsically appropriate to learning which will promote sustainable development is itself developmental, is also open to critique from a number of directions.

Developmental doubts and beyond

First, we should note the caveats which the authors we have cited themselves express. O'Rourke (1998), while positive about learning journals in general, is not blind to their difficulties. These include their labour-intensiveness and issues relating to their subjectivity, authenticity and validity. We might note here, in passing, that objectivity may be problematised by qualitative assessment approaches but this is not the same as abandoning all concern for it.

Taylor and Marienau (1997: 240) raise questions about the ethics of developmental assessment which have particular implications in the context of learning and sustainable development. First, they point out that human developmental growth takes place over many years. It is therefore very difficult to assess learners fairly over relatively short periods. Second, such growth is uneven, giving rise to similar concerns. Finally, and most significantly, they point out that individuals have a choice about whether they want to 'grow' in terms of theoretical schemes of human development or not. This returns us sharply to our discussion at the end of Chapter 7, where we noted the tendency of all our exemplar curriculum innovations to leave no room for rationalities and worldviews other than their own. To put it as starkly as possible, if sustainable development requires that everyone *actually has achieved* (as opposed to being given opportunities for) high order developmental growth then it is a nonsense – since it is in the nature of development that there exists a prior stage from which individuals undergo progression; because whoever happens to be at that prior stage at a particular time cannot be excluded from social, economic and environmental processes; and because some individuals will anyway reject the opportunity to grow in this way. To return to the point made by Christie and Warburton (2001, above), people cannot be compelled to reject affluence in favour of what others think ought to be their 'real satisfactions' and in the end they cannot necessarily be taught to do so either.

Taylor and Marienau (1997: 240–1) conclude their analysis with the suggestion that human developmentally focused assessment, 'focus on "value-added", that is, what is the developmental direction of this group or cohort, and what does that tell us about our programme, curricula, or teaching methodologies?'. In relation to learning and sustainable development this seems to us a suitably cautious formulation, which retains the potential of such assessment as a useful, and sometimes powerful, tool.

Messy assessment: how to tidy it up

We suggested earlier in this chapter that our careful classification of approaches to assessment into the quantitative and the qualitative might not be as absolute as it appeared. It should now be clear that there is, for example, no very obvious reason why a qualitative, developmental approach to assessment, such as a learning journal, could not both record, *inter alia*, the acquisition of facts by the learner and also celebrate this. Presumably no one really doubts the laws of thermo-dynamics, for example, or even those of elementary supply and demand. Presumably no one would want to deny knowledge of these achievements of human understanding to anyone else. Only perhaps the most determined of post-structuralists would dispute that here is knowledge which individuals may perfectly well, and usefully, accumulate, in what looks suspiciously like a positivist fashion. Conversely, it is wrong to assume that the simple act of transferring knowledge of this kind from one mind to another cannot be developmental, since this would assume that the learner her or himself brings nothing to the learning situation. On the contrary, and for example, a simple theoretical understanding of supply and demand might well be highly empowering to a small-scale farmer in a developing country (Ellis, 1993).

This would seem to suggest that there may well be a place for quantitative instruments, for example of the multiple-choice kind, in assessment of learning in relation to sustainable development. Before considering what that place might be, however, let us return to Biggs's (1996) notion of qualitative, ecological assessment, which seeks to test the learner's abilities in a realistic context.

Biggs (p. 8) notes that requiring a test to be in an authentic setting is hardly different from insisting that it should be valid. What he means by this is that one should, for example, test 'problem-solving by giving students the sort of problem they would meet in real life'. This raises again an issue discussed in Chapter 8, where we argued, in apparent contradiction of Biggs's point, that environmental meta-learning should be characterised by a degree of abstraction from context and from decision making. However, it is one thing for assessment to relate to an authentic setting, another for the assessed student to incur, or be influenced by the possibility of, authentic *consequences* of their actions, as appeared to be the case in the WWF example discussed in Chapter 8. We would argue, first, that our approach therefore does not exclude ecological assessment in principle and, second, that such ecological assessment may also be developmental and so associated with declarative as well as procedural knowledge, where our condition of a degree of abstraction is met.

Knowledge of procedures, like knowledge of specific facts, may be uncontroversially useful. This is true whether one is changing a wheel, maintaining a jet engine, or performing heart bypass surgery. Further, and again just as with factual knowledge, procedural knowledge can be developmental if it provides a crucial piece of a personal jigsaw. Knowledge of simple mathematical procedures, for example, may belong in this category. However, complex procedural knowledge tends to be created by communities of practice (Lave and Wenger, 1991; see also Chapter 4). A characteristic of the environmental meta-learning, which we have identified as central to sustainable development, is that it occurs across such communities and their practices and for this a degree of abstraction is necessary. The North Borneo research described in Chapter 8 tested an approach which engaged learners not with one, but with multiple competing procedural knowledges, through simulating a credibly authentic situation from four quite different perspectives. To recap, these perspectives were those of:

• A local manager
• A Ministry of Development official
• A citizen responding to debate in the local paper
• A scenario-writer for a multi-national company.

Assessment of students within the intervention as a whole was:

• Quantitative, in the form of multiple-choice and short-answer responses relating to both management and sustainable development issues
• Qualitative/ecological, in the form of written responses and subsequent focus-group discussions in relation to the simulated situations
• Qualitative/developmental. Evidence was sought that the cohort as a whole evidenced developmental growth in relation to sustainable development *and* learners were required to engage with complex authentic problems from multiple procedural, problem-solving perspectives.

It would be very easy both to understate the difficulties of assessment in relation to sustainable development and to overstate the importance of a single instance of research in a particular context. All we have here is a hypothesis, not a finding. Nevertheless, we would suggest that a productive perspective on appropriate assessment of learning in relation to sustainable development can be derived from Figure 4.2 in the light of the foregoing discussion. Wherever, broadly speaking, 'information' appears to be the appropriate pedagogic strategy, we should expect quantitative evaluation of learning to be useful. Where it is clear that only mediation offers opportunities for appropriate environmental meta-learning, this will be best assessed in terms of evidence of collective, medium- to long-term developmental growth on the part of learners. Where communication is the best approach it will often relate to real and identified situations in which acquisition of procedural knowledge should be assessed along, quite possibly, with elements of both quantitative and developmental learning. It is, we would argue, an approach which respects learners' autonomy while creating opportunities for them, not only to learn things they didn't know, but to explore what they *didn't know they didn't know*. Like the Forum for the Future toolkit, it acknowledges existing values and organisational imperatives but it is also alive to the need for these to be open to challenge by learners themselves.

10 Measuring effectiveness
Monitoring and evaluation

Introduction: learning, efficiency, effectiveness

The wording of the title of this chapter is significant. We have used the word 'effectiveness' in preference to 'efficiency' in identifying the purpose of evaluation. The distinction between these two terms has been elucidated by many people in many ways, some of them rather technical, yet it continues to be a source of confusion. Since our concern here is with learning, own usage draws on learning theory, specifically that of Argyris and Schön (1996), which is represented in chapter 4 of the companion reader. Their work makes the following, crucial distinction:

> By *single-loop learning* we mean instrumental learning that changes strategies of action or assumptions underlying strategies in ways that leave the values of a theory of action unchanged. For example, quality control inspectors who identify a defective product may convey that information to production engineers, who, in turn, may change product specifications and production methods to correct the defect . . . By *double-loop learning* we mean learning that results in a change in the values of the theory-in-use, as well as in its strategies and assumptions.
>
> (Argyris and Schön, 1996: 20–1, original emphasis)

Single-loop learning improves *efficiency*. It results in improvements to the processes through which we seek to achieve what we *know we want* to achieve. This might, sometimes, fit comfortably with the economist's definition, according to which efficiency is improved if either a given output can be produced with fewer inputs, or if with constant inputs more can be produced. On other occasions it might suggest something which is (to many people's minds, anyway) rather more qualitative. For example, we might argue that a given process of institutional change is more efficient, other things been equal, the less resentment it causes among employees and/or the more opportunities it provides for personal career growth. In neither case, however, is there any fundamental intention to make changes to underlying values and purposes.

Double-loop learning improves *effectiveness*. It forces learners to ask whether they are sure that what they *think* they want to do is what they *really do* want to do. As

Argyris and Schön (1996: 23) further write, effectiveness cannot be guaranteed without this fundamental questioning: 'A process of change initiated with an eye to effectiveness under existing norms turns out to yield conflict in the norms themselves'. As we have seen, 'conflict' of this kind is endemic in relation to sustainable development and learning. It is expressed through the sense we have in our lives of complexity, uncertainty, risk and necessity. So, when we evaluate any given instance of environmental learning we must ask whether it is *effective*; whether it takes learners beyond a search for the best *solutions* and helps them instead to (re)consider whether they have really correctly defined the *problems*.

This said, a word needs to be said in defence of efficiency, for as the economist and international development specialist Geof Wood (pers. comm.) remarks, conservation (of, for example, something such as energy) and efficiency are essentially the same thing. Put starkly, once you have decided what you are going to do there is no possible environmental excuse for not doing it as efficiently as you can. *In*efficiency is synonymous with waste. It is for this reason that neo-utopian visions of sustainable development which entail the reordering of social and economic life around self-contained and largely self-sufficient communities (e.g. Trainer, 1990; Fien and Trainer, 1993a; Fien and Trainer, 1993b; Huckle, 1993) should not just be treated with due scepticism, rather they should be firmly rejected; all arguments about their lack of economic and social viability or attractiveness aside, they would be *environmentally* catastrophic. This is because the division of labour, including that associated with the special case of international trade, promotes the more efficient use of environmental resources. Efficiency is thus a necessary but not sufficient condition for effectiveness, but insufficient in and of itself as a focus of evaluation.

Two examples

Readers will find the readings and vignettes which appear in chapter 10 of the companion reader particularly instructive in relation to this discussion of effectiveness as the proper focus of evaluation. The two readings represent very different approaches. Both, it should be said, are excellent given their own purposes and assumptions. The first (Stokking *et al.*, 1999) is centrally concerned with efficiency in two senses. First, in the terms we have used above, it focuses on the evaluation of educational interventions as a way to achieve single-loop learning by educators. Second, it is concerned to promote efficiency in the process of evaluation itself. Both goals are addressed through a clear structure of 'thirteen steps to evaluation'. There is no question that many working in the field of environmental education will find the book extremely useful, that those who read it will almost certainly be led to conduct better evaluations and that the practice of teaching and learning will likely be improved as a result. Further, the authors have a clear sense that evaluation as an activity must compete for resources with other aspects of the teaching and learning process, calling for a proper balance between what evaluation can deliver and what it costs.

Their central focus on the evaluation of single-loop learning is evident from the following:

An activity is always evaluated against certain criteria. Often the most important criteria is whether the activity has any effect. The intended effects are referred to as objectives and the evaluation determines if the objectives were achieved. That can only happen if these objectives have been clearly formulated ... Objectives must not only be clear they must be measurable. For example: 'to contribute to the development of a sustainable society' is not an easily measured objective.

(Stokking *et al.,* 1999: 22)

Double-loop learning involves a change in values. For Stokking *et al.,* evaluation must be against measurable, pre-specified indicators. These can only possibly be derived from existing values. This is not bad evaluation, it is merely narrowly focused and of necessarily limited usefulness. However, anyone taking a wider focus, which recognises issues of complexity, uncertainty, risk and necessity, may well *want* to confront the issue of the contribution of learning to the development of a sustainable society, for which, as Stokking *et al.* quite correctly point out, measurable indicators are hard to establish.

However, as we saw in Chapter 7, some rather sophisticated attempts have been made to develop such indicators, perhaps most notably through 'Learning for sustainable development: a curriculum toolkit' produced by Forum for the Future. However, whether the difficulty of quantification is dealt with by restricting the scope of what is learned and evaluated, or by proposing a set of definitional 'criteria' for sustainable development against which progress can be measured, two inter-connected problems remain. First, the evaluation 'tail' is wagging the learning 'dog' in that what should be learned comes to depend on what can readily be measured. Second, learning is cast as a *means* for the achievement of sustainable development rather than as one of its *key components,* as a co-evolutionary view of the relationship between society and environment requires. Another way of putting this point is that learning cannot be both the means by which we *understand* sustainable development and simultaneously also the way we *implement* it (Foster, 2001 – see also chapter 6 of the companion reader).

A very different approach to evaluation is that taken in a report produced by the World Wildlife Fund (WWF, 1999a) in conjunction with Griffith University and the University of Bath, which examined educational activities across WWF's global network. The work took a participatory approach, citing the following as part of the justification for this:

All actors have a unique perspective on what a problem is, and on what constitutes improvement. As knowledge and understanding are socially constructed, they are functions of each individual's unique context and past. There is, therefore, no single 'correct' understanding. What we take to be true depends on the framework of knowledge and assumptions we bring with us.

(Pimbert and Pretty, 1997: 306)

As a result the internal and external organisational contexts in which WWF's educational effort took place was considered by the evaluation team, along with a wide range of evidence from other sources. Over a period from April 1998 to May 1999 data were collected by interviews with senior WWF staff, a review of documentary evidence from WWF national offices and project teams, a three-part survey and field visits to thirteen countries. To aid the analysis of evidence and elucidation of findings a terminological framework was developed which included the following six categories:

- Conservation outputs: wildlife surveys, detailed biodiversity maps, scientific reports on species loss. *By themselves* these have no intrinsic value, but they provide means whereby progress towards outcomes and impacts can be made

- Conservation outcomes: an improvement in the capacity successfully to plan, implement and/or manage conservation interventions. Cited examples include improved management of an environmental reserve, ISO 14001 accreditation for a company, collaborative agreements with local planners, or new environmental legislation

- Conservation impacts: long-term conservation gains. Cited examples include sustained improvements in stream quality, increased numbers of an endangered species, or improved long-term management of a fishery. Significantly, the authors note (p. 18) that, 'Education can be integrated with other strategies for conservation to achieve these impacts. Indeed, it is very important to recognise that conservation impacts are only feasible where understanding, commitment and other aspects of social capacity have been developed to ensure their sustainability'

- Educational outputs: curriculum materials, posters, kits, teachers' books, stickers, CD-Roms and the like. *By themselves* they provide no evidence at all that learning has occurred, except, perhaps, by those who created the outputs

- Educational outcomes: provide the basis for longer-term learning effects. They may be either people-focused or system-focused, that is, they may represent changes in practices or literacies, or in organisational or cultural institutions. Examples cited in the WWF report include the integration of conservation and sustainable development goals into syllabuses or a National Curriculum, the preparation of guides for professional development by professional associations which support sustainable development, and increased levels of understanding, knowledge and commitment by individuals

- Educational impacts: long-term effects expressed in general terms. Cited examples include the creation through learning of 'cultured individuals' or 'active citizens'. The authors (p. 19) make no apology for this general treatment, arguing that: 'Firstly, it is not possible to specify in advance what such future-oriented goals will mean in any detail because circumstances and contexts change so much over time. Secondly, because so many are value-laden it would be improper to specify what these should be in the many different cultural contexts in which WWF operates'. We should note that this last point is an important one which has been argued in detail by Shaw (1996) in relation to the example of evaluation and evaluation studies in the Middle East.

This framework has a number of advantages. First, it enables discrete evaluation activities to be focused at particular levels. Given a narrow focus it is, in fact, perfectly consistent with the model of Stokking *et al*. If, for example, an environmental interpretation worker in a zoo wants to evaluate awareness-raising work being done with visitors this might be done in terms of: (i) the quality of associated educational outputs; (ii) the achievement of a small number of pre-specified learning outcomes; and, (iii) expressed future intentions of visitors which bear on the realisation of tangible conservation outcomes. Following Stokking *et al*.'s 'thirteen steps' would be rather a good way of going about this. Both the usefulness and the proper limitations of the project would be clear to all involved. Importantly, however, the framework permits attempts to measure long-term, qualitative impacts where these are appropriate.

Second, the WWF terminological framework separates that which is educational from that which is environmental. This is invaluable. All over the world, education systems come under constant pressure from interest groups of all kinds who believe that education is central to the achievement of their goals (Hindson *et al.*, 2001). In this respect, and seen from the point of view of an official in most Ministries of Education around the world, environmentalists are no different from campaigners on issues of health, peace, animal welfare, consumerism, entrepreneurship, national sporting performance, heritage and so on. Environmentalists themselves, of course, consider themselves to have a particular and crucially irrefutable case; but so do all the others. This means that sustainable development is unlikely ever to have more than a token presence in school, higher or vocational education *unless* it can show convincingly that it is a means to improve the quality of educational generally – not according to the standards of environmentalists, but according to those standards which the main stakeholders in education and learning, such as parents, teachers, pupils, government ministers and employers *have arrived at for themselves*. Separating the evaluation of educational outcomes and impacts from that of environmental ones is a key step towards securing this mainstream curriculum presence.

Third, the framework makes a clear link to the organisational context of learning and teaching. This enables it to be not only a basis for evaluation of particular learning interventions, but also for evaluation of the evaluative effort itself, and in this way the WWF evaluation becomes a step to double-loop learning. It encourages evaluators to ask whether they are evaluating the right things. This point is illustrated by Box 10.1, 'The Miller's Tale', which is a reflection by one of the WWF evaluation team on a field visit to the Borjomi-Kharagauli National Park in Georgia in October 1998, drawing additionally on ideas from Lusigi (1994). The thinking behind the challenging questions raised in this extract about the purposes of education in conservation and sustainable development has been, and continues to be, productive for the organisation and its work. It is consistent with the implications of both Figure 4.2, which distinguishes information from communication and mediation as approaches to learning, and sets them in a context of influential external factors. It is also consistent with Figure 6.1, and with the notion of environmental meta-learning across institutions, practices and literacies.

The Miller's Tale: Reflections on the miller, his two cows and the distant pasture: false consciousness, or competing rationalities, and the ends of sustainable development education WWF (1999b: 14).

In the context of the development of the new national park in Borjomi it is clear that in many people's minds the purpose of (environmental) education associated with this programme is to persuade the recipients of the educational intervention (villagers, farmers, herders) that the authority's plan to implement the national park is rational and therefore the only sensible possible development. The proponents of this case (teachers, NGO officials, politicians, bureaucrats) believe in the rationality of the national park programme – even though it means that village people in certain areas will no longer have the possibility of cutting and/or gathering wood, or grazing their cattle in traditional areas. The supporters of this argument believe this because of the higher conservation goal (a 'natural' forest containing newly regenerated land) and its contribution to maintaining biodiversity across the Caucasus. Taxed with the claims of the traditional users, they argue these higher goals and point to alternatives which have been built into the plan (in this case grazing which is at some inconvenient distance from the traditional areas). They believe in the rationality of their case and see education, or perhaps more accurately, information, as the means of either persuading (where successful) or justifying (where unsuccessful) this higher conservation goal. These people are (to various degrees) educated, eloquent, confident, literate – sets of status which bolster their conviction about the plan (and park's) rationality. They probably also believe that theirs is, and can be, the only possible rationality – especially since it is shared by so many other people in powerful and influential positions. The argument of the villagers (who are about to be dispossessed of traditional access and benefits) must seem like an aberration, a special pleading, a disposition which is only possible because of ignorance of the facts and of the value of the wider goal.

However, from the villagers' perspective, one might surmise that their own case is just as rational. Here are traditional rights, enjoyed by generations, which survived the rigours and arbitrariness of collectivisation, which emerged intact into a more democratic future, which are now to be taken away or abridged at any rate by that newly democratic state, aided by the West's most prestigious NGOs and richer governments – and for what: the promise of something in the future and a rather vague conservation ideal (sustainable development). So, when the local miller asks 'why can't this huge national park cope with my two cows?' he doesn't get an answer because it has been decided that the question need not be taken seriously; rather, the question is to be argued away by a process of re-education which, if successful, will resolve the problem; if unsuccessful, it will at least explain the subsequent exercise of state power.

The point here is that it is patronising not to see the Miller's question and the disposition from which it stems as one which in his terms, on his ground, in his time, is quite as rational as the other.

Perhaps there needs to be two kinds of sustainable development education: one form directed at addressing the conservation issues; one form focused at the power groups who sponsor the first. The aim of these two, complementary approaches might be to seek compromise, to find plausible alternatives, to allow everyone to 'win'. The NGOs have a vital role in this. Their unique position can be used to broker a solution, rather than being part of imposing one. Thus the end of environmental education needs to lead to compromise and alternative paths, not coercion to a superior point of view. The error, perhaps, from this perspective, which the powerful groups make is to believe that their own form of rationality lies dormant, untapped, unrealised, within the other – lying masked by feelings, thoughts, passions and convictions which are to be overcome, and that the role of education is to help those individuals see the error of their ways and release them from their false view of the problems and hence the world. And if education fails in this task, well then, compulsion in the name of the higher rationality, is its own form of schooling.

Finally, the framework leads us to expect that, in general, the longer-term, larger-scale and socially and environmentally most significant impacts will be the hardest both to achieve and evaluate. This should come as no surprise perhaps, but it is worth making the point that the relationship between outcomes and impacts is one of *growth*, not aggregation; that is, both conservation and educational impacts are likely to be built through the sustained, iterative use of learning strategies combined with other social and economic strategies. This means that they will *not* just happen automatically once the total of disconnected short-term output targets achieved reaches some kind of critical mass. Rather, this suggests the need for a range of qualitatively different approaches to evaluation capable of providing information about everything from short-term, local outcomes to long-term, international impacts: and indeed this is what the report envisages and what continuing work on evaluation within WWF seeks to create.

Of course, the WWF evaluation did not create, *ab initio*, this discourse of outputs, outcomes and impacts which already existed both within and outwith the organisation. It was the framework that was novel as an heuristic for thinking systematically about the issues and as a means of making progress in practical evaluation. In other contexts slightly different frameworks exist. In 2002 the UK's National Council of Voluntary Organisations (NCVO, 2002) reported on its own consideration of these issues in its attempts to facilitate more effective evaluations of its member organisations' work. This retains the language (inputs – outputs – outcomes – impacts) and sees initiatives as having a series of iterative outcomes (staging posts/ milestones) which allow work to be done, *recognised* and built on. In this framework, what is desired at the end (what we have termed impacts) is actually only the final (desired) outcome, while *impact* refers to everything that accrues whether positive/ negative, desired/undesired or useful/problematic. Thus impacts includes outcomes *together with* everything else that results. This is useful because: (i) it acknowledges that things go awry (and, indeed, might usefully do so), (ii) that what turns out isn't always what is aimed for (but might be the next starting point), and (iii) that it is important to include everything that happens when measuring what's been achieved, and equally important to learn from this.

Sustainable development learning: an example

We might summarise the main points of the foregoing discussion as follows: evaluation of learning activities in relation to sustainable development should:

- Be systematic and efficient in the way it is conducted
- Employ a range of evaluation strategies to establish whether the activities have achieved their stated aims and objectives, disaggregating these into educational and environmental outcomes and impacts
- Provide information and stimulate reflection about the appropriateness of such aims and objectives
- Enable improvements in the design of activities through an examination of the contexts in which both learning takes place and is then applied by learners.

This is to re-assert the value of the Stokking *et al.* approach where it is appropriately targeted, but also to suggest that sustainable development will require double-loop learning and that this, in turn, will require additional types of evaluation input.

To illustrate the implications of these points in a practical setting we now consider a major UK policy initiative in sustainable development and learning which began in November 2001 and culminated in the launch of a major publication in London in September 2002, following hard on the heels of the UN World Summit on Sustainable Development in Johannesburg. This was 'Learning to Last: skills, sustainability and strategy', a project under the auspices of the Learning and Skills Development Agency (LSDA) which focused on the integration of 'sustainability principles and practices into all levels of post-16 learning' (Cohen *et al.*, 2002). LSDA is 'a national, strategic agency for the development of policy and practice in post-16 education and training, with a remit from government to work across the whole learning and skills sector'.

At the publication launch guests received, in addition to the publication itself and information about LSDA, copies of:

- A brochure about Forum for the Future's 'Higher Education Partnership for Sustainability' (HEPS) initiative (see Chapter 7)

- Details from the NCFE (national awarding body) of a national 'Foundation Certificate in Sustainable Development' award aimed at those 'seeking to enhance their employment prospects'. Mandatory units are *Understand the role of the individual in sustainable development* and *How to become an effective participant in sustainable development*
- Copies of the third and fourth annual reports of the UK's Sustainable Development Education Panel (SDEP), produced under the auspices of DEFRA, the government's Department for Environment, Food and Rural Affairs
- 'Changing Business': a publication from Forum for the Future setting out details of that organisation's work with the business community
- 'Towards Sustainability: a guide for colleges', a pamphlet commissioned by SDEP in conjunction with the Further Education Development Agency (FEDA) and the Association of Colleges (AOC)
- A copy of the press release which accompanied the launch, including supportive quotations from Lord Whitty, the senior DEFRA Minister who attended on the day.

One can see, therefore, that a very substantial organisational alliance is assembled around this project. Its intellectual credentials are also impressive. Prior to the launch three seminars had been held in which the distinguished contributors to the publication presented their initial papers. Three papers were presented in each seminar. The themes addressed by the seminars were:

- Seminar 1: Citizenship, Social Inclusion and Environmental Justice
- Seminar 2: Education for Sustainable Economic Development
- Seminar 3: Responsibility and Education in a Risk Society.

One chapter of the project publication provides a helpful initial focus for our discussion of evaluation. In this, Andrew Dobson develops an argument linking social inclusion, environmental sustainability and citizenship (Dobson, 2002; see also chapter 12 of the companion reader). Dobson discusses the social, economic and environmental dimensions of sustainable development through a consideration of factors that can be influenced through learning. How difficult the creation of these linkages is has been a recurring theme of this book and was discussed in some detail in Chapter 7.

In beginning with the notion of citizenship Dobson shares common ground with a long tradition of work in the field of environmental education (e.g. Hungerford *et al.*, 1980; 1983; Hungerford and Volk, 1984). The similarity, however, is superficial since Hungerford, his co-workers and his followers have tended to assume that learners *are* citizens and enjoy citizenship rights. By contrast, Dobson recognises from the outset that many individuals are victims of social exclusion, whose citizenship rights are denied in one way or another. With this in mind, he identifies two related but different ways in which, in Western societies, people have conceived citizenship.

The first of these stresses the rights to which citizens are entitled. Dobson considers the idea that, in addition to social, political and civil rights, people are entitled to environmental rights; and, just as any denial of civil rights, for example, amounts to an instance of civil injustice, so the denial of environmental rights creates environmental injustice. Drawing on evidence from the USA and the UK, Dobson is able to argue that environmental, civil, political and social injustice tend to go hand-in-hand. Those individuals whose rights are abridged in one of these senses are rather likely, as a matter of empirical record, to find their other rights similarly curtailed. Hence, in terms of citizenship-as-rights, 'movements for environmental sustainability are movements for social inclusion' (Dobson, 2002: 45) whether or not, we might add, environmentalists necessarily know or care about this. This conclusion provides a powerful lever for sustainable development by identifying it with another goal – social inclusion – which appears high among the priorities of many stakeholders in education and learning, exactly meeting the requirement we identified earlier in this chapter that learning interventions address *existing* stakeholder concerns.

Declaring that people have rights is one way of telling them that they are entitled to something for nothing; that they are the recipients, in Dobson's (p. 46) words, of 'a right to be consumed rather than a duty to be exercised'. In fact of course, such rights have often been very hard won and may have continuingly to be paid for. We might add that sustainable development, if it ever happens, will not happen in a context in which having anything for nothing is an option. Thus, on its own, and without qualification, the notion of citizenship-as-rights seems inherently unsustainable.

Political institutions, however, may often be quite comfortable with the idea of citizenship-as-rights, for the simple reason that promoting it is likely to make them more popular. Dobson provides an intriguing and all-too-brief analysis of how this bears upon the thinking of one institution, Britain's governing New Labour party, before going on to insist on a second, and perhaps complementary dimension of citizenship: citizenship-as-obligation. This, he argues, can also be linked to environmental justice and so to social inclusion, through the notion of the 'ecological footprint' (Wackernagel, 1995). Further, citizenship-as-obligation is an idea which extends the notion of citizenship to the international stage. This is because the differential impacts made upon a shared, global environment by different groups across the world constitutes an environmental injustice.

It is notable that Dobson himself approaches the notion of the 'ecological footprint' with caution, or at least with a sense that not everyone can be expected to take it entirely seriously. The concept of the 'ecological footprint' uses the quite striking metaphor of a footprint of a particular area of the earth's surface to account for each individual's usage of the earth's limited productive and waste-absorbing capacity. It is open to a number of objections, some of which Dobson briefly acknowledges, and some of which are implicit in arguments within this book, particularly in Chapter 5. Nevertheless, the 'ecological footprint' remains a powerful heuristic for, as Dobson notes: (1) the evidence is that different people and different countries make quite different imprints on a shared global environment to a degree that is unjust; and (2) that, once again, this environmental injustice is likely to be coincident with other forms of injustice. The evidence seems overwhelming regardless of the precise definitions, concepts or measures used to make the point.

However, if linking sustainable development to social inclusion is important in practical terms, linking it to international relations and, implicitly but clearly, through the footprint, to trade, is a potentially hugely significant step because, on any measure of the importance nations *actually* attach to issues, trade is clear by several points at the top of the first division. Hard-come-by money is spent by governments and business in promoting trade, while often only warm words can be spared for sustainable development. International trade has the World Trade Organisation; international sustainable development has (with the greatest respect) UNESCO. Nevertheless, in the autumn of 2002 that link had been made following the World Summit on Sustainable Development in Johannesburg. Thus, at the LSDA's 'Learning to Last' publication launch, Lord Whitty spoke, not only about the importance of sustainable development to the UK government, but also about the imperative to reform the European Union's Common Agricultural Policy (CAP), which is an institution that places significant obstacles in the way of trade with developing-country farmers. The argument for CAP reform goes: 'European farmers are often inefficient. Replace their output with lower-cost produce from the developing world and sustainable development, environmental justice and international citizenship will all be advanced'. This is a sound argument; but at the same moment farmers in Britain and elsewhere in Europe protest about the economic threat this brings to both their traditional lifestyles and livelihoods and many local organisations include the footprint-reducing 'extend local procurement' argument among their preferred sustainable development strategies.

In Chapter 7 we argued that the view of sustainable development as a universally beneficial route to an entirely collaborative social order was naïve because it took no account of other, legitimate rationalities and worldviews. We have also argued throughout this book that these competing rationalities are a *permanent* feature of the sustainable development project, because complexity, uncertainty, risk and necessity are inherent in the relationship between humans and nature. Individualists and hierarchists (see Chapter 1) can be ignored by egalitarian environmentalists but only until the stakes get high; they *cannot* be abolished through legislation, fiscal initiatives or through (re)education.

In October 2002 the EU deferred reform of the CAP for further consultation and extended deliberation. The extent to which this advances the cause of sustainable development remains unclear.

Lessons for evaluation

How might the general points we have made in this chapter be applied to the 'Learning to Last' example? First, we have argued that evaluation should *be systematic and efficient in the way it is conducted*. Where measurable learning objectives can be specified, and where Stokking *et al.*'s 'thirteen steps' *can* be followed, they *should* be followed. So, for example, the NCFE's Foundation Certificate units *Understand the role of the individual in sustainable development* and *How to become an effective participant in sustainable development* would surely include some inputs of information and communication and yield some quantifiable learning outcome measures for evaluation. Further, this might well contribute to social inclusion and environmental justice by providing learners with an asset, that is, information, which they did not previously possess.

Second, there is a need to *enable improvements in the design of activities through an examination of the contexts in which both learning takes place, and is then applied by learners.* Figure 6.1 provides a useful template for the analysis of context. Clearly 'Learning to Last' has been much influenced by organisational alliances, such as those between the Learning and Skills Development Agency (LSDA), Forum for the Future and the Sustainable Development Education Panel (SDEP), but also by wider institutional inter-relations, such as those between the UK government's Department for Environment, Farming and Rural Affairs (DEFRA) and the United Nations. All of these are *organisational institutions* which share a commitment to promoting the status of sustainable development as a *cultural institution.* Andrew Dobson's work provides a useful example of a *practice* which has been influential both on aspects of political and environmental *literacy* and also on other *practices,* such as those of some civil servants and NGO staff. Analysis should also take account of less encouraging aspects if it is to be useful in informing judgements about what has been achieved and what can now best be done, that is, if it is to support both single- and double-loop learning by those involved. At the publication launch of 'Learning to Last', the representative from the UK government's Department for Education and Skills (DfES) did not talk in the wide-ranging global terms of his DEFRA colleague. Rather he noted that sustainable development was relevant to a specific range of priorities and indicators, decided elsewhere. These were: enhancing competitiveness; social inclusion (as we have noted, an important cultural institution); the numbers of young people with and without qualifications; and, making large towns and cities better places to live in. Also, as we have seen, there are voices making themselves heard from quite different perspectives. These include the hierarchical, bureaucratic rationality of the EU. To give a further example of an individualist perspective, an influential (*on a range of practitioners*) organisational institution (*The Economist*), representing an influential literacy (*neo-classical economics*) and an important cultural institution (*meritocratic* rather than *egalitarian* justice) argued on 31 August 2002 that 'no one in their right mind is against "sustainable development"', but that even though 'making the rich poorer will not make the poor richer', it is 'outrageous that rich countries preach free trade to the poor while lavishing over $US300 billion a year on their own farmers'. On 30 November 2002 the same newspaper attacked the irresponsible application of the 'dangerous fashion for corporate social responsibility' following a decision by one company to withdraw work from a factory in Thailand which had a longer working week than the company could conscience even though it was giving its (now unemployed) workers wages and conditions better than the Thai minimum.

What this analysis reveals is that the 'ecological footprint' is only one aspect of sustainable development and, in the same way, environmental rights and obligations are only one part of citizenship. In both cases, enhancing one aspect may involve a trade-off with others. So, for example, the aforementioned company's attempt to demonstrate positive environmental and social values has had the effect of *increasing* economic inequality and *reducing* inclusion for some Thais: and Dayaks of North Borneo (see Chapter 8), many of whom have been displaced by logging and made new lives in coastal towns, are just one of many groups worldwide who, in the here and now, may depend for the most basic of opportunities on the continuing asymmetric ecological footprint of the oil-thirsty West. There is clearly scope for learning in society about the net significance of these issues for global environmental and economic justice, and about the wider meanings of those terms. Any evaluation of such learning, we would argue, is simply meaningless without an understanding of the institutional context in which it will be applied, and so continue to develop.

Third, our evaluation should: *employ a range of strategies to establish whether the activities have achieved their stated aims and objectives, disaggregating these into educational and environmental outcomes and impacts.* It should also: *provide information and stimulate reflection about the appropriateness of such aims and objectives.* Figure 4.2 is useful here since, as we saw in Chapter 9, whether assessment takes the form of a quantitative or a developmental reckoning depends on whether the appropriate pedagogic approach is one of information, communication or mediation. Assessment outcomes, as we also noted, are one important source of data for evaluation. In general, we would expect quantitative assessment to tell us about educational outcomes, while more developmental assessment may be informative about educational impacts and perhaps also about environmental outputs and impacts.

The most difficult kind of evaluation identified through our analysis is of the environmental and educational impacts of learning achieved through mediation in relation to contested issues. It is these impacts which are of the greatest potential significance for citizenship and both social and environmental justice. We would be wrong to pretend that a complete solution is readily to hand, but acknowledging the issue may at least prevent the raising of false hopes through over-simplistic evaluations, or a descent into false gloom through pretending that there is no point in even attempting such evaluations. One approach which appears promising uses metaphor as an evaluative tool (Kemp, 1999). In this, learners are presented with an evaluation instrument which prompts them to express their feelings about aspects of their learning as metaphors or similes of their own creation. The approach is simple to administer, but enables quite complex developments in learners' thinking to be charted over time. It may be used for individual or group evaluations, enables the learner to report changes in feelings as well as knowledge and would seem able to relate equally well to both educational and environmental aspects. Finally, it empowers learners to critique the learning process itself as Kemp (p.87) notes when reporting the following comment from a Social Work student that many will empathise with: 'We've also had a few onslaughts of being brainwashed by radical humanist androids'.

11 Building capacity, developing agency
Evolving a theory of change

Introduction

As we noted at the outset of this book, much has been written about appropriate content, processes and pedagogies for learning in relation to sustainable development. As particular approaches are invented and named, they become attached to particular institutions, which then acquire an interest in their success which goes beyond the purely intellectual. Titles and acronyms are deployed, as are lists of points and principles which, it is argued, capture the wider reality of what happens. As we also noted from the very beginning of this book, even the question of arriving at definitions of terms cuts both ways. On the one hand, continuing debate about definitions seems consistent with the case we have made for the potential contribution of multiple rationalities in the face of uncertainty. An early and still telling discussion of the dangers inherent in definitional standardisation is Robottom's (1987b). On the other hand, if one is trying to persuade people who are busy doing something else of the significance of a concept like sustainable development, then reducing that concept to a portable form has its advantages. Further, it might be argued that a field incapable of establishing agreed definitions of its most basic terminology is unlikely to make any other sort of progress.

At its heart, this is a question about the *theory of change* which informs different approaches to learning and sustainable development. Not all the approaches to sustainable development and/or learning we have discussed have an explicit theory but since sustainable development clearly implies some sort of change from the status quo, all must have at least an implicit theory of how it might happen. In this chapter we examine a number of possible ways of thinking about learning, sustainable development and change. Implicit in our discussion are the questions of:

- How the capacity of society for sustainable development might be enhanced, and
- How individual agency might effectively be energised and channelled.

As we noted in Chapter 10, it is not only those with predominantly environmental concerns who have seen learning as a route to the achievement of their social goals. Of particular interest here are those writers with a broader, but by no means unconnected, focus on education and social policy as a whole. Some of these have argued that meaningful social progress of any kind depends on developing new ways of learning in a rapidly changing world. For Brown and Lauder (2001 – see also chapter 11 of the companion reader), for example, there is now an historic choice to be made between market individualism and 'collective intelligence'. They argue for, 'a proper balance between competition and cooperation, which recognizes our mutual dependence on society'. This is to see things in a very similar way to many of those concerned to promote sustainable development, though within a wider frame of reference.

Existing theories of change: two unsatisfactory approaches

However, it is not, in fact, at all clear how any sort of learning leads to change or whether it does so at all in any predictable or manageable way (Levin and Kelley, 1997). As we have seen, learning always takes place within a pre-existing but often dynamic context of power-relations, rules, expectations, historical narratives and perceptions of group and individual interests, which affect not only what learners learn but what they think it is important to learn and why. A theory which explains how we think learning leads to social change seems indispensable to the planning of any sustainable development project. In Chapters 6 and 8 we began to develop such a theory ourselves, through a focus on the institutional context of change and the notion of Themes for Environmental Meta-Learning (TEMS). Here we initially take a step back, to consider the process of theory formation itself, before continuing this development.

We might conceive of a satisfactory theory linking learning, sustainable development and change in three ways.

In *Type One* theories it is assumed that environmental problems can be solved through appropriate social and environmental measures. In *Type Two* theories there is also confidence in the efficacy of such remedies but the core problems are seen as being *social* rather than environmental, whereas *Type Three* theories see the problem as one of finding appropriate ways forward in a context of social and environmental *co-evolution*. These types, discussed in detail below, largely follow from the analysis first put forward in Figure 1.1.

Type One theories: environmental problems understood; social solutions understood

We might, firstly, suppose that all that is needed is an appropriate educational technology to contribute to the solution of environmental problems which are themselves either well understood or amenable to understanding through science. Approaches of this kind commonly depend upon a notion of environmentally responsible citizenship, so assuming, at least, that countries are run by their citizens and that the role of 'citizen' is of more significance to people than other roles they may have (for example: 'employee', 'parent' or 'business-person') when they are making environmentally significant choices. The 'citizen' is seen as the vector through which objective knowledge is turned into social action. In a recent paper Kollmuss and Aygeman (2002) review selected frameworks for analysing what they term 'pro-environmental behaviour'. Their findings make depressing reading. We quote here an extract at length:

> The oldest and simplest models of pro-environmental behavior were based on a linear progression of environmental knowledge leading to environmental awareness and concern (environmental attitudes), which in turn was thought to lead to pro-environmental behavior. These rationalist models assumed that educating people about environmental issues would automatically result in more pro-environmental behavior, and have been termed (information) 'deficit' models of public understanding and action by Burgess *et al.* (1998: 1447).

Early models of pro-environmental behavior

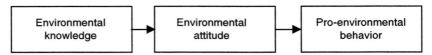

These models from the early 70s were soon proven to be wrong. Research showed that in most cases, increases in knowledge and awareness did not lead to pro-environmental behavior. Yet today, most environmental NGOs still base their communication campaigns and strategies on the simplistic assumption that more knowledge will lead to more enlightened behavior. Owens (2000) points out that even governments use this assumption, for example the UK government's 'Save it' energy conservation campaign in the mid-1970s, and the 'Are You Doing Your Bit?' campaign which was launched in 1998 to develop public understanding of sustainable development.

(Kollmuss and Aygeman, 2002: 241–8)

The reality is worse than even this would suggest (though, as we shall see, not as bad as it could get). First, it emerges plainly from Kollmuss and Aygeman's review that a clear, linear mechanism linking learning to change in a positive way remains elusive and probably doesn't exist. Second, resistance to (one might say denial of) this fact appears to be impervious to contrary evidence. So, for example, in the context of the Learning to Last initiative discussed in Chapter 10, we find one highly distinguished contributor (Sir Bernard Crick) quoting another (Alison West) favourably as follows:

> In other words we should move from rhetoric to prescription and, in terms of lifelong learning, this would enable us to identify the issues that local communities will need information on and the skills they are likely to need.

(Crick, 2002: 38)

This is not to suggest that information is useless or its provision a waste of time. As we made clear in Chapter 4, and have argued consistently since, both information provision and communication are important but are limited strategies which work only under certain circumstances. However, as we have further argued, and as Kollmuss and Aygeman's work confirms, these circumstances are not universally prevalent in relation to sustainable development. What makes the situation particularly strange is that while the view persists that something as complex as sustainable development would happen if only people knew enough facts about it, it is more than fifty years since *anyone* believed that the best way get a person to do something relatively simple, like buy a particular type of car, was to list its specifications. This last point, however, is also a pointer to how things could be even worse. There is a further view according to which environmental problems have scientific solutions and people should be instructed, or manipulated, into doing what is 'good' for 'them' (Wilson, 1975; Ehrlich, 1968; Goodland, 2002; see also Chapter 6). In approaches of this sort there is no obvious place for education, other than that of developing skills in the elite and compliance in the mass which, in our view, would be neither sustainable, nor bring about development.

Type Two theories: social problems understood; social and environmental solutions understood

Second, our theory of change might work from the premise that the problem of sustainable development is not really environmental at all, but social. What is therefore needed is an educational technology through which learners will come properly to understand the social obstacles to sustainable development, so that they can collectively take appropriate social, political and environmental action. This is a view particularly associated, in the field of education at least, with socially critical theory and the idea of an emancipatory curriculum. It has its roots in the work of Friere (1971), Habermas (1978) and Stephen Kemmis (Carr and Kemmis, 1986; Kemmis and Fitzclarence, 1986) and has been influentially developed by Pepper (1989) and John Fien, whose 1993 work (see chapter 6 of the companion reader) is a particularly lucid exposition. Like the work of Dobson (2002 and chapter 12 of the companion reader) which was discussed in Chapter 10, this approach brings together the achievement of social and environmental justice. It is open to critique on the grounds that it oversimplifies the nature and distribution of both environmental and social disadvantage (Gough, 1995), pictures practitioners and students as passive victims of wider economic forces (Robinson, 1994), over-specifies in advance what people are supposed to decide to do when they are 'emancipated' (Scott and Oulton, 1999), lacks an appropriate theory of implementation through which practitioners and researchers can make improvements to their practice (Walker, 1997), and offers little practical educational purchase on a world in which socialism and (particularly) false consciousness now appear widely discredited (Gare, 1995; Robinson, 1993). This last problem was not helped, perhaps, by those who cheered Robert Mugabe at the 2002 World Summit on Sustainable Development, though clearly the approach to learning we are describing here is far more sophisticated than any envisaged by the current President of Zimbabwe. A final point is that socially critical approaches have also been criticised by Bowers (1993; 1995 – see chapter 11 of the companion reader) on the grounds that they have, in principle, exactly the same underlying view of nature as informs the market capitalism they seek to persuade us all to replace.

Type Three theories: co-evolving problems and adaptive solutions

Approaches to developing a theory of change at the above two levels have been very useful in certain circumstances and we have recognised throughout this work that there may very well be instances in which either dissemination (through teaching/ learning) of factual information about environmental variables or facilitation of collective action (through teaching/learning) enables people to solve environmental problems to common advantage.

What we do not accept is that one or other of these approaches is *always* useful, or that, as some have argued (Robottom and Hart, 1993; Huckle, 1993), and others implied (Joseph and Mansell, 1996), they are ideologically and/or paradigmatically incompatible. The nub of the problem is not, we suggest, ideology or paradigm but uncertainty and complexity. In developing this argument we draw on a number of theoretical strands developed in earlier chapters, including our analytical framework of institutions, literacies and practices (Figure 6.1, p. 57). First, however, we revisit 'cultural theory', which was first outlined in Chapter 1.

The minimum claim we wish to make for cultural theory is that it is a useful heuristic in understanding problems relating to complexity, uncertainty, risk and necessity. Whether it is grounded in any sort of universal psychological or anthropological truth remains something of an open question. This is not necessarily a problem as it is quite clear that insisting on the literal truth is not always the most helpful approach to thinking about real problems. We know, for example, that the rate of passage of time *is not* absolute but we do not plan our lives in the expectation that it will vary. More prosaically, we find it convenient to talk about the rising and setting of the sun, though we know that it is really the earth that is turning. What we are saying is this: things do happen quite often *as if* the main claims of cultural theory were true.

The application of cultural theory to particular problems can be traced through the work of, *inter alia,*

- Douglas and Wildavsky (1982), James and Thompson (1989) and Schwarz and Thompson (1990) in cultural anthropology
- Thompson (1990, 1997) in environmental management
- Adams (1995) in the study of risk
- Gough (1995), Gough and Scott (1999), and Gough *et al.* (2000) in environmental education.

To recap, the key proposition of this work as it concerns us here is that it is possible to identify multiple forms of rationality, the possession of any one of which predisposes an individual to particular values, attitudes, interpretations of knowledge, definitions of problems and view of what is in her/his own interest. The last item on this list is, perhaps, of particular significance, since it has been quite common in the literature to assume that people's interests are given and self-evident.

The form of rationality likely to be exhibited by given individuals at given times and places is, we argue, consequent upon logically prior variables relating to their:

- Membership (or not) of bounded social groups
- Freedom of action (or lack of it).

The cultural theory approach has been found to have considerable apparent explanatory power in relation to environmental management and environmental education. Claims concerning its ability accurately to predict the risk perceptions of individuals have, however, been helpfully contested (Wildavsky and Dake, 1990; Sjöberg, 1997) and remain very questionable. However, this is less problematic for the approach as a whole if one accepts that individuals can and do frequently switch between rationalities. To illustrate how this may happen, we might observe a member of a university's Faculty to exhibit, in rapid succession, an egalitarian rationality (say, by arguing for biospheric equality as a guiding principle for sustainable development education programmes), a bureaucratic rationality (say, while conducting a quality assurance review), an individualistic, market rationality (say, while competing with staff of another university for funding or students) and a fatalistic rationality (say, while reflecting on her or his inability to influence the decisions of the university promotions board).

The significance of this for the present discussion is that it opens up the possibility of thinking about learning and change in a quite different way. Approaches at level 1 or level 2 suppose that what counts as 'pro-environmental' or 'pro-sustainable development' behaviour can be specified, and that, through learning, appropriate cognitive (thinking), conative (action) or affective (feeling) skills can be induced which will contribute to bringing this about. The main debate, in this view, is about *which* set of skills should be the primary target for learning. However, where complexity and uncertainty are present it may be more the case that individuals *begin* with a view of pro-environmental or sustainable behaviour which is rooted in their institutional affiliations and *derive* for themselves thoughts, actions and feelings which are consonant with this. Such an explanation has, at least, the powerful advantage of being able to explain why people's opinions, actions and feelings are often confused or contradictory as one would necessarily expect them to differ as the person's context and rationality varies.

It follows that here the role of learning must be quite different and cannot directly help people to adjudicate between sustainable development problem-definitions as in this view, for the time being at least, uncertainty and complexity are irreducible and whoever is responsible for the design of the learning experience (e.g. teachers, trainers) *cannot possibly make this adjudication themselves*. What they can do, however, most productively and creatively, is to confront learners with competing problem definitions: both, for example, those they themselves switch between in different contexts, and those favoured by others.

To illustrate this, we return to the example of the North Borneo research described in Chapter 8. During the *design* case study, which focused on tourism development and environment, the following positions were found among the sample of students:

- *Hierarchical rationality*: regulation is the key to developing the right sort of tourism to attract the right sort of tourists. If this is done properly there is no serious threat to the environment. Indeed, the environment may be enhanced. Established institutions are competent to develop an appropriate regulatory framework, and have already identified both the economic need for tourism development, and the social, cultural and political imperatives which make regulation necessary
- *Individualistic rationality*: information about tourism from both supply-side and demand-side will be most efficiently processed through markets. The price mechanism will determine most effectively which environmental assets are consumed in the development of tourism and which are conserved. Social, political and infrastructural arrangements need to change to allow markets to operate efficiently
- *Egalitarian rationality*: tourism development is tending to destroy or cheapen our traditional lifestyles and disempower us in relation to our environment. A political remedy is needed which achieves a just and democratic solution to this problem
- *Fatalistic rationality*: tourism development is tending to destroy or cheapen our traditional lifestyles and disempower us in relation to our environment. There is nothing we can do about it.

Respondents tended to switch between these rationalities when asked to adopt different roles, for example as a government official, village headman or tourism company employee. As noted in Chapter 9, the learning which occurred through this process was reflected in the achievement of quantitative and qualitative assessment goals. These assessment results were also, of course, educational outcomes (see Chapter 10) for evaluation purposes. The interventions were also evaluated positively by the lecturers whose job it was to teach the programme and by the college administration. An environmental outcome was the engagement of the Ministries of Development and Industry and Primary Resources in a national programme of management training, to both *their* satisfaction and that of the Ministry of Education. In short, the use of *themes for environmental meta-learning* (TEMS, see Chapter 8) resulted in social actors with different rationalities learning from, and with, each other under conditions of uncertainty and complexity.

Type Three: towards a more general theory of change about sustainable development through learning

Sustainable development is widely conceptualised as having three components, the environmental, the social and the economic. This view is represented in Figure 11.1.

It is this formulation which underpins the currently rather fashionable notion that sustainable development has a 'triple bottom line'. It has also been extended in various ways by various organisations. For example, the UNESCO 'Teaching and learning for a sustainable future' multimedia teacher education programme described in Chapter 7 prefers a four-segment approach. The four segments in that

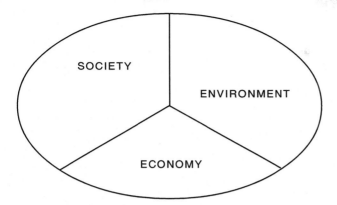

Figure 11.1 Dimensions of sustainable development.

case are social, economic, natural and political. Forum for the Future's 'Learning for sustainable development: a curriculum toolkit' uses the three-segment approach but extends it into five kinds of capital. These are: natural; human; social; manufactured; and financial. However, for our purposes here, the basic three-segment model shown in Figure 11.1 will serve quite well.

Any complex task needs to be broken up in some way before it can be attempted. The three-segment model, and derivations from it, are a way of doing this. What is clear, however, is that although there may be other ways of doing it, this particular way supports, and is supported by, a strong coalition of institutions, literacies and practices. From the various points of view of these institutions, literacies and practices, therefore, the three-segment view of sustainable development is *deeply conservative*, in the sense that it accords with their existing ways of thinking and organising.

To take these two points in order, the three-way division of sustainable development is an artefact of human thought, not an innate property of sustainable development itself. It is not, in fact, possible to have an economy (sustainable or otherwise) without a society and an environment. It is not possible to have a society without an environment or, in any sense meaningful in the modern world, an economy. Most significantly perhaps, while it may be possible to have an environment without a society or an economy, it is not possible to have *the* environment without these. It is *the* environment because of the significance it acquires for us through our building of social and economic relations with it. Without humans there can be no basis for preferring the present environment (itself an artefact of co-evolution) to any other – that of Jupiter, say, or that which would follow any species of 'environmental' catastrophe. This means that there is potential for social learning, broadly consistent with that advocated by Brown and Lauder (2001) and others such as Elliott (1998, and chapter 4 of the companion reader) and Young (1998, and chapter 7 of the companion reader), through asking: what are the common elements of economy, society and environment? In the present context this might be restated as, 'what constitutes the lines in Figure 11.1?'

Whatever their potential educational power, however, these questions have little currency in the context of contemporary educational and social policy formation which brings us to the second point above. Discrete literacies (for example those of the economist, the sociologist, and the biologist) exist to focus on and extol the central importance of their own particular segment of concern. This is true whatever organisational institution the specialists in question work for: whether it is, for example, a mining company, an environmental NGO or a government agency. Hence, while protagonists to the debate about sustainable development may disagree strongly about *solutions*, they share an interest in seeing the *problem* in a particular way. Further, each literacy supports and is supported by a set of practices and these in turn are consistent with the way organisational institutions structure themselves (so, for example, governments have ministries of finance, of environment, of development). School curricula are organised into subjects that are defined by existing literacies and prioritised by policy makers on the basis of needs identified in relation to existing institutional structures, both organisational and cultural. Students who are successful are inducted into appropriate practices. It is thus difficult for anything *really* new to emerge.

We have suggested in this book that, faced with the necessity to act under conditions of complexity, uncertainty and risk, there is merit in encouraging learners to re-think the categories through which society typically conceives its relationship with the non-human world. One obstacle to this is the inertia possessed by existing institutions, literacies and practices. A second is the attachment these have to different rationalities, each of which is capable of making sense of our relationship with the non-human world *in a different way*.

There is, however, a significant third obstacle. This is the existence, in Western thought at least, of a form of meta-literacy that takes for granted the appropriateness of 'competition' and 'cooperation' as ultimate, opposed categories of social analysis. Hence, diverse organisational institutions, cultural institutions, literacies and practices are grouped into coherent 'worldviews' or 'paradigms' which are seen as necessarily in opposition to each other. Some people favour cooperation and equality, so this line of reasoning goes, and some favour competition and merit-ocracy. The two worldviews compete directly with each other, and also compete, in terms of our cultural theory analysis, both to influence the decisions of bureaucrats and to recruit fatalists to their cause. As we have seen, Brown and Lauder have made a case for 'balance' between these worldviews in relation to learning. Others, such as Christie and Warburton (2001) have done so in relation to sustainable development. An implication of our argument is that this entire conceptual edifice is ultimately *conservative* because its locks us endlessly into the same debates. We might, therefore, question the appeal to 'balance'. In the natural world, plants and animals are both interdependent and in competition, full-on, all the time. In social affairs individuals and groups, whatever their espoused 'worldview', plot and scheme even as they form alliances and keep their promises. There *is no* either/or.

We have argued that the challenge for learning in relation to sustainable development is to confront learners with competing accounts of human and environmental reality wherever complexity and uncertainty mean that it is possible for competing rationalities to yield competing versions of the truth. This, we have suggested, radically revises our view of learning: from a process which acts on individuals' characteristics in order to change the world to one which challenges individuals' views of the world as a means of influencing their characteristics and hence ways of thinking and living. Following the work of cultural theorists, we have proposed a minimum framework for classifying the different rationalities which people may use to make sense of complexity, uncertainty, risk and necessity. We have argued that the choice of rationality under these circumstances is likely to be a product of the individual's institutional context in relation to the problem.

Finally, we have argued that the 'dichotomy' between competition and cooperation as organising principles is not an innate characteristic of societies, but only an artefact of thought. It is, therefore, unlikely to be helpful to seek to promote 'balance' between competition and cooperation. They are not different solutions to social and environmental problems, but rather alternative (but not the only) ways of *defining* such problems. Balance is not possible between two people sitting on different see-saws. If we are going to build new capacity and create individual agency for radical change then, to persist with the metaphor, we need to encourage and help learners to look around the playground.

12 Economic behaviour
Value and values

Introduction

In Chapter 11 we argued that achieving sustainable development is not about achieving a triumph of collaboration and egalitarianism, on the one hand, over competition and market individualism on the other, nor an equally triumphal reverse of this, nor, again, a state of balance between the two. However, it is not surprising that debates about sustainable development seem so often to be framed in terms of this 'dichotomy'. As the psychologist Helen Haste (2000 and chapter 12 of the companion reader) points out, dichotomous thinking, according to which a given entity at a given time cannot simultaneously *be* in a given state and also *not be* in that state, is very deeply rooted in Western minds. Whether this Aristotelian precept is ultimately true or not, it clearly leads to faulty thinking when applied to something like 'society', the nature of which is conceptual, not physical. So, if we consider two archetypes, one of a 'competitive' society (say, the United States of America) and the other one founded on principles of cooperation and equality (say, Soviet-era Russia), what we actually find in both *at the micro-level* is abundant evidence of *both* competitive and collaborative social interaction. Where people cannot compete through markets they usually find other ways to compete for favour and favours. When they are required to compete through markets they often look for collaborative ways to achieve advantage, or take comfort in non-competitive relationships and alliances. In both cases they may well appeal to, make, break, uphold or seek to change systems of rules which they find helpful, or value for their own sakes. Our question would therefore be not: 'what balance of competition and collaboration is compatible with sustainable development?' but rather 'how do we make sustainable development happen where both are constantly present?' In seeking an answer, we need to explore the issue of the relationship between, on the one hand, human values and, on the other, what *has* value in the economic sense.

A search for 'compromise'

In fact, although we have argued it is fundamental misconceived, there is at the time of writing considerable evidence of a search for compromise between the advocates of competition and collaboration. In Chapter 3 we considered the language of sustainable development. We now suggest that sustainable development requires, if not a new language, at least a new word or two which can liberate us from the limiting notion of compromise, and from the inadequate metaphors we are accustomed to use ('this way or that'; 'either/or'; 'more or less'). To do this we consider two recent examples which start from one particular viewpoint and seek to compromise with the 'other'. In doing this, as so often in this book, we seek to build on constructive thinking from different perspectives, not to adjudicate between them.

The Real World Coalition (Christie and Warburton, 2001; see also Jacobs, 1996) is an association of campaigning organisations in the United Kingdom. It lists its objectives as: environmental sustainability; social justice; eradication of poverty; peace and security; and, democratic renewal, describing these collectively as the 'key policy constituencies of sustainable development' (Christie and Warburton, 2001: vi). These goals are similar to those of the Forum for the Future curriculum toolkit described and discussed in Chapter 7 and it should be no surprise that the Chair of the Real World Coalition is a prominent member of the Forum.

It would, of course, be hard to find anyone who is explicitly *opposed* to the goals of the Real World Coalition as set out above. However, the predisposition of its members to an egalitarian rationality and to collaborative problem solving is apparent from the 'five areas for action' (Christie and Warburton, 2001: 20–1) it sets out for the achievement of the goals, each of which is developed through sophisticated arguments in the rest of the book. These appeal to both evidence and experience, drawn from both the United Kingdom and the rest of the world, and make practical proposals for the improvement of policy. The 'five areas' are shown in Box 12.1.

This is an articulate and extremely well informed response to conditions of complexity, uncertainty, risk and necessity, written wholly from the perspective of an egalitarian rationality (See Chapter 1, and Chapter 1 of the companion reader). Things social, economic and environmental will be all right, we are being reassured here, if they are *fair*: and assuredly there is something in this. Equally certainly, there is more to it than this. Among the objections someone approaching the same complexities and uncertainties from an individualistic, competitive rationality might raise (perhaps before passing on, muttering *sotto voce* about 'do-gooders') are the following:

1   If we can achieve a tenfold productivity increase why not use it for our own competitive advantage and distribute a proportion of the increased profits to the socially disadvantaged through the tax system? Surely, arguments which depend on the notion of 'environmental limits' have often been proven to be dubious or downright wrong?

2   Surely the only possible way to make everyone better off is through economic growth? If a massive global income redistribution is being proposed then this should be made clear to people in developed countries, who may not consider themselves to be particularly rich but would surely be net losers. The history of attempts at income redistribution is hardly encouraging. Also, what about people who abuse citizenship rights or don't want to make a social contribution?

3   Who is going to do this? Isn't 'democracy' better served by having something as complex as international trade overseen by the World Trade Organisation,

rather than by special-interest campaigners? Shouldn't we focus on getting developing countries to grow at all before we insist they do it 'equitably'? Isn't the whole point about market forces that they serve the public good best when no one interferes with them?

4   Shouldn't debt relief for developing countries, and strengthening the United Nations be conditional on their performance? Wouldn't firms stop making arms if governments stopped buying them? Then there would be less need for peacekeeping too.

5   In this 'democratic' future, are we allowed to choose something else?

In an analogous way issues could be raised from a hierarchical, bureaucratic rationality.

Box 12.1 The Real World Coalition: five areas for action

1. *Making a Low Carbon, High Value Economy*: promoting business innovation in technology to achieve a tenfold increase in the productivity of our energy and material use, dramatically reducing waste, pollution and greenhouse gas emissions, in order to respect the environmental limits we are already, or are in danger of breaching.

2. *Reducing poverty and key inequalities at home and abroad*: attacking the causes and consequences for individuals, families and communities (including whole regions and countries) of persistent poverty and social exclusion – lack of access to the resources, services and rights which make full citizenship and social contribution possible.

3. *Promoting sustainable development in the international economic system*: reforming global economic governance – above all the trade system – to ensure that developing countries can grow equitably and in an environmentally sound way; leadership from the rich world in reducing resource consumption, and in redesigning debt and aid strategies to promote sustainable and fair globalization that ensures that market forces serve the public good in the rich and developing worlds alike.

4. *Promoting security, peace and conflict prevention*: seeing sustainable development strategies as a vital force for long-term international security and prevention of conflicts; and helping promote security through debt relief, strengthening of the UN, curbs on arms production and the arms trade, better development and humanitarian aid, and peacekeeping.

5. *Renewing democracy for richer choices*: innovating in democratic processes at local, national, and international/global levels, in order to improve public engagement in decision making and to foster national and international debate on innovations, risks, and long-term impacts of our choices as consumers and citizens.

Source: Christie and Warburton, 2001: 20–1.

The issue here is that, first, these points are *also* valid, based on the assumption that things make sense not if they are fair but if they are *successful*. The focus is not on social and environmental justice outcomes but on what seems to work in the here and now. Adversarial debate between this view and that of the Real World Coalition is ultimately unlikely to be productive and compromise may well be seen as the worst of all worlds from both points of view. Quite simply, the protagonists cannot agree, or compromise, on a solution because they are not debating from the same definition of the problem. Note, however, that even the most apparently incompatible institutions may find reasons to build alliances from time to time and have need to explain them by reference to compromises over budding, not-very-clearly-defined cultural institutions such as sustainable development. This is a different matter entirely and sometimes results in the strangest of bedfellows.

However, there is no need to depend on a straw man of our own creation to put the individualist/ competitive case in relation to sustainable development. An actual example is readily to hand in the shape of *The Economist* weekly newspaper. The difference in its underlying rationality from that of the Real World Coalition is at once apparent in the way each assesses its own constituency. Real World (Christie and Warburton, 2001: xi) tells us of its conviction that 'there is a hunger in the public at large for a politics that takes seriously the great challenges of environmental sustainability, democratic regeneration, inequality, and the revitalisation of community life'. *The Economist*, on the other hand, just sells a lot of copies round the world.

In its 31 August 2002 edition, *The Economist* led on the World Summit on Sustainable Development and also ran a three-page special feature on sustainable development. *Inter alia* it argued that:

- In spite of the non-attendance of George W. Bush, the United States had been 'constructive' in relation to the Summit. South Africa's president Thabo Mbeki, on the other hand, was inaccurate and unhelpful in giving succour to the 'anti-growth lobby'.
- Since the 1992 Earth Summit in Rio de Janeiro there has been much progress in enhancing human welfare, especially in the world's most populous countries, through globalisation and economic liberalisation. In countries which have elected not to participate in this process, suffering has increased. It is domestic policies in developing countries that make the most difference.
- There is a need to make sure that where poor countries benefit from economic growth this does not exacerbate global warming. World leaders could use the Summit to agree to phase out subsidies on coal and other dirty fuels as the best means to advance a green agenda.
- Rich countries should abolish, or at least dramatically reduce, farm subsidies to give the poor a chance to compete in world markets.
- Aid should be focused primarily on the issue of disease because that is an area in which poor countries face the greatest difficulties in helping themselves. 'Type 2' partnerships which link governments, NGOs, community groups and businesses are a promising way of setting about this.

Once again, this is a well informed case. There is certainly some truth in it. This time, however, it is egalitarians who are likely to be outraged. From their perspective the whole point has been missed. *Equality*, as a primary principle of social organisation, is nowhere to be seen.

It may be useful at this point to summarise the relevant part of our argument, developing in particular, but in our own way and for our own purposes, some of the ideas of Richard Norgaard and Michael Thompson, and their co-workers, which have been referred to elsewhere in this book – and see chapters 1 and 12 of the companion reader. The argument goes:

- The human relationship with nature is co-evolutionary: society adapts to its environment; the environment responds to human activity and both shift over time
- Society's adaptations are influenced by, and assessed in terms of, human values and knowledge. Values can change. Knowledge can be gained or lost, but it cannot be *complete* in any imaginable time frame. Of course, more knowledge is better than less: but nevertheless uncertainty and complexity are often inherent and inescapable – indeed, this is one of the most potentially useful things we *know*
- However, in order to live (well or otherwise), humans cannot escape the necessity both to face up to this uncertainty and complexity *and* to deal with risk which derives from it. Learning is integral in such processes
- The environment's responses to human activity are value-free in the sense of being indifferent to humans and their interests
- Both social and environmental processes are continuous, though each may be more or less rapid and dramatic at different times and places. This means that human learning, managed or unmanaged, is a centrally constituent part of the process
- Sustainable development cannot possibly mean an 'end state' to be achieved, because there *are no* 'end states': if sustainable development means anything it can only be a way of describing an adaptive approach to managing human-environment co-evolution
- However, when faced with uncertainty, people typically try to resolve it through the application of a particular rationality, a way of making sense of things. There appears to be convincing evidence that at least four of these rationalities can co-exist in relation to a problem: the *individualistic*; the *egalitarian*; the *hierarchical* and the *fatalistic*
- The particular rationalities which given individuals apply vary from problem to problem, context to context, and over time
- The rationality employed depends on the person's institutional affiliations (that is, their attachments to organisational institutions, cultural institutions, literacies and practices) in relation to that problem and context. This results in competing *problem definitions*, each of which, in turn, suggests a particular type of solution
- Advocates of these preferred 'solutions' often propose educational or other means by which such solutions may be implemented. However, the proper role

of educators (teachers/ trainers/facilitators/curriculum designers/policy experts/ etc.) in these circumstances has to be to help learners confront the generic underlying uncertainty and complexity through engagement with multiple credible problem definitions, and hence *learn* – though what they learn will not necessarily be what some others might wish

- Finally, important though the foregoing is, it is also crucial not to forget that there will be many occasions where uncertainty and complexity are absent or manageable and determining what is to be learned will therefore be more or less straightforward (see Chapter 4).

It follows from the above that neither the Real World Coalition, nor *The Economist*, has it quite right in relation to sustainable development: equally, neither has it entirely wrong. Neither is appealing to more accurate facts: neither is appealing to superior values. Compromise will not necessarily result in either being closer to the truth. They might learn from each other: and indeed, in a largely serendipitous and unplanned way they probably do, sometimes. What would be helpful would be to set an overall goal for learning which defines it clearly as *part of the process* of sustainable development, rather than *a means of implementing* it.

Society, economy and environment: once again

However, it is all very well for academics to declare sustainable development to be a shifting, indefinable and contingent concept. Academics are not (or, at least should not be) under professional pressure to settle matters of definition. Rather, they are there to ask critical questions for as long as there are critical questions to ask. However, sustainable development has not found its way onto the agendas of many important and influential organisations principally because it is of abstract interest to academics. Significant numbers of other people now have jobs which require them, in one way or another, to engage with the notion of sustainable development. They may work in national or local government, the private sector or the NGO sector, perhaps having responsibility for environmental management systems, green procurement, social inclusion, waste management, water quality or any of a host of other matters. They may be policy makers, engineers or teachers. Whoever they are, they will typically work with colleagues who to a greater or lesser degree do not share their focal concern with sustainable development. They are also likely themselves to have a professional identity, an allegiance to a practice and/or a literacy, to which the concept of sustainable development is in no way intrinsic. They may, for instance, be physicists or educationalists; administrators or personnel officers; French teachers or civil engineers; health and safety officers or landscape architects. Finally, these individuals will be concerned with sustainable development in one or both of two quite different dimensions. First, they may be concerned with the promotion of sustainable development through actions which are essentially internal to their own organisations (say through in-house energy management or, more broadly, through the pursuit of ISO 14001 accreditation). Second, they may be responsible for bringing about more sustainable outcomes of one sort or another outside their own organisations. For example: a local government officer may seek to increase energy efficiency among local residents; a manager with a multi-national company may wish to improve the emissions standards of suppliers in under-regulated developing countries; and a teacher may aim to teach children (and through them, their families) about biodiversity conservation. All of these undertakings would seem to involve learning by someone to a greater or lesser degree, though those involved may prefer to talk about 'education', or 'training', or 'communication', or 'awareness-raising' or even 'capacity building'.

All these people have a need to attach a meaning to the term sustainable development if they are to do their jobs. It is therefore unsurprising that there is a ready market for formulations such as Forum for the Future's 'Twelve Principles' and 'Five Capitals', or *The Economist*'s more *laissez-faire* approach: promote growth and internal reform; target disease; abolish damaging subsidies. As we saw in Chapter 11, one particularly influential conceptualisation of sustainable development sees it as a whole made up of three segments – economy, environment and society (Figure 11.1, p. 117).

We return to this now to explore how useful opportunities for learning might be created. In Chapter 11 we asked what the lines in Figure 11.1 consisted of. What exactly is it that demarcates, for example, the economic from the environmental? On a journey across the boundary from one to the other, what would we pass through? There may well be many answers to this, but here we suggest four, each with its own implications and opportunities for the design of learning experiences.

First, there is *culture*. A cultural imperative to *save*, to take just one example, is important in each of the domains of society, economy and environment and is clearly in some sense their joint *product*. Exploring the ways in which aspects of culture are interwoven with society, economy and environment is likely to be itself a learning experience, to reveal opportunities for learning by others and to facilitate the better management of learning. To continue with the example, the notion of things being saved (and its opposite) is fundamental to conservation, capitalism, science, religion, history, love, war and, therefore, literature. It clearly permeates the content (and methods) of education (and training, communication and so on) already, without its significance or ubiquitousness being recognised or exploited in any systematic way. If this could be done, and the society/economy/environment segments thus re-merged along this particular cross-section, sustainable development learning might result. By identifying 'culture' as an element of all three segments, we have been able to further identify '*Saving*' as a theme for environmental meta-learning (TEM) similar to those described in a practical setting in Chapter 8. This TEM would be employed not as an element within discrete subject disciplines (as, of course, already happens) but as a cross-cutting and simultaneously unifying focus. In the example above, learners would engage with what both the Real World Coalition and *The Economist* think is important about the idea of 'saving'. This conceptual-isation bears similarities to Young's (1998, and chapter 7 of the companion reader) notion of a 'connective curriculum', particularly insofar as its integrative approach is balanced by a recognition of the continuing significance of existing disciplines. We are proposing TEMs to complement, not replace, these disciplines.

Second, and as we have already made clear, *institutions* are important. Like 'culture', their influence pervades the three separate 'segments' of sustainable development. All the significant social actors mentioned above belong to institutions. They will certainly have personal agendas (concerning promotion, for example, or the control of resources) in relation to those institutions. The institutions themselves will be engaged in competition and collaboration, deal making and breaking, with other institutions. Since these institutional machinations may be expected significantly to influence both the priority accorded to sustainable development at particular times and places, and the resources devoted to its pursuit, all of this bears strongly on what people in institutions *actually do*. Often, none of it features in *accounts of* what is being done. Institutions disappear from the story. It is told instead about principles and citizens, as if history was everywhere and always shaped by citizens acting on principle. An important sustainable development learning opportunity lies in always insisting that the pursuit of principles by institutions is mirrored by their pursuit of advantage and resources. This is not to suggest that all institutions are somehow dishonest: rather, it is to insist that what they do is *integral* to social, economic and environmental processes, not detached from them.

Third, we are far from being the first to note that *history* provides our most abundant, most fundamental resource for learning. In the context of sustainable development this is not so much because it tells us how society, economy and environment came to be as they are but because of the light it can shed on why we perceive them as we do – and why others may perceive them differently. In its way, the past may often turn out to be as complex and uncertain as the future and just as amenable to inflexible interpretation from pre-determined perspectives.

Finally, there is biogeophysical *nature* itself, which clearly impinges on society, on economy and on environment and, like each of the preceding three factors, is implicated in the creation of both value and values. We would not go as far as Greenall Gough (1993 and chapter 12 of the companion reader) in critiquing scientific approaches to the study of nature. In our view science is vitally important because, as we have said, it is much better to know more than to know less. However, if our learning is to be effective, nature should be seen as a wellspring of surprises as much as an object of prediction and as a source of value and values as much as a reservoir of facts.

To illustrate all of this in concrete terms we might consider the example of Charterhouse in the English Mendip Hills. Here, lead mining took place in Roman and quite possibly pre-Roman times. Lead was an economic resource because the Romans both had uses for it and knew how to extract it. The process of production created lead-rich soils – contaminated land in modern parlance – which over time became home to lead-tolerant plants. Meanwhile, the lead that remained ceased to be an economic resource because no one thought it worth their while to exploit it any more. After a very long time (by human standards) the resulting landscape was thought interesting and beautiful enough to be declared a nature reserve. Now it is a tourist attraction and so has once again become an economic resource, though this time in a fashion the Romans might have found hard to conceive. What is striking about this instance of unplanned outcomes is not that the elements of society, economy and environment can be so well combined through it, but that they are so difficult to unpick in the first place. It is an example which seems to offer a basis for worthwhile learning opportunities relating to sustainable development for just about any interested (or co-opted) person regardless of age, or disciplinary or core professional interest. It *could* be used for purely scientific learning – in chemistry, say. It could also be the basis for a learning exploration of the ways in which culture, institutions, history and nature each provides a unique perspective on *the integrated whole* which we normally divide into society, economy and environment.

A goal for learning: a 'real options' metaphor

With the foregoing in mind, we return now to the problem of finding an overall goal for learning which defines it clearly as *part of the process* of sustainable development, rather than a *means of implementing* it. If the meaning of sustainable development is largely provisional, how might one know whether any particular learning process was tending to promote it? To attempt to answer this we draw on a metaphor from what may seem a rather improbable source, financial economics. However, the ability to link things which are apparently very different is precisely where the power of metaphors lies. Further, their importance in influencing our thinking about our relationship with our environment is clear (Bowers, 2002).

Our metaphoric focus is 'Real Options Theory' (Amram and Kulatilaka, 1999). This is an economic theory concerned with the evaluation of investment projects. It seeks to replace an existing, long-established model, the capital-asset pricing model or CAPM, which has been influential in efforts to value the environment. Real options theory takes techniques used in the pricing of financial options, and other still more arcane instruments, and seeks to apply them to the valuation of projects, real assets and future returns. We should note in passing that environmental economists have been much concerned with the valuation of the environment. It is here that the interesting linguistic divergence which appears in the title of this chapter may be seen to good effect, since it has been suggested that putting a value on parts of the environment is somehow improper, on the grounds that, for example, to do so is inherently anthropocentric (which it clearly is). In other words, our values should be such as to preclude certain things being accorded a value. Whatever one makes of this, it does seem impossible to live anything approaching a normal life without placing at least implicit value on aspects of the environment and using these as guides to action.

In following the approach of the capital-asset pricing model (CAPM), it is normal to value (by whatever means) environmental costs and benefits expected to arise in the future and then discount these at a rate which depends upon the extent of preference for present over future returns, the degree of expected risk and uncertainty, the alternatives available in the present, and other factors. It is not at all surprising that this procedure has attracted criticism from environmentalists and others. The higher the rate of discount, the greater is the discrimination against future generations and the lower the chances of projects with anticipated high future social returns being adopted. However, adopting a low rate of discount does not solve the problem in a satisfactory way. Even very low rates of discount will have a powerful effect on costs and benefits which are far in the future. A rate of discount of 0 per cent implies that there is no reason to prefer present to future consumption over any time period and a negative discount rate implies a preference for distant future consumption over present consumption. All this simply fails to describe the human world in a credible way. If, as a general rule to guide action, we value the future equally or more than the present, then this implies indifference or aversion to satisfying human needs through consumption now. The choice, then, is between any positive rate of discount which will seem to undervalue the future and zero or negative rates which cannot provide a credible basis for analysis or policy. See Pearce and Kerry Turner (1990: chapter 14) for an extended discussion of this complex issue.

A parallel seems to exist between CAPM and most existing approaches to learning and sustainable development. If a secondary school chemistry teacher, a local government executive or the manager of a medium-sized manufacturing business (to take just three examples of the kind we mentioned earlier in this chapter) are informed (or attempts are made to educate/train them) that they must radically change what they do in the name of sustainable development, they will want to know why. The answer, and therefore what they, and by extension the stakeholders in their work, are supposed to learn, is essentially that there are very large future costs associated with unsustainable development and correspondingly large benefits to be had from sustainability. Both the Real World Coalition and *The Economist* advance arguments of this general kind.

However, in the situation in which they find themselves, each of our three exemplar individuals is likely to be subject to immediate pressures which are not directly related to the achievement of sustainable development. The teacher's pupils may have exams coming up based on a somewhat traditional and hierarchically prescribed syllabus; the local government executive may have central government house-building targets to meet, despite local opposition from environmentalists; and the manager may be worried about cash-flow and jobs. Each may also have a good part of their self-esteem invested in professional accomplishments which, according to thinking on sustainable development, are of questionable merit (say, the business has secured a profitable contract to supply spare parts for petrol pumps). Each is likely to heavily discount the already clearly very small contribution they can personally make to ameliorating long-term, uncertain, global sustainable development costs and benefits. At the margin, the choice to carry on with the existing syllabus, build the houses or supply the parts looks only rational. To say this is simply to concur with evidence from behavioural studies (Krause, 1996) which have shown that consequences which are soon, certain and positive are stronger motivators of behaviour than those which are deferred, uncertain and negative. As a result it is even possible that our three individuals will choose to reject the learning opportunity they are being offered.

Interestingly, the CAPM approach tends to be unpopular with managers as well as with environmentalists. This is because it allows little scope for the exercise of their professional skills. In large part this follows from the fact that the model can only use information which is already known. Since (as with environmental decision making) this information is often incomplete or uncertain, discount rates may be correspondingly high. Hence, promising projects which call for innovative and adaptive implementation may well be rejected.

The real options approach, by contrast, starts from the idea that investment decisions have embedded within them a series of managerial options. Rather than seeking to arrive a firm valuation of expected returns, the approach instead seeks to value the *options* implicit in the project *at each stage of its life*. Hence, to take an environmental example, rather than trying to arrive at a valuation of an area of rainforest and then discounting that figure over whatever was judged to be an appropriate time-period, one would try instead to calculate the *option-value* of having the rainforest intact at different decision points, using a range of contingencies, over the same time-period. We should stress that this is *not* the same as a policy of 'keeping options open'. In particular circumstances it might theoretically be the case that the greatest option-value was obtained by keeping available only one option which precluded all others.

The option-value would tend to *increase* the longer the time-period under consideration and the greater the inherent uncertainty. By contrast CAPM increases its discount rate in response to long time-horizons and high levels of uncertainty. The option-value would be compared with immediate net benefits and future option-values arising from possible alternative deployments of the asset, such as chopping down the trees for timber. Thus, the higher the option-value attached to the forest, the more likely would be its survival.

This *is* a metaphorical discussion. It is not proposed that a form of calculus is at hand which will enable the precise quantitative evaluation of different episodes of learning. However, to continue, option-values might be increased by:

- Increasing the number of available options
- Increasing levels of human skill at recognising and managing such options
- Changing perceptions so that options which were previously little valued become more highly valued.

Learning is one vehicle by which all of these might be achieved. Hence, whether one was talking about, for example: (a) in-service training relating to sustainable development in the curriculum for chemistry teachers; (b) in-house professional development in sustainable development management for local government executives; or, (c) training as part of environmental management system accreditation for private sector managers, the aim would in each case be to bring about learning which tended to *increase the future option-value* of the environment. Since, as we have seen, the environment, and the values we attach to it, are inseparably entwined with social and economic considerations through (at least) culture, institutions, history and the biogeophysical properties of nature, the actual focus of any such learning episode might be chosen from a wide menu. The criteria for its selection would be as follows. It should tend to present opportunities for learning *in context* and *at the margin*. These must tend to increase learners' awareness of their own professional work as being pregnant with implications for future choices which they, and those upon whom their work impacts, may have to make.

In this conceptualisation of sustainable development learning, our chemistry teacher, local government executive and business manager no longer appear as people who thought they were doing a good job but must now, at someone else's behest, think again. Instead, they are viewed as having an indispensable contribution to make to our wider understanding of society's options, and how these become available or are foreclosed. In a given context of time or place, environmental option value might be increased by teaching a narrowly academic chemistry curriculum, exceeding the proposed housing target, and expanding production of petrol pump parts. This might be true if, for example, these actions resulted in, respectively:

- More access to higher education in a poor country with a shortage of local administrative, management and technical skills
- Reductions in the numbers of families living in squatter settlements
- Economies of scale leading to less wasteful use of energy and raw materials.

At another time and place the appropriate measures might instead be an integrated curriculum, a campaign to alter housing preferences among the public and a programme to move production into different lines. It is hard to see how the best decisions for sustainable development could be reached without learning by our three actors. Equally, it is just as hard to see how such decisions might be reached without their involvement. If the day came when they and others were routinely learning and contributing in this way, sustainable development would be happening.

A wider picture: 'Development as Freedom'

If the foregoing arguments are complex, they are hardly more complex than those one might expect to encounter in other disciplines which bear on environmental, social and economic issues. Nevertheless, experience suggests that we will continue to see learning interventions which attempt to promote sustainable development through either the unadorned provision of information or the proselytisation of particular points of view: and indeed these may sometimes be useful. However, we conclude this chapter by looking, briefly but hopefully, to a recent work which seems, in a wider context, to promote an approach compatible with our own. Further, this work carries great status in terms of relevant institutions and literacies, and as a source of information, having been written by a Nobel Laureate in Economics, Amartya Sen.

In his book *Development as Freedom*, Sen (1999: 3) argues for a definition of development as 'a process of expanding the real freedoms that people enjoy'. Sen does not use the term sustainable development, nor does he focus in any narrow sense specifically on environmental issues. Nevertheless, his concerns – with development, justice, poverty, democracy, famines, markets, population, social change and so on – reflect many of those touched on throughout this book. It would clearly be both presumptuous and pointless to attempt to summarise Sen's case but we conclude this chapter with two short quotations which seem particularly appropriate to its discussion of economic behaviour, value and values. The first relates to markets, to their advocates and detractors, and to our search for an inclusive underlying principle for learning:

> It is hard to think that any process of substantial development can do without very extensive use of markets, but that does not preclude the role of social support, public regulation or statecraft when they can enrich – rather than impoverish – human lives. The approach used here provides a broader and more inclusive perspective on markets than is frequently invoked in *either* defending *or* chastising the market mechanism.
>
> (Sen, 1999: 7, original emphasis)

The second quotation suggests what this underlying principle for learning might be, in terms not obviously incompatible with our notion of sustainable development learning as a means to increase the metaphoric 'option-value' of the environment. Sen (p. 74) writes of the importance to development of:

> The substantive freedoms – the capabilities – to choose a life one has reason to value.

13 Globalisation and fragmentation
Science and self

Globalisation

According to Christie and Warburton (2001, 25):

> Sustainable development requires that we *learn to govern* the globalization of markets, rather than letting it dominate societies the world over.
>
> (emphasis added)

'Globalisation' is a word which has passed into everyday parlance, if only because millions of viewers around the world have seen television news pictures of anti-globalisation protesters at one international function or another. 'Postmodernism' trips off fewer tongues but deserves to be mentioned in the same breath at least once in any discussion, because it draws attention to the fact that even as globalisation leads to greater standardisation across the globe, so it also tends to undermine established elements of the structure of societies. These include family, religion, school, local community, geographical setting and type of employment (Payne, 1997). The result may be resistance, as people unite in the attempt to uphold and celebrate the local and/or the traditional; alternatively, it may be social disintegration; finally, it may be both at once, as groups coalesce around social micro-narratives (Lyotard, 1984). All these possible secondary outcomes seem to be evidence of *fragmentation* and so contrary to globalisation itself.

Farrell (2001) helpfully notes that postmodernism may take the form of a claim either about history or about knowledge. To illustrate this with an example relevant to the theme of this chapter, postmodernists are generally dismissive of the 'grand narrative' that progress is achieved through rationality and science. This can mean both that: (a) there is no credible basis in logic for this grand narrative (a claim about knowledge); and (b) whether or not there is such a logical basis, people generally have now widely ceased to believe in the ability of rationality and science to deliver progress (a claim about history). In terms of the claim about knowledge, the continuing potential efficacy of science as a means to progress has been a significant thread throughout this book. We have tried to argue that progress though the acquisition, dissemination and application of knowledge is perfectly possible; but that, at the margins of complexity, uncertainty, risk and necessity, it is likely to be an incremental, non-linear and surprise-prone enterprise. In terms of the postmodern claim about history, this is of course self-fulfilling to the extent that postmodernism succeeds in attracting new converts. There does also appear to be some evidence (Scott, 2001) that public trust in science has been reduced following its apparent implication in a number of environmental incidents, such as the Chernobyl explosion of 1986. To this, three different responses may be made. First, Lucas (1980) has pointed out that however much science may be responsible for the creation of environmental problems, it appears to remain a necessary tool for their resolution. Second, Beck (1992 and chapter 1 of the companion reader) has argued that in contemporary society science is fundamentally implicated in the creation and management of risk for commercial exploitation. One might therefore expect apprehension and trust to go hand-in-hand. Finally, it is quite possible to argue that, far from being a spent force, science and technology are the principal drivers of economic growth and therefore of globalisation (Dicken, 1998).

The wider literature of globalisation is similarly contested, as is shown by a useful overview by Jemmott (2002: 47–62), on which we draw extensively here. Only two things are absolutely clear: first, fairly recently, a lot of people have come to attach importance to the *word* 'globalisation' (Giddens, 1999; Robertson, 1992); second, this word is used from different perspectives to try to come to terms with an extremely complex set of phenomena.

Supporters of globalisation (Ohmae, 1990; Reich, 1991) tend to be enthusiasts for markets, competition and individualism. They argue that three major changes have re-shaped the world. First, technological advances have resulted in the faster, cheaper transfer across space of goods, people and ideas. This has created a global economy and marginalized nation-states, which increasingly find it convenient to cede power to supranational organisations of one sort or another. Second, multi-national corporations (MNCs) have become trans-national corporations (TNCs), that is, there has been a shift from nationally based and financed companies, which operate within and between countries, to truly international organisations with international workforces and investors. Third, increasingly free international capital flows mean a shift of global production and employment opportunities, mediated through markets, which theory predicts will be of universal benefit. Fairly clearly, the implication of this view for formal education is that it should prepare learners to participate in the global economy. Many national governments take this as a basis for their education policy (Spring, 1998). However, the facility with which national governments – which globalisers predict to be marginalised – have popped back into the picture illustrates a more general difficulty. This is that, even if information is now following freely across the globe, the articulation between the economy and the education system is complex and problematical (Jamieson, 1996). To highlight just two difficulties (or sources of market imperfection): first, presently available information about the demand for human resource inputs produces educated human resources only after a considerable time-lag, by which time market signals may have changed; and, second, teachers may refuse to accept, or be – by virtue of their own training – unable to fulfil their designated role as conveyors of market signals. It is partly because of this that the pro-globalisation case also involves an appeal to lifelong learning. As Edwards (1997: 174) notes:

Central to a learning society is the proposition that the economic, social and cultural challenges confronting individuals and social formations in the late twentieth into the twenty-first century make reliance on initial education as a preparation for the full extent of adult life unsustainable. The capacity to meet those challenges requires continuing learning and recurrent opportunities to learn.

Against this case there are two broad arguments, both typically informed by an underlying focus on justice and equality. One is that globalisation is a myth (Hirst and Thompson, 1999). The other is that it exists but is malign. In this latter view, it tends to create cultural standardisation across the globe (Pieterse, 1995), of a type symbolised for many by the McDonalds fast-food chain, which provides poor compensation for the fragmenting of established communities which tends to accompany it. Further, rather than providing the world's poor with a route to prosperity, globalisation offers them little or nothing at all (Martin and Schumann, 1997; UNDP, 1999). Clearly this also has implications for both formal education and learning more widely, which are in this case seen as a means to resist the damaging effects of globalisation or, at the local level, as a means to survive in spite of them. Educational activities consistent with this view include, for example:

- The work of co-operatives internationally (Couchman, 2002), for whom education is integral to the creation of self-supporting communities
- Approaches to adult learning which focus on the achievement of improvements in quality of life through meeting needs rather than consuming goods and services (Leveson-Gower, 2002)
- The work of NGOs such as ActionAid which has, for instance, effected locally appropriate educational improvements in Pakistan through the facilitation of local women's groups (Hindson *et al*, 2001).

The examples described in Chapter 12 illustrate well the implications for sustainable development of these opposed views of globalisation. For *The Economist*, the economic and social advantages of globalisation are manifest and there is a need to manage any unfortunate environmental consequences that might follow. For the Real World Coalition, it is obvious that globalisation has unacceptable environmental and social costs, so the economic forces which drive it need to be managed. In both cases, the proper role of learning is arrived at by derivation from the main argument.

It is possible to argue that what is really being globalised here are particular problem definitions. This is unhelpful only to the extent that it also entails the attempt to exclude other credible problem definitions. Dicken (1998) is one who has suggested that the polarisation of thinking on globalisation is unjustified. Forces which promote globalisation are at work, but their operation is not uniform or complete. Consequences vary from one setting to another. Nor are we necessarily helpless before such forces, or compelled to embrace or reject them entirely. As Sen (1999: 240–1) writes:

The threat to native cultures in the globalizing world of today is, to a considerable extent, inescapable . . . This is a problem, but not just a problem, since global trade and commerce can bring with it – as Adam Smith foresaw – greater economic prosperity for each nation. But there can be losers as well as gainers, even if in the net the aggregate figures move up rather than down. In the context of economic disparities, the appropriate response has to include concerted efforts to make the form of globalization less destructive of employment and traditional livelihood . . . it is up to the society to determine what, if anything, it wants to do to preserve old forms of living, perhaps even at significant economic cost.

An aside: globalisation and the globe

One image has perhaps been influential on both pro- and anti-globalisation thinking. This is the picture, taken from space, of the blue planet rising over the cratered surface of the moon; sailing through space with all of us on board. There are two sets of inferences we might draw from this image, both of them false. They are illustrated by Figure 13.1

One way of seeing this is that the human species has stepped outside of its environment and is capable of viewing it with detachment, comprehending it, mastering it and managing it. The other is that human society is revealed as being contained within an environment which is finite and given. This is spaceship earth, and we need to look after it. Both these conceptualisations make the mistake of supposing that even rocketry gives us the power to see ourselves from the outside. As we argued in Chapter 11, what makes our environment *the* environment are the meanings we give to it. This goes just as much for astronauts as for anyone else. We can't step outside our environment to fix it. Equally, as we showed in Chapter 5, this environment is not given but co-evolving. It can even sometimes be locally negentropic from the human point of view, that is, over quite long periods of time

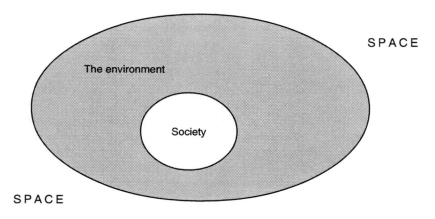

Figure 13.1 The alien's view.

and from a uniquely human perspective, the useful environment can get *bigger*, rather than just be depleted. The remote, disengaged 'view from space' is, literally, alien. The only place we can have any view from is *inside* the circle labelled 'society'.

Example of a globalised space: the Chihuahuan Desert

To illustrate some of the foregoing in the context of learning, we turn now to the example of a region which exhibits many of the characteristics associated, one way or another, with globalisation.

According to staff of the World Wildlife Fund, the Chihuahuan Desert is one of the three most biologically rich and diverse desert ecoregions in the world. It covers 629,000 square kilometres, stretching across the border between Mexico and the United States of America. It exhibits a wide diversity of plant communities, particularly cacti, and of land and freshwater invertebrates. It also supports a large number of mammals, including pronghorns, jaguars and many species of rodent. Even more remarkable is the diversity of reptiles, which is among the highest of all desert regions. In keeping with this species diversity, the Chihuahuan also has a wide variety of habitats including the Rio Grande system, other rivers which drain inland to produce isolated freshwater habitats and forested 'sky islands'.

The Chihuahuan is badly degraded. Before the 1850s it lay entirely inside Mexico. Thereafter, the pace of development increased. Today, economic activity is varied. The *maquiladora* system, through which labour-intensive assembly or manufacturing plants process US products in Mexico for re-export to the United States, has led to population growth in the border cities. There are mines producing significant quantities of silver, lead, zinc, copper and other metals. Various crops are grown and are heavily dependent on irrigation. Livestock farming, which requires much land and little manpower, is much practised and very profitable. Water resources are heavily exploited and are subject to different jurisdictions. Most of the flow of the Rio Grande is consumed by the time it gets to El Paso.

Among the people of the Mexican Chihuahuan the standard of living is on average higher than the rest of Mexico. Average levels of literacy and participation in basic education are high. However, these average figures hide quite wide disparities in both literacy levels and access to basic services such as piped water, drainage, sewage treatment and electricity. On both sides of the border, the Chihuahuan is home to indigenous peoples. For example, in south-west Chihuahua between forty and fifty thousand Tarahumaras live as semi-nomadic herdsmen or farmers.

To summarise, the Chihuahuan is an ecologically and, in some ways, a socially coherent space. It forms part of a developing country and also part of the world's most developed country. It is illustrative of the processes and consequences of globalisation. Indeed, if one sees globalisation as a primarily US-driven process, one might almost argue that the Chihuahuan is the site of its birth. Development has been socially and economically beneficial for large numbers of people. It has marginalised others and has, in general, done little to increase social equality. National governments remain significant and yet at the same time economic activities, in particular, show strong linkages across the border, particularly since the implementation of the

North American Free Trade Agreement (NAFTA). Indigenous populations survive alongside national identities. The predominant traditional cultural form on the Mexican side of the border is characterised not by harmony and stability but by historically rooted difference and to some extent distrust, both of the residents of southern Mexico and of the United States, who tend to be both resented and admired. On the US side of the border there are nationally high concentrations of unemployment and poverty. Environmental sustainability is absent. The Desert and its biodiversity are endangered. A crucial issue in this respect, and for wider conceptions of sustainable development, is the management of water resources. Of course, many economic and social influences on the course of events in the Chihuahuan have their origins elsewhere: in the wider United States, in Mexico and (for example with regard to commodity prices) internationally.

This example illustrates the inadequacy of one-size-fits-all sustainable development solutions. The operation of market forces clearly produces patchy results. So, for example in relation to water resources, does regulation of markets. Indeed, because of the very nature of riparian systems, state-level regulation (let alone anything *more* local) tends to amplify conflicts of interest and give unfair advantage to upstream users. There is plenty of evidence of social exclusion and injustice but it is difficult to see how any attempt at redistribution would operate, at even the most basic level. Who should give and who should receive? Who should decide? If Americans generally begin to satisfy their needs without the benefit of the goods produced by the *maquiladora* industry will that promote sustainable development? Or social justice? And yet, to continue as at present seems to exclude the possibility of sustainable development entirely.

This is not intended to be a council of despair. Rather, we wish to draw attention to the true complexity of the sustainable development challenge. Complex problems may well be amenable to amelioration by quite simple actions. As Sen (1999) notes, there are plenty of instances of successful change and, failing that, plenty of scope for learning from mistakes without causing too much damage. However, even where simple solutions are possible, they will not be discovered by simplistic analysis.

Promoting sustainable development in the Chihuahuan Desert ecoregion, and the role that learning might have in this, are far from being simple matters. There are, however, a number of relatively straightforward observations that can be made. First, it seems quite clear that learning can *only* have an effective role in conjunction with other social and economic policy actions which tend jointly to build capacity for sustainable development. This is clear, as a general principle, from Figure 4.2 (see p. 38) and in this case will involve a coordinated approach in terms of, for example, taxation, water regulation, land management, transport policy, urban planning and so on, as well as learning. This means that, second, there is a need for environmental meta-learning across those responsible for all these different aspects, even if this is only initially in the form of occasional facilitated exchanges at a senior level around simple core themes, such as the value of particular environmental assets or the nature of 'quality' outcomes, from different perspectives. A third point follows from the first two: learning interventions, and sustainable development interventions as a whole, need to be informed by an analysis of the main organisational and cultural institutions, literacies and practices which are implicated in the development process in the Chihuahuan. There are many of these, but the analysis need not be massively complicated if it is done as a simple SWOT under each of the four institutional headings. Fourth, appropriate learning interventions need to be designed by sector (e.g. formal primary and secondary, non-formal and training), by context (e.g. Mexican/US/urban/rural/non-Chihuahuan), and using information, communication and mediation according to the degree of uncertainty and complexity entailed in particular cases (see Chapter 4). Ultimately this is to say no more than that learning needs to be 'situated' in a context and that the transfer of knowledge from one context to another requires pedagogic skill, as well as the voluntary engagement of learners. Appropriate learning will not necessarily be 'about' sustainable development in any transmissive sense. As the authors of Chapter 36 of Agenda 21 recognised, for example, basic literacy and numeracy are essential in themselves. In some settings sustainable development may be promoted by learning which enables some groups to compete more effectively, perhaps by developing marketing skills for traditional craft products. In other cases learning may promote collaborative behaviour, for example to improve the local quality of drinking water. Learning may help people increase their incomes, so that they can *afford* to protect their environment: it may also help them avoid waste or meet needs directly. As we argued in Chapter 12, in each context the question should be this: how, at the margin, might learning either, (a) create new options for people in the way they live in their environment; and/or, (b) increase their skill at recognising and managing such options; and/or (c) change perceptions so that more sustainable options which were previously less valued become more highly valued? Such learning will not be a tool to implement sustainable development. It will be an integral and indispensable part of the process of sustainable development.

Examples of contributions to sustainable development learning in the context of globalisation

To conclude this chapter we consider two examples from recent research. The first of these relates to the general skill, 'learning-to-learn'. As part of a wider project focusing on employability skills formation in Barbados, Jemmott (2002) conducted two case studies in businesses in the service sector. The research was supported by the World Bank, the Barbados Community College and the Barbados Ministry of Education. Barbados is a relatively developed country with, in 2001, a slowing rate of economic growth and a strong dependency on tourism. Tourism growth is, of course, itself an aspect of a globalised economy. It is also a route to development for which the issue of sustainability is immediate. As Cater and Goodall (1992) point out, its resource base is also its product. Jemmott notes that Barbados is additionally subject to other globalised influences, including trade liberalisation, and attempts to regulate the international financial services industry. The case study businesses were a telecommunications company and an hotel. In both instances there was a focus on frontline employees. In the case of the telecommunications company these were 'outside plant technicians' (OPTs) who conduct maintenance and repairs for businesses and private customers, as well as maintaining the infrastructure. At the hotel, they were waiters and waitresses. In both cases data were also collected from managers/supervisors, and by observation.

'Learning-to-learn' is the process by which an individual acquires the knowledge and skills necessary to be able to learn in any context or setting. There is no doubt that the development of this skill is widely seen as central to human resources management (HRM) in general and corporate environmental management in particular. As Barrett and Murphy (1996: 92) have written:

> The organisation needs to develop a culture that empowers staff to respond to an ever-changing external environment . . . The implications for HRM and environmental policy are that companies must begin to place greater emphasis upon investment in organisational 'learners' as opposed to plant infrastructure, for example . . . Traditional ways of thinking about education and training, therefore, need to be challenged. As well as formal training relating to procedures, people need to be equipped to participate in the overall change process.

Jemmott found that in both businesses globalisation was identified by employees as a factor leading to changes in the workplace. Also in both cases, learning-to-learn was identified as a key skill. Jemmott (2002: 220) notes that the wider benefits of this skill include:

> The business having the capability to adapt to changes at local and international levels. Managers in both companies were of the opinion that employees who knew how to learn and who could benefit from the learning opportunities they encountered were helpful to the companies in times of change.

There is wider evidence of the importance of this skill (Stasz, 2001). Jemmott therefore suggests that formal, school-based education should be based on constructivist approaches which develop, *inter alia*, skills of team working, problem solving and communication. Again, there is substantial recent evidence (Hindson *et al.*, 2001) that environmental learning can be a powerful tool for the reform of curriculum development and implementation procedures where these are, for example, highly centralised, heavily bureaucratic and/or characterised by pedagogic conservatism on the part of teachers.

We may conclude that the skill of learning-to-learn will merit consideration as a focus for learning interventions which aim to promote sustainable development, in both the formal and non-formal sectors, and in a range of contexts where uncertainty and complexity are present. The skill is not directly *about* sustainable development but it could fairly readily be given a sustainable development context; it seems in any case to be indispensable *to* sustainable development. Learning-to-learn will fit comfortably within many institutional contexts. It is a skill that many people *want* to acquire. It facilitates learning across literacies and practices. It is appropriate to both collaborative and competitive action. It enables people better to exercise the options inherent in their environment in an adaptive way.

Our second example draws on work by Reid *et al.* (2002) which, as part of the preparations for the UN Summit on Sustainable Development in Johannesburg in 2002, examined educational responses in the United Kingdom to Agenda 21. The work contributed to a submission by the UK's *Council for Environmental Education* to the House of Commons' Environmental Audit Committee. The globalisation context in this case, therefore, is that of the implementation of supra-national policy at the national level.

There have been suggestions (for example, Sterling, 2001) that little was done in the United Kingdom in response to Chapter 36 of Agenda 21 in the ten years following the 1992 Rio Summit. Reid *et al.* reject this, pointing out a significant range of activities conducted under the auspices of central government and its agencies, local authorities, NGOs and others. Within formal education, revisions to the national curriculum created space for innovation and sustainable development was identified as an important aspect of both general curriculum aims and particular subject focuses. Schools remained centrally concerned with a 'basics agenda' set by the central government Department for Education and Science, but to the extent that this agenda stressed literacy, numeracy and ICT skills it was itself consistent with the achievement of sustainable development (Hopkins *et al.,* 1996). Sustainable development initiatives were also attempted in further and higher education. In the non-formal sector, a number of NGOs did (and continue to do) exemplary work in advancing understanding of sustainable development and the role of education and learning within it, and in bringing about increased visibility for such issues in policy circles (CEE, 2002). Within non-formal education, two major public awareness campaigns were conducted and a statutory framework was established to create opportunities for the development of lifelong learning initiatives, focused on sustainable development. Also, the Department for International Development took an international lead in commissioning research into the role of environmental learning in achieving sustainable development.

Against this, however, Reid *et al.* point out that, although there were many initiatives, they lacked an overall strategic focus. In terms of learning and sustainable development many initiatives which were of value in themselves were not linked to advantage. Often this was because teachers, local government officers, NGO employees and others lacked the understanding and/or infrastructural support to realise such integration. Examples were the development of parallel unconnected sustainable development and lifelong learning initiatives in some local authorities, uncertainty within schools and NGOs regarding funding mechanisms and funding priorities (for example, for environmental education, development education, sustainable development, social inclusion and so on) and a lack of integration between school curriculum development and Local Agenda 21 work. A further point was that sustainable development learning was often seen as an expensive bolt-on to existing programmes, rather than as a means and opportunity better to meet existing goals for *both* learning *and* sustainable development.

Two points are particularly illustrated by this second example. The first is the importance of an initial analysis which identifies the institutional players and their inter-relationships. The second is that sharing that analysis with those players would be a first step towards initiating a process of environmental meta-learning, which would contribute to the maximisation of benefits from the good work which clearly goes on. As we noted in Chapter 10, inefficiency is incompatible with sustainable development. This is as true for learning as for anything else. In discussing ideas around a self-directing society Lindblom (1992, and chapter 11 of the companion reader) uses the term 'disjointed incrementalism' to describe change which is erratic, evolutionary and iterative. There seems no doubt that change through learning towards sustainable development will occur in this way but that does not imply a need to be any more 'disjointed' than one can help.

14　What happens next?

It is an appropriately historic moment to ask the question 'what happens next?' in relation to sustainable development and learning. The United Nations World Summit on Sustainable Development has happened. In its aftermath, as we also note in Chapter 14 of the companion reader, conspicuous evidence of any widespread belief that learning is in some way central to the achievement of sustainable development is hard to find. Yet, it is hard to see how the ambitious goals which have been set can be achieved without a great deal of learning across all sectors.

Key outcomes from Johannesburg (see Reading 1 in Chapter 14 of the companion reader)

Sustainable development and poverty eradication

Perhaps *the* key outcome of the summit has been the linking of sustainable development to poverty eradication. This has the effect, in terms of international institutional agendas at least, of re-instating 'sustainable development' over 'sustainability' as the term of choice. There are dangers in this, of course, as 'sustainable development' too easily becomes re-interpreted and tacitly re-understood as 'sustainable economic growth'. On the other hand, 'sustainability' too easily becomes a justification not only for denying the poor the right to choose anything other than a 'traditional' lifestyle, but, it would seem, sometimes also an excuse for denying *everyone* the most basic rights, particularly the right of free exchange (Fien and Trainer, 1993a; 1993b; Trainer, 1990). As writers such as Sen (1999) and Hill (1989) have in different ways suggested, exchange is simply part of the way in which free people live and interact.

One of the 'key commitments' emerging from the Summit reads as follows: 'By 2020, achieve a significant improvement in the lives of at least 100 million slum dwellers'. It really is difficult to see how this will be achieved *without* learning by those 100 million people: and even if that learning relates *simply* to the acquisition of skills of literacy and numeracy, that is, to goals of basic education, we may still ask whether learning will not be needed by others elsewhere in the world as a result of the coming into existence, over a relatively short period, of an extra 100 million literate, numerate individuals with incomes to spend and expectations and hopes to fulfil. We have argued that such learning can be made both more efficient and more effective if it is planned and managed, taking care to match the complexity of the pedagogy employed to the degree of uncertainty inherent in the subject matter, and context of the learning (see especially Chapter 4).

The 'understanding of sustainable development'

A second claimed key outcome of the Summit was that 'understanding of sustainable development was strengthened and broadened . . . particularly the important linkages between poverty, the environment and the use of natural resources'. At one level one can question whether this is really true. For all the progress made in different disciplines over the years in understanding elements of the human/nature relationship, it continues to be characterised, as we have argued throughout this book, by complexity, uncertainty, risk and necessity, by competing perceptions, disciplinary chauvinism and the not-infrequent re-invention of conceptual wheels. Yet, in another sense, this claim seems to be substantiated and to offer evidence that learning has been taking place.

The UK's *Sunday Times* newspaper of 1 September 2002 featured two particular stories side-by-side. The first was headlined: *World Bank does a U-turn: obsession with austerity gives way to concern for the poor*. The second appeared under the heading: *Greens change tack and join forces with the poor*. The following are extracts from these stories:

World Bank does a U-turn

'We have come to understand that economic growth, though necessary, is not enough to deal with poverty', explains the Bank's director of development policy, Ian Goldin . . . Gone is the advocacy of private-sector driven growth with minimal state participation. In comes a new drive aimed at encouraging the involvement of the state in unleashing human potential and distributing assets fairly to benefit all . . . 'There is better understanding now of the role of the market and of public policy and the need for strong and clear public policy,' says Goldin.

Greens change tack

Green groups have abandoned their hardline approach to environmental affairs and joined forces with social and civil society to tackle the impact of economic globalisation. Groups like Friends of the Earth International, Greenpeace and the World Wildlife Fund used to be in conflict with poor communities over environmental and wildlife conservation methods. But in the 10 years since the Earth Summit in Rio de Janeiro environmentalists have moved closer to left wing groups and their agendas of combating poverty, tackling trade imbalances and developing mechanisms to aid the involvement of communities in decision-making.

Things, then, are clear. In a world where policy actions are either left-wing or right-wing, pro-poor or pro-rich, for private good or for public good, and determined by either the market or public policy, everyone has suddenly become more left-wing. This is true, it seems, to the point where apparently even the World Bank (but not *The Economist*: see Chapter 12 and Chapter 14 of the companion reader) is persuaded of the truth of the egalitarian notion that redistributing more equally resources which are at present distributed unequally will 'benefit all'. What is the principal policy-change through which this change of heart has been produced? The answer, according to the World Bank, and appearing within the same article is:

> Trade reforms, which we believe are absolutely fundamental. There cannot be equity at a global level if one group of countries is spending more on subsidies than the total income of Africa.

The crucial purpose of this cross-cutting move to the political left turns out to be a freeing-up of international markets.

Our point here is not that the above extracts fail to make collective sense but that they make excellent sense. First, they illustrate very clearly the pervasiveness of the meta-literacy, discussed in Chapter 11, that takes for granted the appropriateness of 'competition' and 'cooperation' as ultimate, opposed categories of social analysis. To their very great credit, both the World Bank and the NGOs, confronted with the inadequacy of this conceptualisation on a day-to-day basis, have done some practical, collaborative learning. We would argue that approaches described in this book suggest how this learning could be further stimulated, managed and enhanced. Second, the above extracts provide at least a glimpse of the institutional manoeuvrings which underlie public debate about points of principle. Again, it would be better if these were in the open, understood as a part of the necessary context of sustainable development and not, as at present, a secret sub-text to it.

'Concrete commitments' for sustainable development

The Johannesburg Summit led to a number of further long-term commitments in relation to:

- Water and sanitation. For example, there is a new commitment to halve the number of people in the world who do not have access to basic sanitation by 2015
- Sustainable production and consumption. A ten-year framework to promote this is to be developed
- Energy. For example: 'Improve access to reliable, affordable, economically viable, socially acceptable and environmentally sound energy services and resources . . .'
- Chemicals. For example, by 2020 these are to be used and produced in ways that do not lead to significant adverse effects on human health and the environment
- Natural resource management. For example, 'on an urgent basis and where possible by 2015, maintain or restore depleted fish stocks to levels that can produce the maximum sustainable yield'

- Corporate responsibility. Plans to enhance this are strongly linked to the Summit's emphasis on the development of partnerships (see below)
- Health. Health education is to be 'enhanced'
- Small-island states. Of particular interest, community-based initiatives on sustainable tourism are to be developed by 2004
- Africa. For example, there is to be support for the development and implementation of food security strategies by 2005.

All of the above will involve learning by a wide range of people. Many of those people will have much to teach others too. In each case there will be simple things to be done and simple information which has value as soon as it is disseminated. In each case there will be complexities of context, trades-off between different objectives and a need for complex learning which collaboratively creates new knowledge, so actually *constituting* sustainable development as it happens.

Civil society and partnerships

The Summit recognised the 'key role of civil society'. Over 8,000 'civil society participants' attended and groups within civil society that were represented included NGOs, women, indigenous people, youth, farmers, trades union leaders, scientists and so on. As already noted, partnerships between business, governments and civil society were seen as a particularly promising way forward. Under none of these headings does one find homogeneity. One wonders, for example, how 'youth' or 'farmers' were 'represented' in any meaningful sense of the word. Partnerships of the kind described, by the same token, will always be between *particular* businesses, governments and elements of civil society and they will be formed in a particular context. Two points follow. First, the involvement of (effectively) everybody in sustainable development under some kind of (organisational or cultural) institutional heading suggests both the opportunity and need for environmental meta-learning. Second, every instance of such learning needs to be managed, pragmatically and adaptively, with regard to its own unique context.

What has happened: what will happen: what might happen?

We noted in Chapter 2 that policy making is as much a response to what has already happened as it is a determinant of what will happen. It is not possible for those living in the present reliably to discern the long-term, or even the medium-term, historical influences that shape the events they experience. However, it is at least possible that future historians will identify the Johannesburg Summit as evidence for a thesis that, by the beginning of the twenty-first century, a critical mass of people living in rich countries had come to feel ashamed and/or threatened because of the sheer numbers of the world's poor and because of globalising tendencies which tended to bring the poor, conceptually and physically, closer to home. This (for now, at least) entirely unsubstantiated hypothesis has the merit of explaining why the Summit linked sustainable development so strongly to the issue of poverty while to some degree uncoupling it, if not from the environment, at least from a focus on 'nature'. Unless something else happens to change policy, officials at the United Nations, in government ministries and at the local government level will try to implement the outcomes of the Summit. They will have some successes and some failures and while they are doing so they will also, because they are human, pursue personal and organisational agendas which may, in themselves, either move sustainable development forward or retard it.

But the Summit, though important, is only a bureaucratic, hierarchical response. It makes sense if sustainable development is about rules, plans and procedures: as, in part, it surely is. Others, from an egalitarian perspective, will seek to promote social and/or environmental justice by direct means of one sort or another, from political action to teaching children in a particular way. Individualists will seek to escape poverty and/or improve their environments through their own actions, or will try to give others the opportunity to do so. Fatalists will throw up their hands. Some people will do all these things, at different times, in different social roles and in different places.

None of this is in any doubt: but what the outcome will be in terms of sustainable development, nobody knows, and nobody can. What might happen, however, is that by learning throughout our lives we equip ourselves to choose most advantageously as the future unfolds. This would not bring about sustainable development. Rather, it would be evidence that sustainable development was happening.

References

Adams J. (1995) *Risk*, London, University College London Press.

Amram M. and Kulatilaka N. (1999) *Real Options: Managing Strategic Investment in an Uncertain World*, Harvard Business School Press.

Argyris C. and Schön D. (1978) *Organisational Learning in Action: A Theory in Action Perspective*, Boston, MA, Addison-Wesley.

Argyris C. and Schön D. (1996) *Organisational Learning II: Theory, Method and Practice*, Reading, MA, Addison-Wesley.

Bak N. (1995) 'Green doesn't always mean "Go": possible tensions in the desirability and implementation of environmental education', *Environmental Education Research*, 1(3), 345–52.

Ballantyne R., Connell S. and Fien J. (1998a) 'Students as catalysts of environmental change: a framework for researching intergenerational influence through environmental education', *Environmental Education Research*, 4(3), 285–98.

Ballantyne R., Connell S. and Fien J. (1998b) 'Factors contributing to intergenerational communication regarding environmental programmes: preliminary research findings', *Australian Journal of Environmental Education*, 14, 1–10.

Ballantyne R., Fien J. and Packer J. (2001) 'School environmental education programme impacts upon school and family learning: a case study analysis', *Environmental Education Research*, 7(1), 23–37.

Barrett S. and Murphy D. (1996) 'Managing corporate environmental policy: a process of complex change', in W. Wehrmeyer (ed.) *Greening People: Human Resources and Environmental Management*, Sheffield, Greenleaf, 75–98.

Beck U. (1992) *Risk Society: Towards a New Modernity*, London, Sage.

Berlin I. (1990) 'The decline of utopian ideas in the West', in I. Berlin *The Crooked Timber of Humanity*, London, Fontana.

Bhargava S. and Welford R. (1996) 'Corporate strategy and the environment: the theory', in R. Welford (ed.) *Corporate Environmental Management: Systems and Strategies*, London, Earthscan, 13–34.

Biggs J. (1996) 'Assessing learning quality: reconciling institutional, staff and educational demands', *Assessment and Evaluation in Higher Education*, 21(1), 5–15.

Blaikie P. and Brookfield H. (1987) *Land Degradation and Society*, London, Methuen.

Blenkin G. V., Edwards G. and Kelly A. V. (1997) 'Perspectives on educational change', in A. Harris, N. Bennett and M. Preedy (eds) *Organizational Effectiveness and Improvement in Education*, Buckingham, Open University Press, 216–30.

Boserup E. (1965) *The Conditions of Agricultural Growth: The Economics of Agrarian Change under Population Pressure*, Chicago, IL, Aldine.

Bowers C. A. (1993) *Critical Essays on Education, Modernity, and the Recovery of the Ecological Imperative*, New York, Teachers College Press.

Bowers C. A. (1995) 'Toward an ecological perspective', in Kohl W. (ed.) *Critical Conversations in Philosophy of Education*, New York, Routledge.

Bowers C. A. (2001) *Educating for Eco-Justice and Community*, Athens, GA, University of Georgia Press.

Bowers C. A. (2002) 'Towards an eco-justice pedagogy', *Environmental Education Research* 8(1), 21–34.

Bray M. (1999) *The Shadow Education System: Private Tutoring and its Implications for Planners*, Paris, UNESCO.

Braybrooke D. (1987) *Philosophy of Social Science*, Englewood Cliffs, NJ, Prentice-Hall.

Brown P. and Lauder H. (2001) *Capitalism and Social Progress: The Future of Society in a Global Economy*, Basingstoke, Palgrave.

Brunei Government (1996) *Summary Record of the First ACCSQ-CER Meeting*, Bandar Seri Begawan, ASEAN Consultative Committee on Standards and Quality.

Buell L. (1995) *The Environmental Imagination: Thoreau, Nature Writing and the Formation of American Culture*, Cambridge, MA, Belknep Press of Harvard University.

Burgess J., Harrison C. and Filius P. (1998) 'Environmental communication and cultural politics of environmental citizenship', *Environment and Planning A*, 30, 1445–60.

Carley M. and Christie I. (1992) *Managing Sustainable Development*, London, Earthscan.

Carr W. and Kemmis S. (1986) *Becoming Critical: Education, Knowledge and Action Research*, Lewes, Falmer.

Cater E. and Goodall B. (1992) 'Must tourism destroy its resource base?', in A. M. Mannion and S. R. Bowlby (eds) *Environmental Issues in the 1990s*, Chichester, John Wiley, 309–24.

CEE (2002) 'Reports from the CEE National Conference 2001: the power of place in learning for sustainable development', http://www.cee.org.uk/news/conf2001.html, accessed March 2002.

Chalmers N. (2002) 'Science, sustainability and education', in J. Cohen, S. James and J. Blewitt (eds) *Learning to Last: Skills, Sustainability and Strategy*, London, Learning and Skills Development Agency, 95–113.

Charter M. (1992) 'Emerging concepts in a greener world', in M. Charter (ed.) *Greener Marketing: A Responsible Approach to Business*, Sheffield, Greenleaf.

Christie I. and Warburton D. (2001) *From Here to Sustainability: Politics in the Real World*, London, Earthscan.

Clark M. E. (1989) *Ariadne's Thread*, New York, St Martin's Press.

Cohen J., James S. and Blewitt J. (2002) *Learning to Last: Skills, Sustainability and Strategy*, London, Learning and Skills Development Agency.

Colchester M. (1992) *Pirates, Squatters and Poachers*, 2nd edn, London/Selangor, Survival International/INSAN.

Cole N. S. (1990) 'Conceptions of educational achievement', *Educational Researcher*, 19(3), 2–7.

Connell S. (1997) 'Empirical-analytical methodological research in environmental education: response to negative trend in methodological and ideological discussions', *Environmental Education Research*, 3(2), 117–32.

Couchman P. (2002) 'Education for sustainable development: a co-operative perspective', in J. Cohen, S. James and J. Blewitt (eds) *Learning to Last: Skills, Sustainability and Strategy*, London, Learning and Skills Development Agency, 67–78.

Crick B. (2002) 'Citizenship and sustainable development', in J. Cohen, S. James and J. Blewitt (eds) *Learning to Last: Skills, Sustainability and Strategy*, London, Learning and Skills Development Agency, 31–9.

Cronon W. (1990) 'Modes of prophecy and production: placing nature in history', *Journal of American History*, 76, 1122–31.

Da Silva C. (1996) 'Building bridges: traditional environmental knowledge and environmental education in Tanzanian secondary schools', in W. Leal Filho, Z. Murphy and K. O'Loan (eds) *A Sourcebook for Environmental Education: A Practical Review Based on the Belgrade Charter*, Carnforth and New York, Parthenon and University of Bradford Press, 112–34.

Daly H. E. (1973) 'The steady-state economy: toward a political economy of biophysical equilibrium and moral growth', in H. E. Daly (ed.) *Economics, Ecology and Ethics: Essays Towards a Steady-state Economy*, San Francisco, CA, W. H. Freeman.

Devall B. and Sessions G. (1985) *Deep Ecology: Living as if Nature Mattered*, Salt Lake City, UT, Peregrine Smith.

Dicken P. (1998) *Global Shift: Transforming the World Economy*, 3rd edn, London, Paul Chapman.

Disinger J. F. and Roth C. E. (1992) *Environmental Literacy*, Columbus, OH, ERIC/SMEAC Information Reference Center.

Dobson A. (1996) 'Environmental sustainabilities: an analysis and a typology', *Environmental Politics*, 5(3), 401–28.

Dobson A. (2002) 'Social inclusion, environmental sustainability and citizenship', in J. Cohen, S. James and J. Blewitt (eds) *Learning to Last: Skills, Sustainability and Strategy*, London, Learning and Skills Development Agency, 41–51.

Douglas M. and Wildavsky A. (1982) *Risk and Culture: An Essay on the Selection of Technological and Environmental Dangers*, Berkeley, CA, University of California Press.

Drew K. (2000) 'Creating a community of learners: the experiences of one Wiltshire primary school', unpublished dissertation, University of Bath.

Edelman G (1987) *Neural Darwinism: The Theory of Neuronal Group Selection*, New York: Basic Books.

Edwards R. (1997) *Changing Places? Flexibility, Lifelong Learning and a Learning Society*, London, Routledge.

Ehrenfeld D. (1995) *Beginning Again*, Oxford, Oxford University Press.

Ehrlich P. R. (1968) *The Population Bomb*, New York, Ballantyne.

Ekins P. (1997) 'The Kuznets Curve for the environment and economic growth: examining the evidence', *Environment and Planning*, 29(5), 805–30.

Elliott J. (1998) *The Curriculum Experiment: Meeting the Challenge of Social Change*, Buckingham, Open University Press.

Ellis F. (1993) *Peasant Economics: Farm Households and Agrarian Development*, 2nd edn, Cambridge, Cambridge University Press.

Engestrom Y. (1994) *Training for Change: A New Approach to Instruction and Learning in Working Life*, Geneva, ILO.

European Commission (1996) *Teaching and Learning: Towards the Learning Society*, Luxembourg, Office for Official Publications.

Falconer L. (1998) 'A review of fuzzy decision-making and its application to managing occupational risks', *Journal of the Institution of Occupational Safety and Health*, 2(1), 29–36.

Falconer L., Ford N. J., Ray K. and Rennie D. M. (1999) 'Risk assessment and risk management', in W. H. Bassett (ed.) *Clay's Handbook of Environmental Health*, 18th edn, London, E & FN Spon, 196–213.

Farrell F. (2001) 'Postmodernism and educational marketing', *Educational Management and Administration*, 29(2), 169–80.

Fay B. (1987) *Critical Social Science: Liberation and its Limits*, London, Polity Press.

Fennell D. A. (1999) *Ecotourism*, London, Routledge.

Field J. (2000) 'Governing the ungovernable: why lifelong learning policies promise so much yet deliver so little', *Educational Management and Administration*, 28(3), 249–61.

Fien J. (1993) *Education for the Environment: Critical Curriculum Theorising and Environmental Education*, Geelong, Deakin University Press.

Fien J. (2002) 'Advancing sustainability in higher education: issues and opportunities for research', *Higher Education Policy*, 15(2), 143–52.

Fien J. and Trainer T. (1993a) 'Education for sustainability', in J. Fien (ed.) *Environmental Education: A Pathway to Sustainability*, Geelong, Deakin University Press, 11–23.

Fien J. and Trainer T. (1993b) 'A vision of sustainability', in J. Fien (ed.) *Environmental Education: A Pathway to Sustainability*, Geelong, Deakin University Press, 24–42.

Foster J. (2001) 'Education as sustainability', *Environmental Education Research*, 7(2), 153–65.

Foucault M. (1981) *The History of Sexuality, Volume 1: An Introduction*, Harmondsworth, Penguin.

Fox S. (2000) 'Communities of practice: Foucault and actor-network theory', *Journal of Management Studies*, 37(6), 853–67.

Friere P. (1971) *Pedagogy of the Oppressed*, Harmondsworth, Penguin.

Fullan M. (2001) *The New Meaning of Educational Change*, 3rd edn, London, RoutledgeFalmer.

Gare A. E. (1995) *Postmodernism and the Environmental Crisis*, London, RoutledgeFalmer.

Garrod B. (2003) 'Defining marine ecotourism: a Delphi study', in B. Garrod and J. C. Wilson (eds) *Marine Ecotourism: Issues and Experiences*, Clevedon, Channel View Publications (in press).

GECP (1999) *The Politics of GM Food: Risk, Science and Public Trust*, Brighton, GECP/ESRC.

Giddens A. (1999) *Runaway World: How Globalisation is Reshaping our Lives*, London, Profile Books.

Goodland R. (2002) 'Sustainability: human, social, economic and environmental', in *Encyclopaedia of Global Environmental Change*, London, John Wiley, and http://www.wiley.co.uk/wileychi/egec/accessed 22.12.2002.

Gore J. (1993) *The Struggle of Pedagogies: Critical and Feminist Pedagogies as Regimes of Truth*, London, Routledge.

Gough A. (1997) *Education and the Environment: Policy, Trends, and the Problems of Marginalisation*, Melbourne, Australian Council for Educational Research

Gough N. (2002) 'Ignorance in environmental education research', *Australian Journal of Environmental Education*, 18, 19–26.

Gough S. R. (1995) 'Environmental education in a region of rapid development: the case of Sarawak', *Environmental Education Research*, 1(3), 327–36.

Gough S. R. and Scott W. A. H. (1999) 'Education and training for sustainable tourism: problems, possibilities and cautious first steps', *Canadian Journal of Environmental Education*, 4, 193–212.

Gough S. R. and Scott W. A. H. (2000) 'Exploring the purposes of qualitative data coding in educational enquiry: insights from recent research', *Educational Studies*, 26(3), 339–54.

Gough S. R. and Scott W. A. H. (2001) 'Curriculum development and sustainable development: practices, institutions and literacies', *Educational Philosophy & Theory*, 33(2), 137–52.

Gough S. R., Scott W. A. H. and Oulton C. R. (1998) 'Environmental education, management education and sustainability: exploring the use of adaptive concepts', *International Journal of Environmental Education and Information*, 17(4), 367–80

Gough S. R., Scott W. A. H. and Stables A. W. G. (2000) 'Beyond O'Riordan: balancing anthropocentrism and ecocentrism', *International Research in Geographical and Environmental Education*, 9(1), 36–47.

Gough S. R., Walker K. E. and Scott W. A. H. (2001) 'Lifelong learning: towards a theory of practice for formal and non-formal environmental education and training', *Canadian Journal of Environmental Education*, 6, 178–96.

Gray J., Hopkins D., Reynolds D., Wilcox B., Farrell, S. and Jesson D. (1999) *Improving Schools Performance and Potential*, Buckingham, Open University Press.

Greenall Gough A. (1993) *Founders in Environmental Education*, Geelong, Deakin University Press.

Group of Eight (1999) *Köln Charter: Aims and Ambitions for Lifelong Learning*, 18 June 1999, Cologne, G8.

Habermas J. (1978) *Knowledge and Human Interests*, 2nd edn, translated J. J. Shapiro, London, Heinemann.

Hamilton I. (2001) 'An evaluation of the Motorola UK graduate development programme', unpublished dissertation, University of Bath.

Harrisson T. (1959) *World Within: A Borneo Story*, reprinted 1986, Singapore, Oxford University Press.

Hart P. and Nolan K. (1999) 'A critical analysis of research in environmental education', *Studies in Science Education*, 34, 1–69.

Haste H. (2000) 'Are women human?', in N. Roughley (ed.) *Being Human*, Cambridge, Cambridge University Press.

Haste H. (2001) 'Ambiguity, autonomy and agency; psychological challenges to new competence', in D. S. Rychen and L. H. Salganik (eds) *Defining and Selecting Key Competencies*, Seattle, WA, Hogrefe & Huber, 93–120.

Hedstrom G. S. (1996) 'Foreword', in W. Wehrmeyer (ed.) *Greening People: Human Resources and Environmental Management*, Sheffield, Greenleaf, 9–10.

Hill P. (1989) 'Market places', in J. Eatwell, M. Milgate and P. Newman (eds) *The New Palgrave: Economic Development*, London, Macmillan, 238–42.

Hindson J., Dillon J., Gough S., Scott W. and Teamey K. (2001) *Mainstreaming Environmental Education: A Report with Recommendations for DFID*, Field Studies Council, Shrewsbury.

Hines J. (1985) 'An analysis and synthesis of research on responsible environmental behavior', doctoral dissertation, Southern Illinois University at Carbondale, 1984, *Dissertation Abstracts International*, 46(3), 665–A. UMI No. DER85-10027.

Hirst P. and Thompson G. (1999) *Globalisation in Question*, 2nd edn, Cambridge, Polity Press.

Hlebowitsch P. (1999) 'The burdens of the new curricularist', *Curriculum Inquiry*, 29(3), 369–73.

Holland A. (1994) 'Natural capital', in R. Attfield and A. Belsey (eds) *Philosophy and the Natural Environment*, Cambridge, Cambridge University Press.

Holland G. (2002) 'Working towards sustainability: the business case for sustainable development education', in J. Cohen, S. James and J. Blewitt (eds) *Learning to Last: Skills, Sustainability and Strategy*, London, Learning and Skills Development Agency, 55–66.

Holling C. S. (1995) 'Sustainability: the cross-scale dimension', in M. Munasinghe and W. Shearer (eds) *Defining and Measuring Sustainability: The Biogeophysical Foundations*, Washington DC, United Nations University/World Bank, 65–75.

Hong E. (1987) *Natives of Sarawak: Survival in Borneo's Vanishing Forests*, 2nd edn, Penang, Institut Masyarakat.

Hopkins C., Damlamian J. and López-Ospina G. (1996) 'Evolving towards education for sustainable development: an international perspective', *Nature and Resources*, 32(3), 2–11.

Huckle J. (1983a) 'Environmental education', in J. Huckle (ed.) *Geographical Education: Reflection and Action*, Oxford: Oxford University Press.

Huckle, J. (1983b) 'Values education through geography: a radical critique', *Journal of Geography*, 82(2), 59–63.

Huckle J. (1991) 'Education for sustainability: assessing pathways to the future', *Australian Journal of Environmental Education*, 7, 43–62.

Huckle J. (1993) 'Environmental education and sustainability: a view from critical theory', in J. Fien (ed.) *Environmental Education: A Pathway to Sustainability*, Geelong, Deakin University Press, 43–68.

Huckle J. (1996) 'Realizing sustainability in changing times', in J. Huckle and S. Sterling (eds) *Education for Sustainability*, London, Earthscan, 3–17.

Huckle J. (1998) 'Locating environmental education – between modern capitalism and postmodern socialism: a reply to Lucie Sauvé', in A. Jarnet, B. Jickling, L. Sauvé, A. Wals and P. Clarkin (eds) *Colloquium on the Future of Environmental Education in a Postmodern World*, Whitehorse, Yukon College, 71–5.

Hughes C. and Tight M. (1995) 'The myth of the learning society', *British Journal of Educational Studies*, 43(3), 209–304.

Hungerford H. and Volk T. (1984) 'The challenges of K–12 environmental education', in A. B. Sacks (ed.) *Monographs in Environmental Education and Environmental Studies*, Vol. 1, Troy, OH, NAAEE, 5–16, 26–30.

Hungerford H. and Volk T. (1990) 'Changing learner behaviour through environmental education', *Journal of Environmental Education*, 21(3), 8–21.

Hungerford H., Peyton R. and Wilke R. (1980) 'Goals for curriculum development in environmental education', *Journal of Environmental Education*, 11(3), 42–7.

Hungerford H., Peyton R. and Wilke R. (1983) 'Yes, EE does have definition and structure', *Journal of Environmental Education*, 14(3), 1–2.

Hungerford H., Volk T., Dixon B., MarcinKowski T. and Sia A. (1988) 'Goals and allied topics', in *An Environmental Education Approach to the Training of Elementary Teachers: A Teacher Education Programme*, Paris, UNESCO–UNEP, Environmental Series 27, International Environmental Programme, 1–10.

Hungerford H., Volk T. and Ramsey J. (2000) 'Instructional impacts of environmental education on citizenship behavior and student achievement: research on investigating and evaluating environmental issues and actions, 1979–2000', paper presented at the 29th Annual Conference of the North American Association for Environmental Education, South Padre Island, TX, 17–21 October.

Inayatullah S. (1993) 'A response to Zia Sardar's "Colonising the Future"', *Futures*, 25(2), 190–5.

Jacobs M. (1996) *The Politics of the Real World*, London, Earthscan.

James P. and Thompson M. (1989) 'The plural rationality approach', in J. Brown (ed.) *Environmental Threats: Perception, Analysis and Management*, London, Belhaven, 87–94.

Jamieson I. (1996) 'Education and business: converging models', in C. Pole and R. Chawla-Duggan (eds) *Reshaping Education in the 1990s: Perspectives on Secondary Schooling*, London, Falmer, 26–39.

Jansen S. C. (1990) 'Is science a man? New feminist epistemologies and reconstructions of knowledge', *Theory and Society*, 19, 235–46.

Jemmott H. (2002) 'Employability skills formation in the service sector in Barbados: implications for education and training', unpublished PhD thesis, University of Bath.

Jensen B. B. (2002) 'Knowledge, action and pro-environmental behaviour', *Environmental Education Research*, 8(3), 325–34.

Jensen B. B. and Schnack K. (1997) 'The action competence approach in environmental education', *Environmental Education Research*, 3(2), 163–78.

Jickling B. (1992) 'Why I don't want my children to be educated for sustainable development', *Journal of Environmental Education*, 23(4), 5–8.

Jickling B. and Spork H. (1998) 'Education for the environment: a critique', *Environmental Education Research*, 4(3), 309–28.

Jones M. (1997) 'The role of stakeholder participation: linkages to stakeholder impact assessment and social capital in Camisea, Peru', *Greener Management International*, 19, 87–98.

Joseph J. B. and Mansell M. G. (1996) 'Trends in environmental engineering education', *Environmental Education Research*, 2(2), 215–26.

Jules C. and Cowling M. (1999) 'From environmental blight to model disposal sites: the solid waste disposal experience in St Lucia, West Indies', paper to the Millennium Conference on Environmental Education and Communication.

Kasimov N., Malkhazova S. and Romanova E. (2002) 'The role of environmental education for sustainable development in Russian universities', *Planet*, Special Edition 4, 24–5.

Kegan R. (1994) *In Over Our Heads: The Mental Demands of Modern Life*, Cambridge MA, Harvard University Press.

Kemmis D. (1990) *Community and the Politics of Place*, Norman, OK, University of Oklahoma Press.

Kemmis S. and Fitzclarence L. (1986) *Curriculum Theorizing: Beyond Reproduction Theory*, Geelong, Deakin University Press.

Kemp E. (1999) 'Metaphor as a tool for evaluation', *Assessment and Evaluation in Higher Education*, 24(1), 81–90.

Kerry Turner R. (ed.) (1993) *Sustainable Environmental Economics and Management: Principles and Practice*, London, Belhaven.

Kollmuss A. and Aygeman J. (2002) 'Mind the gap: why do people act environmentally and what are the barriers to pro-environmental behaviour?', *Environmental Education Research*, 8(3), 239–60.

Krause T. H. (1996) *The Behavior-based Safety Process*, 2nd edn, London, John Wiley.

Kuhn T. S. (1996) *The Structure of Scientific Revolutions*, 3rd edn, Chicago, IL, University of Chicago Press.

Lauder H. and Brown P. (2000) *Capitalism and Social Progress: The Future of Society in a Global Economy*, Basingstoke, Palgrave.

Laurillard D. (2002) *Rethinking University Teaching: A Conversational Framework for the Effective Use of Learning Technologies*, London, RoutledgeFalmer.

Lave J. (1988) *Cognition in Practice: Mind, Mathematics and Culture in Everyday Life*, Cambridge, Cambridge University Press.

Lave J. and Wenger E. (1991) *Situated Learning: Legitimate Peripheral Participation*, Cambridge, Cambridge University Press.

Leinan M. (2001) 'Keynote address to the annual conference of the North American Association for Environmental Education', Little Rock, Arkansas.

Lele S. and Norgaard R. (1995) 'Sustainability and the scientists burden', *Conservation Biology*, 10(2), 354–65.

Lelliott A., Pendlebury S. and Enslin P. (2000) 'Promises of access and inclusion: online education in Africa', *Journal of Philosophy of Education*, 34(1), 41–52.

Leveson-Gower H. (2002) 'Sustainable economic development: learning to satisfy real needs without costing the earth', in J. Cohen, S. James and J. Blewitt (eds) *Learning to Last: Skills, Sustainability and Strategy*, London, Learning and Skills Development Agency, 79–81.

Levin H. M. and Kelley C. (1997) 'Can education do it alone', in A. H. Halsey, H. Lauder, P. Brown and A. Stuart Wells (eds) *Education: Culture, Economy, Society*, Oxford, Oxford University Press, 240–52.

Levinson A. (2000) 'The ups and downs of the environmental Kuznets curve', paper prepared for the UCF/CentER conference on Environment, 30 November–2 December, Orlando, FL.   http://216.239.37.100/search?q=cache:5f0dOsDyBDcC:www.georgetown.edu/

faculty/aml6/pdfs%26zips/ups%2520and%2520downs.PDF+Environmental+Kuznets +Curve&hl=en&ie=UTF-8, accessed 19 December 2002.

Lewontin R. (2000) 'The triple helix: gene, organism and environment', Cambridge, MA, Harvard University Press.

Lindblom C. E. (1992) 'Inquiry and change: the troubled attempt to understand and shape society', New Haven, CT, Yale University Press.

Linke R. D. (1976) 'A case for indoctrination in environmental education', *South Pacific Journal of Teacher Education*, 4(2), 125–9.

Löfstedt R. and Frewer L. (eds) (1998) *Risk and Modern Society*, London, Earthscan.

Lomborg B. (2001) *The Skeptical Environmentalist: Measuring the Real State of the World*, Cambridge, Cambridge University Press. See also: http://www.lomborg.org

Lovelock J. (1979) *Gaia: A New Look at Life on Earth*, Oxford, Oxford University Press.

Lucas A. M. (1979) *Environment and Environmental Education: Conceptual Issues and Curriculum Implications*, Melbourne, Australian International Press and Publications.

Lucas A. M. (1980) 'Science and environmental education: pious hopes, self praise and disciplinary chauvinism', *Studies in Science Education*, 7, 1–21.

Luke T. (1988) 'The dreams of deep ecology', *Telos*, (Summer), 65–92.

Lundgren U. P. (1991) 'Between education and schooling: outlines of a diachronic curriculum theory', Geelong, Deakin University Press.

Lusigi W. (1994) 'Socioeconomic and ecological prospects for multiple use of protected areas in Africa', in M. Munasinghe and J. A. McNeely (eds) *Protected Area Economics and Policy: Linking Conservation and Sustainable Development*, Washington, DC, World Bank/IUCN.

Lyotard J. -F. (1984) *The Postmodern Condition: A Report on Knowledge*, Manchester, Manchester University Press.

MacIntyre A. (1981) *After Virtue: A Study in Moral Theory*, London, Duckworth.

Marcinkowski T. (2001) 'Predictors of responsible environmental behavior: a review of three dissertation studies', in H. Hungerford, W. Bluhm, T. Volk and J. Ramsey (eds) *Essential Readings in Environmental Education*, Champaign, IL, Stipes, 247–77.

Martin H. P. and Schumann H. (1997) *The Global Trap: Globalization and the Assault on Prosperity and Democracy*, London, Zed Books.

Maslow A. (1943) 'A theory of human motivation', *Psychological Review*, 50.

McKenzie-Mohr D. and Smith W. (1999) *Fostering Sustainable Behaviour: An Introduction to Community-based Social Marketing*, Gabrioloa Island, New Society.

Meadows D. H., Meadows D. L., Randers J. and Behrens III W. W. (1972) *The Limits to Growth*, New York, Universe Books.

Merchant C. (1990) *The Death of Nature: Women, Ecology and the Scientific Revolution*, rev. edn, San Francisco, CA and New York, Harper.

Mies M. and Shiva V. (1993) *EcoFeminism*, London: Zed Books.

Müller J. (1997) 'Literacy and non-formal (basic) education: still a donors' priority?', *Adult Education and Development*, 47, 37–60.

Munasinghe M. and Shearer W. (1995) 'An introduction to the definition and measurement of biogeophysical sustainability', in M. Munasinghe and W. Shearer (eds) *Defining and Measuring Sustainability: The Biogeophysical Foundations*, Washington DC, United Nations University/World Bank, xviii–xxxiii.

NCVO (2002) *Measuring Impact*, London, National Council of Voluntary Organisations.

Norgaard R. (1984) 'Coevolutionary development', *Economic Development and Cultural Change*, 32(2), 525–46.

Norgaard R. (1994) *Development Betrayed: The End of Progress and a Coevolutionary Revisioning of the Future*, London, Routledge.

North R. D. (1995) *Life on a Modern Planet: A Manifesto for Progress*, Manchester and New York, Manchester University Press.

O'Riordan T. (1981) *Environmentalism*, London, Pion-Methuen.

O'Riordan T. (1989) 'The challenge for environmentalism', in R. Peet and N. Thrift (eds) *New Models in Geography*, London, Unwin Hyman, 77–102.

O'Riordan T. (1990) 'On the greening of major projects', *Geographical Journal*, 156(2), 141–8.

O'Rourke R. (1998) 'The learning journal: from chaos to coherence', *Assessment and Evaluation in Higher Education*, 23(4), 403–14.

Oakland J. S. (1993) 'Total quality management', in D. Lock (ed.) *Handbook of Management*, 3rd edn, Aldershot, Gower, 82–99.

OECD (1996) *Lifelong Learning for All*, Paris, Organisation for Economic Co-operation and Development.

Ohmae K. (1990) *The Borderless World: Power and Strategy for the Interlinked Economy*, London, Collins.

Orr D. (1992) *Ecological Literacy, Education and the Transition to a Postmodern World*, New York, University of New York Press.

Orr D. (2001) 'Foreword', in S. Sterling, *Sustainable Education: Revisioning Learning and Change*, Totnes: Green Books.

Owens S. (2000) 'Engaging the public: information and deliberation in environmental policy', *Environment and Planning A*, 32, 141–1148.

Payne P. (1997) 'Embodiment and environmental education', *Environmental Education Research*, 3(2), 133–54.

Pearce D. and Kerry Turner R. (1990) *Economics of Natural Resources and the Environment*, Hemel Hempstead, Harvester Wheatsheaf.

Pepper D. (1989) 'Red and green, educational perspectives', in D. Randle (ed.) *Teaching Green*, London, Green Print, 85–91.

Pezzoli K. (1997) 'Sustainable development literature: a transdisciplinary bibliography', *Journal of Environmental Planning and Management*, 40(5), 575–602.

Pieterse J. N. (1995) 'Globalization and hybridization', in M. Featherstone, S. Lash and R. Robertson (eds), *Global Modernities*, London, Sage, 45–68.

Pimbert M. and Pretty J. (1997) 'Parks, people and professionals', in K. Ghimire and M. Pimbert (eds) *Social Change and Conservation*, London, Earthscan/UNRISD.

Rao P. K. (2000) *Sustainable Development: Economics and Policy*, Oxford, Blackwell.

Ravenscroft N., Curry N. and Markwell S. (2002) 'Outdoor recreation and participative democracy in England and Wales', *Journal of Environmental Planning and Management*, 45(5), 715–34.

Redclift M. (1987) *Sustainable Development: Exploring the Contradictions*, London and New York, Methuen, reprinted by Routledge (1989).

Reich R. (1991) *The Work of Nations: A Blueprint for the Future*, New York, Vintage.

Reid A. D. and Gough S. R. (2000) 'Guidelines for reporting and evaluating qualitative research: what are the alternatives?', *Environmental Education Research*, 6(1), 59–91.

Reid A. D., Scott W. A. H. and Gough S. R. (2002) 'Education and sustainable development in the UK: an exploration of progress since Rio', *Geography*, 87(3), 247–55.

Reid W. A. (1999) *Curriculum as Institution and Practice: Essays in the Deliberative Tradition*, Mahwah, NJ, Lawrence Erlbaum.

Rickinson M. (2001) 'Learners and learning in environmental education: a critical review of the evidence', *Environmental Education Research*, 7(3), 208–320.

Robertson R. (1992) *Globalization: Social Theory and Global Culture*, London, Sage.

Robinson V. M. J. (1993) *Problem-based Methodology: Research for the Improvement of Practice*, Oxford, Pergamon.

Robinson V. M. J. (1994) 'The practical promise of critical research in educational administration', *Educational Administrative Quarterly*, 30(1), 56–76.

Robottom I. (1987a) 'Towards inquiry-based professional development in environmental education', in I. Robottom (ed.) *Environmental Education: Practice and Possibility*, Geelong, Deakin University Press, 83–120.

Robottom I. (1987b) 'Contestation and consensus in environmental education', *Curriculum Perspectives*, 7(1), 23–6.

Robottom I. and Hart P. (1993) *Research in Environmental Education: Engaging the Debate*, Geelong, Deakin University Press.

Rogers E. (1995) *Diffusion of Innovations*, 4th edn, New York: The Free Press.

Rosa E. A. (2000) 'Modern theories of society and the environment: the risk society', in G. Spaargaren, A. Mol and F. Buttel (eds) *Environment and Global Modernity*, London, Sage.

Ross A. (1994) *The Chicago Gangster Theory of Life: Nature's Debt to Society*, New York, Verso.

Roth R. E. (1970) 'Fundamental concepts for environmental management education', *Journal of Environmental Education*, 1(3), 65–74.

Rothery B. (1993) *BS7750: Implementing the Environmental Management Standard and the EC Eco-Management Scheme*, Aldershot, Gower.

Sachs W. (1991) 'Environment and development: the story of a dangerous liaison', *The Ecologist*, 21(6), 252–7.

Said E. (1985) 'Orientalism reconsidered', *Cultural Critique*, 1, 89–107.

Sauvé L. and Berryman T. (2003) 'Researchers and research in environmental education: a critical review essay on Mark Rickinson's report on learners and learning', *Environmental Education Research*, 9(2).

Schwab J. J. (1978) 'The "impossible" role of the teacher in progressive education', in I. Westbury and N. J. Wilkof (eds) *Science, Curriculum and Liberal Education*, Chicago, IL, University of Chicago Press, 170–1.

Schwarz M. and Thompson M. (1990) *Divided We Stand: Redefining Politics, Technology and Social Choice*, Philadelphia, PA, University of Pennsylvania Press.

Scott A. (2001) 'Technological risk, scientific advice and public "education": groping for an adequate language in the case of GM foods', *Environmental Education Research*, 7(2), 129–39.

Scott W. A. H. and Oulton C. R. (1999) 'Environmental education: arguing the case for multiple approaches', *Educational Studies*, 25(1), 119–25.

Sen A. (1999) *Development as Freedom*, Oxford, Oxford University Press.

Senge P. (1992) *The Fifth Discipline: The Art and Practice of the Learning Organisation*, London, Doubleday/Century Business.

Sharp R. (1992) 'Organizing for change: people power and the role of institutions', in J. Holmberg (ed.) *Policies for a Small Planet*, London, Earthscan, 39–64.

Shaw K. E. (1996) 'Cultural issues in evaluation studies of Middle Eastern higher education', *Assessment and Evaluation in Higher Education*, 21(4), 313–24.

Shiva V. (1989) *Staying Alive: Women, Ecology and Development*, London, Zed Books.

Simon J. L. (1977) *The Economics of Population Growth*, Princeton, NJ, Princeton University Press.

Sjöberg L. (1997) 'Explaining risk perception: an empirical evaluation of cultural theory', *Risk Decision and Policy*, 2(2), 113–30.

Skolimowski H. (1982) 'Knowledge and values', *The Ecologist*, 5(1), 8–15.

Southgate V. R. (1997) 'Schistosomiasis in the Senegal River basin: before and after the construction of the dams at Diama, Senegal and Manantali, Mali and future prospects', *Journal of Helminthology*, 71, 125–32.

Spretnak C. (1990) 'Ecofeminism: our roots and flowering', in I. Diamond and G. F. Orenstein (eds) *Reweaving the World: The Emergence of Ecofeminism*, San Francisco, CA: Sierra Club Books.

Spring J. (1998) *Education and the Rise of the Global Economy*, Mahwah, NJ, Lawrence Erlbaum.

Stables A. W. G. (1996) 'Reading the environment as text: literary theory and environmental education', *Environmental Education Research*, 2(2), 189–95.

Stables A. W. G. (1997) 'The landscape and "the death of the author"', *Canadian Journal of Environmental Education*, 2, 104–13.

Stables A. W. G. (1998) 'Environmental literacy: functional, cultural, critical: the case of the SCAA guidelines', *Environmental Education Research*, 4(2), 155–64.

Stables A. W. G. (2001a) 'Who drew the sky? Conflicting assumptions in environmental education', *Educational Philosophy and Theory*, 33(2), 245–56.

Stables A. W. G. (2001b) 'Language and meaning in environmental education: an overview', *Environmental Education Research*, 7(2), 121–8.

Stables A. W. G. (2002) 'Environmental education and the arts/science divide: the case for a disciplined environmental literacy', in J. Siddall (ed.) *Towards an Advanced Environmental Research Agenda*, Basingstoke, Macmillan.

Stables A. W. G. and Bishop K. N. (2001) 'Weak and strong conceptions of environmental literacy: implications for environmental education', *Environmental Education Research*, 7(1), 89–97.

Stables A. W. G. and Scott W. A. H. (2001) 'Disciplined environmental literacies', *Environmental Education*, 68, 14–16.

Stables A. W. G. and Scott W. A. H. (2001) 'Post-humanist liberal pragmatism: environmental education out of modernity', *Journal of Philosophy of Education*, 35(2), 269–80.

Stasz C. (2001) 'Assessing skills for work', *Oxford Economic Papers*, 53(3), 385–405.

Sterling S. (1993) 'Environmental education and sustainability: a view from holistic ethics', in J. Fien (ed.) *Environmental Education: A Pathway to Sustainability*, Geelong, Deakin University Press, 69–98.

Sterling S. (1998) 'WWF and sustainable development – *inspiration!*', Godalming, WWF–UK (on behalf of the WWF family).

Sterling S. (2001) *Sustainable Education: Revisioning Learning and Change*, Totnes, Green Books.

Stern P. (2000) 'Toward a coherent theory of environmentally significant behavior', *Journal of Social Issues*, 56(3), 407–24.

Stokking H., van Aert L., Meijberg W. and Kaskens A. (1999) *Evaluating Environmental Education*, Gland and Cambridge, IUCN.

Strain M. (2000) 'Editorial', *Educational Management and Administration*, 28(3), 243–7.

Sustainable Development Education Panel (2001) *Education for Sustainable Development – More Relevant than Ever: The Third Annual Report*, London, DETR/DEFRA.

Tanner T. (1998) 'On the origins of SLE research, questions outstanding and other research traditions', *Environmental Education Research*, 4(4), 419–23.

Taylor K. and Marienau C. (1997) 'Constructive-development theory as a framework for assessment in higher education', *Assessment and Evaluation in Higher Education*, 22(2), 233–44.

Tesh S. N. (1988) 'Hidden arguments: political ideology and disease prevention policy', New Brunswick, NY, Rutgers University Press.

Thompson M. (1990) 'Policy making in the face of uncertainty', *Concepts of the Environment in the Social Sciences: Readings 3*, London, Wye College, 161–87.

Thompson M. (1997) 'Security and solidarity: an anti-reductionist framework for thinking about the relationship between us and the rest of nature', *The Geographical Journal*, 163(2), 141–9.

Thompson M., Ellis R. and Wildavsky A. (1990) *Cultural Theory*, Boulder, CO and Oxford, Westview.

Townsend A. (1999) *Global Classrooms: Activities for Engaging Students in Third Millennium Schools*, Melbourne, Hawker Brownlow.

Townsend A., Clarke P. and Ainscow M. (1999) *Third Millennium Schools: A World of Difference in Effectiveness and Improvement*, Melbourne, Swets and Zeitlinger.

Trainer T. (1990) 'Towards an ecological philosophy of education', *Discourse*, 10(2), 92–117.

Tyler Miller Jnr., G. (1990) *Living in the Environment*, 6th edn, Belmont, CA, Wadsworth.

UNCED (1992) *Agenda 21*, UNCED, Rio de Janeiro, Brazil.

UNDP (1999) *Human Development Report*, New York, Oxford University Press.

UNESCO (2001) *Improving Performance in Primary Education – A Challenge to Education for All Goals*, International Workshop TOR.

UNESCO/UNEP (1977) 'The Tbilisi Declaration', *Connect*, 3(1), 1–8.

Uzzell D. (1999) 'Education for environmental action in the community: new roles and relationships', *Cambridge Journal of Education*, 29(3), 397–413.

Uzzell D., Davallon J., Fontes P. J., Gottesdiener H., Jensen B. B., Kofoed J., Uhrenholdt G. and Vognsen C. (1994) *Children as Catalysts of Environmental Change: Report of an Investigation on Environmental Education. Final Report*, Brussels, European Commission.

Wackernagel M. (1995) *Our Ecological Footprint: Reducing Human Impact on the Earth*, Canada, New Society.

Walker K. E. (1997) 'Challenging critical theory in environmental education', *Environmental Education Research*, 3(2), 155–62.

WCED (1987) *Our Common Future: World Commission on Environment and Development*, Oxford, Oxford University Press.

Wehrmeyer W. (ed.) (1996) *Greening People: Human Resources and Environmental Management*, Sheffield, Greenleaf.

Weick K. (1976) 'Educational organisations as loosely coupled systems', *Administrative Science Quarterly*, 21, 1–19.

Westbury I. (1999) 'The burdens and excitement of the "new" curriculum research: a response to Hlebowitsh's "The Burdens of the New Curricularist"', *Curriculum Inquiry*, 29(3), 355–64.

Wildavsky A. and Dake K. (1990) 'Theories of risk perception: who fears what and why?', *Daedalus*, 4(119), 41–60.

Wilkinson R. G. (1973) *Poverty and Progress: An Ecological Perspective on Economic Development*, New York, Praeger.

Wilson E. O. (1975) *Sociobiology: The New Synthesis*, Cambridge, MA, Harvard University Press.

WWF (1999a) 'Education and conservation: an evaluation of the contributions of educational programmes to conservation within the WWF Network', WWF-International and WWF-US, Gland and Washington DC, 35.

WWF (1999b) 'Education and conservation: an evaluation of the contributions of education programmes to conservation within the WWF Network', Reference Volume to the Final Report, Gland and Washington DC, WWF International and WWF-US, 40.

WWF International (1996) *Changing Worlds: 35 Years of Conservation Achievement*, Gland, Worldwide Fund for Nature, 27.

Young M. F. D. (1998) *The Curriculum of the Future: From the 'New Sociology of Education' to a Critical Theory of Learning*, London, Falmer.

Index